Identity, Crime, and Legal Responsibility
in Eighteenth-Century England

Identity, Crime, and Legal Responsibility in Eighteenth-Century England

Dana Y. Rabin

First published 2004 by
PALGRAVE MACMILLAN
Houndmills, Basingstoke, Hampshire RG21 6XS and
175 Fifth Avenue, New York, N.Y. 10010
Companies and representatives throughout the world.

PALGRAVE MACMILLAN is the global academic imprint of the Palgrave Macmillan division of St. Martin's Press, LLC and of Palgrave Macmillan Ltd. Macmillan® is a registered trademark in the United States, United Kingdom and other countries. Palgrave is a registered trademark in the European Union and other countries.

ISBN 1–4039–3444–4 hardback

This book is printed on paper suitable for recycling and made from fully managed and sustained forest sources.

A catalogue record for this book is available from the British Library.

Library of Congress Cataloging-in-Publication Data

Rabin, Dana Y., 1965–
    Identity, crime, and legal responsibility in eighteenth-century England / Dana Y. Rabin.
        p. cm.
    Includes bibliographical references and index.
    ISBN 1–4039–3444–4 (cloth)
        1. Insanity–Jurisprudence–England–History–18th century.
    I. Title.

KD7897.R33 2004
345.42'04—dc22   2004050533

10 9 8 7 6 5 4 3 2 1
13 12 11 10 09 08 07 06 05 04

Printed and bound in Great Britain by
Antony Rowe Ltd, Chippenham and Eastbourne.

For Craig

Contents

Acknowledgments

It is gratifying to be able to thank the many individuals and institutions who have helped to make this book possible. Tom Green and Michael MacDonald guided the research for this project through the dissertation stage. As I reconceptualized the project and wrote the book, Tom Green was a constant source of knowledge, support, and friendship.

I would like to thank the librarians and archivists at the Public Record Office, the Corporation of London Record Office, Westminster Abbey Muniments Room and Library, the Guildhall Library, the British Library, and Lincoln's Inn Library. The staff at the Newberry Library, the Huntington Library, and the library at University of Illinois, Urbana-Champaign did all they could to help me to track down the sources I needed.

A fellowship from the National Endowment for the Humanities funded a summer in Cambridge where I participated in an interdisciplinary seminar on 'The Enlightenment Invention of the Modern Self' directed by Leo Damrosch at Harvard University. A fellowship from the American Society for Eighteenth-Century Studies and the Newberry Library and a Littleton-Griswold Research grant from the American Historical Association funded a summer in Chicago at the Newberry Library. Financial support from the University of Illinois, Urbana-Champaign Research Board funded research trips to England. A good deal of the writing was done in the beautiful setting of the Huntington Library supported by a Barbara Thom Postdoctoral Fellowship.

The University of Illinois has been my intellectual home since 1997. Formal departmental colloquia as well as countless reading groups and coffees provided friendly and challenging discussions of crime, responsibility, and the self.

Scholars from various institutions and disciplines have discussed my ideas with me and improved this study with their comments and suggestions. I would like to thank Amanda Bailey, J. S. Cockburn, Leo Damrosch, Barbara Donegan, Joel Eigen, Jim Epstein, Bob Frank, Amy Froide, Jeffrey Gossman, Bob Griffin, Cynthia Herrup, Caroline Hibbard, Rab Houston, Margaret Hunt, Mark Jackson, Mark Micale, Marilyn Morris, Carol Neely, Steve Pincus, Nick Rogers, Tom Tentler, Jennifer Thorn, Martha Umphrey, Joe Ward, the members of the first annual Bloomington Eighteenth-Century Studies Workshop on the 'Signs of the

Self' at Indiana University, and the members of the University of Illinois early Europe group. I very much appreciate the time and effort of the anonymous reviewers who engaged with the manuscript and gave me invaluable comments and suggestions. Special thanks go to my editor at Palgrave Macmillan, Luciana O'Flaherty.

To friends and family, I would like to express my special gratitude. Antoinette Burton has believed in me and encouraged me with a friendship I cherish. Amy Masciola discussed defendants and selves with me in countless long-distance phone calls, visits, and vacations in Maine. Susanne Pohl and Clare Crowston encouraged me to be bold. Kathy Oberdeck gave sensitive, nuanced suggestions. Becky Conekin provided friendship, advice, and laughter across the pond. The memory of my father, David, inspired me. My mother, Pauline, my sisters Roni and Leora, and my brother Michael, always gave their love and support. My children, Jonah and Eve, gave me new perspectives on life, Lego, and love.

The biggest thanks of all go to Craig Koslofsky who read each word of this book in its every incarnation and never stopped believing in the project or in me. His heroic efforts on my behalf cannot be detailed here, but they are never forgotten, and so it is to him that I dedicate this book.

1
Crime, Culture, and the Self

Introduction

On the evening of May 15, 1800 James Hadfield (1771–1841) waited in the Drury Lane Theatre wearing an officer's waistcoat and armed with a horse pistol. As George III entered the royal box and bowed to the crowd, Hadfield fired at the king, but missed. When apprehended and asked why he shot at the king, Hadfield replied that he was 'tired of life' and that he had come to the theater 'to take the life of some other person, with a view to forfeit his own.'[1] At Hadfield's trial for treason in June of the same year defense counsel Thomas Erskine (1750–1823) argued that his client suffered from delusions caused by injuries he had sustained while a soldier in the Flanders campaign.[2] Erskine explained that although Hadfield knew the difference between good and evil, his disease prompted uncontrolled, passionate violence. The jury found Hadfield 'Not guilty; he being under the influence of insanity at the time the act was committed.'[3] A month later Parliament passed 'The Act for the Safe Custody of Insane Persons Charged with Offenses' (39&40 Geo. III, c. 94) mandating the incarceration of anyone acquitted by reason of insanity for treason, murder, or any other felony. Hadfield's crime resulted in both his acquittal and his life-long confinement. How did English law arrive at mandating the confinement of a defendant found innocent?

The Hadfield case brings to a close a century in which English defendants, victims, witnesses, judges, and jurors spoke a language of the mind. This language of emotion and excuse expressed a desire on the part of the speaker to diminish or deny responsibility for crime. Participants in the legal process mentioned 'confusion,' 'distemper,' 'melancholy,' or 'passion' to refer to psychological and social pressures that interfered with the offender's moral judgment and self-restraint. With their

1

reputations or lives at stake, men and women presented their complex emotions and passions as grounds for acquittal or mitigation of punishment. These states of mind were described and deployed in order to persuade the judge and jury to consider the crime an aberration, committed without criminal intent. These excuses were not new to the eighteenth century. In some ways they were as old as the jury trial itself. By the eighteenth century their consistent appearance in the legal record ranged from 5 to 9 percent of all cases. Nigel Walker found that between 1740 and 1800 the frequency of 'obvious' insanity defenses remained stable at about 4.5 percent of criminal cases except for a rise in the period between 1755 and 1769.[4] I argue that this increase in the number of clear cases of insanity accompanied the elaboration and amplification of a wider set of mental excuses as defendants stretched the boundaries of the insanity defense to include various mental states that ranged from delirium to confusion. Inside the courtroom the language of excuse reshaped crimes and punishments, signaling a shift in the age-old negotiation of mitigation. Outside the courtroom the language of the mind reflected society's preoccupation with questions of sensibility, responsibility, and the self.

I will refer to the descriptions of mental states by defendants, witnesses, jurors, and judges as the language of the mind, the language of mental states, the language of mental excuse, the language of emotion, the language of excuse, the language of non-responsibility, and the language of diminished responsibility. While each of these 'languages' employed the same vocabulary of the mind, the context will determine the label I will use in each particular instance. The terms excuse, non-responsibility, and diminished responsibility are appropriate for a specifically legal discussion, but in a cultural context emotion, mind, mental excuse, and mental states are more precise. This vocabulary of the mind was never regularized and the words themselves suggested only partial images as they often implied an association with mental confusion rather than elaborating with a detailed description. The word language as used here refers to a vocabulary, single words and phrases, rather than an effort to weave a narrative from it: in so far as defendants introduced evidence about their mental states, one can call this a language of the mind inflected with a vocabulary of emotion and excuse.[5]

I argue that the language of the mind was 'stable enough to be available for the use of more than one discussant and to present the character of games defined by a structure of rules for more than one player.'[6] In their choice of words, deponents drew on well-known images or fragments of stories about mental confusion. They often included the 'formulaic but adaptable anecdote or the memorable, serviceable phrase.'[7] The justices of the peace who conducted the examinations and the clerks who recorded them doubtless aided in fashioning this vocabulary as they recast the deponent's words to fit the format dictated by legal conventions and institutions.[8] Although some cases featured extensive and detailed descriptions of the defendant's peculiar behavior, these were the exceptions. More often brief suggestions were used to associate the crime and the accused with more substantiated cases of insanity. In their representations of mental states defendants and witnesses alluded to common preconceptions about insanity that enabled others in the courtroom to connect the dots on their own and envision the scene. The speakers left it to their listeners to create a story, a scenario, or a narrative of events from the pieces of evidence woven into pre-trial depositions or courtroom testimony.[9]

Defendants represented themselves to the authorities as less than fully accountable for their behavior, admitting they had committed crimes but denying responsibility for their actions. These defendants spoke about mental distress, drunkenness, the pain of childbirth, and financial hardship as forces that overcame them and caused them to commit a variety of crimes, from sedition to murder. In the courtroom dialogue, defendants and witnesses tried to portray the confused, drunk, or impoverished offender and the repentant, sober defendant as two distinctly different selves. Their testimony distanced the 'true self' from the criminal act, often juxtaposing the defendant's crime and his or her usual, upstanding character. In the face of a legal system that assumed a coherent and cohesive self and accepted only the single narrowly defined exception of 'total' or 'perfect' insanity, defendants used the language of the mind to bridge the gap between insanity and mental distress, redraw the legal definition of self, and plead for their lives.

This book tracks ideas about the self and emotion as they played out in eighteenth-century society, specifically in the criminal trial. During the eighteenth century the mind, the self, and responsibility for crime were the focus of tremendous intellectual ferment, discussion, and analysis. Chapter 3 examines the cultural forces of moral philosophy, the burgeoning field of psychology, and contemporary concerns with the self, emotion, sensation, and sensibility. Setting legal cases that made more tenuous claims of mental distress beside eighteenth-century conceptions of responsibility and the self that circulated in philosophy, literature, and the popular press, I attempt to show that these excuses, though not unique to the eighteenth century, took on a different meaning in the cultural context of the age of sensibility.[10] Although this is a difficult case to prove, an analysis of the self is organic to this study because perceptions of the self shaped the way in which defendants, witnesses, judges, and jurors defined responsibility and formed the basis for the assessment of guilt in the criminal trial.[11] The language of the mind and its reception grew out of new ideas about a sensible self that actively sought sensation and emotion as a means of enacting a higher set of morals and virtues.

The concern about the relationship between emotion and morality within the context of sensibility propelled gender into the center of the definition of the eighteenth-century self. Gender became an essential component of the negotiation of responsibility in the courtroom. While insanity had been gendered as both masculine and feminine, different features of the diseased mind were thought typical of men or women. Melancholia, with its symptoms of withdrawn, quiet, impenetrable depression, and violent dangerousness, had traditionally been ascribed to men, while women's lunacy was associated with dazzling outbursts of singing and dancing as well as uncontrolled talking.[12] The language of the mind mixed the two kinds of insanity, making them difficult to gender and confusing those mental states deemed legally exculpatory and those that were not. Simultaneously, the era of sensibility blurred the line between masculine and feminine by praising the emotional sensitivity and expression for which women had long been criticized and disparaging the emotional restraint that had been lauded as a splendidly admirable masculine trait. These concurrent developments caused anxiety about the efficacy of law and the definition of manhood.

Within the legal system the anxiety about the boundaries of masculinity and the authority of the law manifested itself in the discussion of the parameters of legal responsibility, the role of compassion in the courtroom, and the appropriate proximity of emotion and justice. Both poor men and women used the language of the mind to represent themselves as less accountable for their crimes: chapter 5 demonstrates how elite men attempted to reclaim and reinvigorate traditional masculinity and reassert the distinction between male and female, popular and elite, by alleging their superior self-control and pathologizing the mental states described in court as the domain of weak men and all women.[13]

This study reconstructs the courtroom as a site of cultural production with special attention to the role of emotion in the criminal trial. As scholars of law and culture have established, 'in a trial, as in other crucial legal encounters, external beliefs, interest, and other forces are siphoned through the peculiar rules, practices, words, and institutions of the law' in an attempt to circumscribe the kind of evidence that can be presented and guide the way verdicts are reached.[14] But these legal 'rules, practices, words, and institutions' did not exist in isolation from the culture that produced them. Despite an ideology of legal autonomy, the people who implemented and enforced them were just as subject to cultural forces as anyone else in eighteenth-century England.

The criminal trial created a conversation (between men and women, patrician and plebeian, young and old), but the meeting in the courtroom was not a chance encounter. It was a tense and freighted exchange whose outcome determined the lives of some of the participants. These encounters exposed the social rifts and cultural commonalties among these groups. A study of these interactions within the legal context enables scholars to imagine relationships between social and economic groups: this study aims to do that without presenting the rigid divide between popular and elite culture that characterizes many descriptions of the eighteenth century.[15] In order to reconceptualize these relationships, we must consider the ways in which each group imprinted the other. Instead of envisioning an active source of culture and a passive recipient, we must consider multiple points of origin and a dynamic process of changing and exchanging attitudes and ways of thinking, in this case about responsibility, crime, sensibility, and the self.

This is not a case study based on a single renowned 'trial of the century.' While the trial of the century may be a 'culture-shaping and culture disclosing event,' each of these well-known trials is itself shaped by the many routine and unnoticed trials that precede it.[16] The degree to which a case study represents the anxieties and preoccupations of an age depends on the questions and debates identified and provisionally resolved by countless ordinary cases.

This book, based on depositions taken in criminal trials of the Northern Circuit and trial transcripts from the *Old Bailey Sessions Papers*, examines the language of the mind in hundreds of brief exchanges that formed the criminal trial in the eighteenth century. These two sets of records document different stages of criminal legal process: the depositions from the Northern Circuit assizes (Yorkshire, Northumberland, Cumberland and Westmorland) between 1660 and 1800 provide pretrial testimony from the victims, witnesses to the crime, and defendants while a sample of the voluminous *Old Bailey Sessions Papers* (OBSP) records the trials at London's central criminal court.[17] To offset the anonymity of the statistical study and its tendency to efface the agency and variation of individuals, this study lingers over particular examples to discuss the circumstances that surrounded a defendant or framed a specific trial.[18]

The depositions contain the results of an examination of the victim, the accused, and the witnesses to the crime. This apparently seamless narrative emerged from unrecorded questions posed by the justice of the peace and the answers as summarized by his clerk. Depositions were usually taken soon after the discovery of the crime and are closest in time to the events recounted. In addition to reconstructing the events surrounding the crime, the depositions often offer some assessment of the character and disposition of the accused and the victim. Although the question of who actually articulated the mental state of the accused is difficult to answer, the varied vocabulary and the nuanced descriptions point to rich and wide-ranging understandings of emotional states of mind.[19]

The fascination with crime and the profits of its narration created an industry of popular literature which included the *Old Bailey Sessions Papers*, as well as chapbooks, broadsides, and pamphlets.[20] Beginning in the 1670s, published accounts of the work of the Old Bailey, the *OBSP*, reported the trials held in the court in pamphlets issued at the end of each session. Produced as both entertainment and news, the reports gave sensational trials the best coverage, but for ordinary cases they accurately recorded the basic facts of the crime, the indictment, and the verdict. Other pamphlet accounts of crime, written by anonymous authors or sometimes attributed to the Ordinary (chaplain) of Newgate Gaol, recounted the lives of condemned prisoners, including detailed descriptions of the prisoners' last days and their confessions and repentance. Some pamphlets claimed to be autobiographies written by prisoners awaiting their death. Others reconstructed crimes that had been described in newspaper accounts or in the *OBSP*. They also drew on published trial transcripts, scaffold speeches, and confessions. Although not every detail they relate can be substantiated, the events they recount have been found generally consistent with information in indictments and other legal records, and they often provide insight into aspects of the legal process otherwise obscured.[21] These sources, produced in response to the detection, prosecution, and punishment of crime, shaped and reflected popular conceptions of the law in the eighteenth century.[22]

Despite the number of cases examined here (about 10,000), this is not a quantitative study of crime and legal administration. With the exception of my examination of the language of the mind in cases of infanticide in chapter 4, I have not attempted to measure the incidence of this language or to prove its efficacy or lack thereof by correlating evidence to verdicts. There are several reasons for this. Foremost among them is the fact that the legal process did not demand or provide for the documentation of jury deliberations, so there is no way to explain how a jury reached a particular verdict. Sources do detail the concerns of judges, legal commentators, and observers of England's legal system who wrote at great length about the appropriate place of emotion and compassion in the courtroom. This anxiety is the focus of discussions in chapters 2 and 5, but obviously this evidence cannot be used to reconstruct the exact factors that swayed jurors in specific cases.

More important than the pragmatic constraints of the correlation of evidence and verdicts, however, is a larger point about the place of verdicts in any legal study. As Cynthia Herrup has argued:

> A verdict is the clearest point of a trial's history, but the weakest focus for an historian. It is a filter built from artificial materials and one that obscures as much as it clarifies, reinforcing rather than upsetting the notion of a trial as a story with an objective ending.[23]

For this study, the outcome of a given case is less important than the presence or perceived presence of the language of mental excuse and anxiety about its possible impact on judicial authorities and institutions. Herrup asserts that a focus on the verdict 'sets the law above rather than within society.'[24] My analysis emphasizes the formation and response to these stories as a cultural phenomenon because they served as explanations regardless of whether they succeeded in court as excuses. In the eighteenth century the language of excuse reflected and created attitudes toward law, responsibility, and self and the cultural work of these pleas was in their conception and deployment rather than just their efficacy.

Natalie Davis has suggested that 'turning a terrible action into a story is a way to distance oneself from it, at worst a form of self-deception, at best a way to pardon the self.'[25] The distance created by the language of mental excuse enabled the defendant to come to some understanding of the crime he or she had committed and began the process of reconciliation with self, kin, and community. To quote Davis again, these stories may allow us to glean some insight about 'how [early modern people] accounted for motive, and how through narrative they made sense of the unexpected and built coherence into immediate experience.'[26] But this was not language used lightly, and the stakes were high. The suspects who used the language of the mind reveal a knowledge of legal precedent that allowed for the exculpation of the insane, but this refusal of responsibility for crime also incorporated an admission of guilt.

This study examines the language of excuse from the perspective of different participants in the legal conversation. The evidence from legal records reveals what Davis described as 'a cultural exchange' rather than 'an impermeable "official culture" imposing its criteria on "popular culture."' While 'the stakes were different for supplicants, listeners, and pardoners ... they were all implicated in a common discourse.'[27] Tracing the language and its effects on different participants in the legal process allows us to reassess several key assumptions about early modern English law and society: the polarization of popular and elite culture, the association of femininity and emotion, and the question of defendant agency.

As a cultural history of the law, this book will show how ideas about the self, reason, and emotion permeated the English courtroom in the eighteenth century and provoked a debate about the limits of the language of excuse. The language of the mind destabilized the definition and determination of *mens rea*, criminal intent, the basis of all criminal law. Although insanity had long been acknowledged as an excuse for crime, the language of emotion and excuse broadened this exculpatory category in unpredictable and uncontrollable ways. English legal culture struggled not only to contain and to direct the 'ungovernable passions' but also to define the integrated, controlled, and controllable self: what scholars would later call the modern subject.

Historiography

Setting out the questions of method and historiography that shape this study is less straightforward than one might think. Although questions of self, reason, sensibility, and responsibility were of fundamental importance to men and women in the eighteenth century, modern scholarship has not examined them together. Beyond the scholarship on crime and law out of which this study grew, I will survey work on the self, insanity pleas, and sensibility.

Recent studies of early modern English law have concluded that the criminal trial came at the end of a long, subtle process of selection in which jurors and judges, prosecutors and witnesses decided which accused offenders would be punished and how severely. In the eighteenth century England's 'bloody code,' which grew to prescribe the death penalty for over 200 offenses (from arson, murder, and riot to smuggling and poaching), served as the backdrop for every investigation of serious felony. These harsh criminal statutes created a judicial system in which mitigation was essential and could be applied at any time, from the discovery of the crime up to the moment of execution.[28]

As social historians have shown, the men who created and enforced England's harsh criminal statutes tempered their conceptions of justice, which translated into the threat of the death penalty, with mercy. As the need for mitigation increased in the eighteenth century, extenuating circumstances such as the defendant's gender, age, character, and reputation were critically important to the criminal legal process.[29] My study seeks to focus on the agency of defendants and the initiative they took in shaping their own fates. I do so by investigating the mechanisms of their intervention with an analysis of the words left to us in the legal records (however mediated) that survive.

Inspired by the approach taken by Davis in *Fiction in the Archives: Pardon Tales and Their Tellers in Sixteenth-Century France*, I argue that defendants, their families, and their communities exerted a significant and direct influence on the negotiation of mitigation and discuss how their strategies for mitigation functioned both culturally and legally. While Davis' sources were turned into tales by notaries, I consider to what extent depositions and trial transcripts reflect the words defendants spoke to the authorities, always keeping in sight the real context of the criminal trial and the high stakes borne by these narratives. This book analyzes the language of excuse in terms of its relationship to law and crime, gender and identity, self and responsibility. Firm conclusions about identity and self are difficult to make and the sources for a 'history from below' leave only suggestions of common people's perceptions of themselves. Nonetheless, in court people from all walks of life relied on skillful self-presentation. A study of the self screened by legal evidence reveals understandings of psychological motivation among ordinary people, popular and elite, as well as the strategies developed by the poor 'at an individual rather than a collective level' to negotiate the 'networks of authority that shaped their lives.'[30]

When we examine the history of the self in the West, the eighteenth century emerges as a unique period of contingency and instability in the history of the modern self.[31] During the seventeenth century the Christian doctrines of universal human depravity defined the self in terms of its sinful nature. Life was a struggle against sin that one could win only with divine grace.[32] By the mid-nineteenth century it has been argued that medicine and science essentialized the self by defining insanity, homosexuality, and criminality as pathologies that encompassed one's entire identity.[33] In the eighteenth century I will show that a window of opportunity existed when the self could be contingent: the displacement caused by emotion and passion was imagined as coexisting with a reasoned and moral self. The self was conceived with a flexibility that defined it as an ongoing project shaped by experience and developed throughout one's life without denying a central, continuous element.

In the 25 years since the publication of Michel Foucault's *Discipline and Punish: The Birth of the Prison*, the question of the relationship between power, culture, the state, and the self has engaged every discipline of the humanities and the social sciences. This book speaks directly to the questions raised by Foucault when he called the individual both 'the fictitious atom of an "ideological" representation of society' and 'a reality fabricated by this specific technology of power ... called discipline.'[34] This study examines the process by which the self, that representation of the individual, was created and deployed in the courtroom. What emerges is the story of the very success of the self as a fictitious, mutable legal entity and the state's response: the momentary consolidation of a unified subject. When the courts acknowledged the displaced self as less than perfectly accountable for its behavior, an alternative was sought in a person's subjectivity, upon which the state was empowered to exact corporeal punishment. Although the subjectivity was itself unstable, contested, and always in the process of being reconsolidated by uncoordinated, multidirectional forces, it was ultimately held accountable to legal mechanisms of mental and physical discipline and violence through the body.

The legal system depended on a true and coherent self that could be held responsible for its behavior and misbehavior. The *Oxford English Dictionary* defines the self as 'that which in a person is really and intrinsically he.' In their study of the self, Raymond Martin and John Barresi explain that ideas about sensational psychology developed during the seventeenth century began the eighteenth century 'revolution in personal identity theory.'[35] This cultural transformation radically changed definitions of the self by questioning the self's immortality, indivisibility, and immateriality. For the first time philosophers in the West posed the question about the continuity of self and its very existence. This discussion of the self, examined at greater length in chapter 3, had very important and concrete effects on the courtroom.

The one exception to the coherent self that the legal system recognized was the insanity plea, which became the cultural and legal basis of pleas of the mind. My book seeks to bridge the gap between popular, in the sense of lay, conceptions of mental illness and legal studies of the insanity plea.[36] Legal historians have demonstrated that while there were few pleas of insanity in criminal cases before 1740, the number of pleas rose in the last 60 years of the eighteenth century.[37] This phenomenon has been explained as the consequence of 'social structural changes brought about by the Industrial Revolution,'[38] a growing awareness of mental impairment and mental illness,[39] empire-building within the medical profession,[40] and the emergence of the disciplines of psychology and psychiatry.[41]

Chapter 2 examines the range of insanity defenses in the eighteenth century by including informal pleas that made a more or less direct comparison with insanity even though they did not meet the rather vague and often inconsistently applied 'standard of proof' for such a defense. Unlike earlier studies of the insanity plea, this is not a study of precedent and I do not restrict myself exclusively to 'obvious' insanity pleas. Like eighteenth-century defendants, in chapter 3, I broaden my focus to include mental states such as drunkenness, poverty, passion, and compulsion that did not qualify as legal insanity in any way.[42]

The language of the mind reflects the broader discussion of self, identity, and 'psychology' that permeated eighteenth-century English culture. Eighteenth-century ideas about the self were deeply inflected with the culture of sensibility and changing ideas about masculinity and emotion. The culture of sensibility urged both men and women to regard the emotional component of identity and the self as integral to every person. The culture of sensibility that emerged in contemporary literature and intellectual discussion construed sensibility, a special and admirable susceptibility to one's own feelings and the feelings of others, as a moral faculty that would preserve humanity from the forces of secularization, industrialization, and consumerism.[43]

In response to the true self assumed and demanded by the law, defendants invented a displaced self. This self was strategically consolidated by both court officials and 'criminals' in an attempt to explain aberrant behavior to themselves and to each other and to try to control the outcome of judicial process. But the vocabulary of the mind and the compassion it elicited in jurors exposed a contradiction in eighteenth century conceptions of the self, justice, and emotion. The ethos of sensibility implied a destabilized self. By definition the good, sensible self responded to passion with compassion. Applied consistently, this interpretation of sensibility connected those tempted to crime and those listening to their narratives of excuse in ways that undermined existing definitions of responsibility and the means of assigning accountability, namely the jury trial.

My analysis suggests that during the eighteenth century elite and popular culture alike posited a 'true' self, innately inclined toward the good, but displaced by experience and behavior. Writings about the self and the words of defendants both represented the true self as vulnerable to external manipulation. Criminal defendants and these authors accounted for unusual behavior in similar terms: by pointing to passions and mental distress – powerful forces beyond their rational control. Although this displacement might mask certain qualities and highlight others, it did not necessarily define one's entire identity.

By the end of the century finding the true self became the goal of legal interrogation, law reform, and criminal rehabilitation. The Hadfield case in 1800 marked the court's recognition of a contingent self; Parliament responded to the jury's verdict of 'Not guilty; he being under the influence of insanity at the time the act was committed'[44] with 'The Act for the Safe Custody of Insane Persons Charged with Offenses.'[45] In Hadfield's trial the self was acknowledged as circumstantial and mercurial, and the parameters of the legal subject were momentarily fixed and determined. In contrast to the psychological self, the modern subject was material, possessed of an embodied person whom the state could punish, confine, and (attempt to) rehabilitate. The invention of the modern subject redeemed the revered place of English law and consolidated an alliance between elite and middling men.

Sin, crime, and the self in the seventeenth century

What preceded the permeable, experiential self described by John Locke (1632–1704) in *An Essay Concerning Human Understanding* (1689), elaborated by scholars of the Scottish Enlightenment, and put into play in the eighteenth-century courtroom? In the seventeenth century we can see one prominent representation of the self in pamphlets that portrayed crime and deviance as signs of the inherent wickedness of human nature. This representation posited crime as the clear and predictable result of sins such as Sabbath-breaking, swearing, and drunkenness. These manifestations of evil exposed one's inherently depraved human nature while their detection and punishment revealed the hand of divine providence intervening to right these wrongs.[46] While the pamphlets mention various explanations for crime that traced its origins to poverty, a lack of parental guidance, or bad company, these factors are generally subordinated to or made a part of the narrative of sin.[47] In order to serve its didactic purpose, the genre allowed only stark lines between right and wrong, with the self described in Reformed Christian terms as weak and sinful.

For the authors of seventeenth-century murder pamphlets, the slippery slope from sin to crime generally began with Sabbath breaking and swearing and ended with murder and suicide. One author captured the sentiment when he traced crime to 'ambition, lust, covetousness, envy, murder, sloth, or any vice whereto he sees a man or a woman most inclined unto.'[48] Peter Lake has argued that in their portrayal of sin and crime writers appealed to a wide variety of readers – among them audiences who were not necessarily fervent Puritans. In their efforts to understand the ultimate crime of murder, these pamphlets sought the source of unlawful behavior and expounded on its broader implications for society by pointing to the seemingly less serious transgressions that fractured the social order and foreshadowed serious crimes.[49]

The well-born man who fell victim to his sensual appetites featured prominently in these pamphlets. *The Bloody Booke* (1606) recounted the story of John Fitz, the knighted son of a gentleman, whose 'careless' and 'desolate' life led to adultery, poverty, a 'dispersed and molested mind,' and finally murder.[50] According to the pamphlet's author, the sinful life of one of its most prominent citizens brought the town of Tavistocke, 'otherwise orderly governed with sobriety, and wisdome of grave magistrates,' into 'the corruption of drunkenness'[51] as Fitz presided over 'riotous surfettinge.' He harbored a wild and disorderly gang:

> beinge drunke they blaspheme and sweare, and in their blasphemy, they teare the divine name of their almighty creator into a thousand pieces, neither regardinge hope of redemption, or dreading feare of damnation, pluckinge men by night out of their beddes, violently breaking windowes, quarrelling with ale-conners, fighting in private brabbles amongst themselves.[52]

In case the threat to the social order posed by this outlawry might be lost on the reader, the author stated quite clearly that these men 'neither worshipping God nor honuringe prince' were 'wholye subjecte to theyr contents alone.'[53] As a prominent member of the community, Fitz neither fulfilled his obligations 'to benefite his country by being a profitable member of the common-weale' nor did he behave as 'a good subject, by observing the peaceable statutes of his prince.'[54] Fitz's failure to provide leadership, and his behavior as a negative role model, threatened the very existence of the social order by questioning every value of the early modern community.

In *The Unnatural Father*, John Taylor's account of John Rowse's murder of his two daughters in 1621, the author described the chain of sins with which 'Satan doth bind and manacle us.' Through these 'infernal fetters' one descended into sin and crime 'for sloth is linked with drunkenness,

drunkenness with fornication and adultery, and adultery with murder.'[55] Rowse's sins began with an adulterous affair with his maidservant, and quickly led to 'daily riot, excessive drinking, and unproportionable spending' that resulted in the loss of his estate, credit, and standing.[56] He explained that he murdered his two daughters 'because he was not able to keep them, and that he was loth they should go about the town a begging.'[57] Taylor signaled Rowse's criminal disposition and sinful nature with reference to drunkenness. At his trial Rowse confessed 'declaring the manner of his life, his odious drinking, his abominable whoring, his cruel murder and the false dealing of his deceitful friend, which was the cause of his final wreck.'[58]

As dangerous as the threat posed by the sins of prominent men, the disorder of those from more humble backgrounds also appeared in pamphlets. When Nathaniel Butler killed his fellow apprentice, John Knight, in 1657, the authors of *Heavens Cry Against Murder* attributed his crime to 'lewd and lascivious courses,' 'not being guided by good counsel, nor the spirit of God.'[59] The pamphlet blamed his master, 'not keeping him as Christian and religious masters ought to do their servants, within order, discipline, and obedience,' as well as Butler's 'loose and dissolute' character evidenced by his proclivity for 'drinking and gaming, the two infallible symptoms of destruction, especially to unbridled youth.'[60] The seriousness of Butler's sinful behavior and 'ungodly wayes' was evident in his imperviousness to 'all fears, obedience, and reverence.'[61] The pamphlet asserted that Butler's 'drinking and gaming' was not simply the idle diversion of youth, but a sign of his criminal nature. Whether committed by a man of substance like John Rowse or a youthful apprentice like Butler, drunkenness shook the social structure and was condemned equally in both instances. This representation of sin unified the view of social order and clearly defined the criminal threats to it.[62]

The serious ramifications of such sinful behavior justified the severe punishment of the crimes that followed with no room for mitigation or pardon.[63] This secular treatment at the hands of the law had religious sanction according to Puritan writers like Taylor who commented that 'by this man's fall, we may see an example of God's justice against drunkenness, whoredome, and murder.'[64] To corroborate this interpretation each of these seventeenth-century pamphlets discussed the perpetrator's disturbed state of mind as a prelude to the final crime or as its consequence. Impoverished and alone, John Rowse was 'much perplexed in his conscience.'[65] 'Tormented and tost with restless imaginations' he killed his two daughters.[66] The language of mental states is more pronounced in the case of John Fitz who 'flying into the sanctuary of a dispersed and molested mind, was amidst his quiet followed and affrighted, by the officers of vengeance, guilt, and terror.'[67] Witnesses remarked that he had 'a certain wild and stearne looke in his countenance,' and Fitz himself admitted before his final murderous act 'I am in minde troubled, I am disquieted.'[68] Nathaniel Butler's 'distracted, disturbed and disquieted' soul prompted his immediate confession after the murder of John Knight.[69] These descriptions of criminal minds did not offer insanity as an excuse or an explanation. Rather the perpetrator's guilt about past sinful and criminal behavior disturbed the mind and led to more crime followed by confession and repentance. This depiction of insanity as an effect of sin reinforced the message about the dangers of sin, its inevitable link to crime, and the absolute necessity of the ultimate punishment, death.

In light of this portrayal of human nature as sinful and ever-susceptible to temptation, the belief in providence could serve to offset the weak and depraved self. Seventeenth-century writers left a variety of sources in which they traced the hand of providence. In her study of the topic Alexandra Walsham shows that cautionary tales, borrowed from a wide variety of texts including ancient authors, Italian humanists, and various Lutheran scholars, filled pamphlets and books. A famous example, Thomas Beard's *The Theatre of God's Judgements* (editions, in 1597, 1612, 1631) recorded the sins and crimes of the poor and the wealthy alike. These narratives meticulously retold the details of the crime as well as the violent, divine, and providential punishment suffered by its perpetrators.[70] Recording the hand of providence provided a semblance of control and reminded everyone of the moral code and the risks for its violators without questioning the idea of a depraved and irredeemable self.[71]

Religious leaders encouraged their congregants to track providence in their own lives. Nehemiah Wallington (1598–1658) Ralph Josselin (1618–1683), Lucy Hutchison (1620?–1680), Oliver Heywood (1630–1702), and Ralph Thoresby (1658–1725) – among others – kept copious notes and diaries in which they recorded the details of their experiences, interactions, thoughts, feelings, and beliefs as testimony of their spiritual journey and the intervention of providence.[72] These diaries often mentioned the providential discovery of crime. In 1630, when Wallington found that his journeyman, Roberts, had pilfered from the business for two years, he celebrated God's 'great mercy ... in bringing this to light' and prayed that God would 'restore unto me double and if it be for my glory and good.'[73] When his son's shop was robbed in 1669, Ralph Josselin noted that he 'providentially heard of them [the thieves] and pursued.'[74] With the thieves apprehended, Josselin happily remarked 'blessing mine this day, those that robbed us were first found,' and when the goods were returned, he pronounced 'god alone have the glory.'[75]

But even the most valiant in faith were sometimes led to doubt the workings of providence when facing personal tragedy. Wallington's introspection offered him little comfort when his children died. Upon the death of his daughter Elizabeth in 1625, Nehemiah wrote that he 'was beside himself with grief.' As he confessed, he '"forgot himself" so much that he broke all his "purposes, promises, and covenants" with God and refused all comfort from men.'[76] Despite his wife's reprimand ('husband, I am persuaded you offend God in grieving for this child so much'), the pious response to such hardship and suffering, as defined in Puritan doctrine by prayer and acceptance, did not always provide Wallington with sufficient resolution or consolation.[77] Ralph Josselin usually responded to the tragedies in his life with acceptance and submission, but when his friend Mary Church died in 1650, he too expressed anguish and doubt.

> When Mrs Mary dyed, my heart trembled, and was perplexed in the dealings of the lord so sadly with us, and desiring God not to proceed on against us with his darts and arrows; looking backe into my wayes, and observing why God hath thus dealt with me.[78]

Even among the godly, providentialism did not always offer solace or a satisfying explanation for tragic events.

The growth of introspection encouraged by diary-keeping may have caused some to supplement their religious search for divine intervention with self-examination that allowed for the possibility that the self might grow, change, and improve. At the end of the seventeenth century one sees tremendous interest in the individual conscience and new ways of approaching age-old issues of character, self, and responsibility. The concern about human motivation and accountability unfolded in popular journals such as *The Athenian Mercury*, edited by John Dunton (1659–1733). Published between 1690 and 1697, this periodical featured letters composed and answered by its editors, among them Daniel Defoe (1660–1731). Dunton's original periodical was so popular that a three-volume collection, the *Athenian Oracle*, was reprinted in 1704.[79]

The genre of autobiography, philosophical treatises on self, the interest in casuistry, along with the scientific revolution, and the enlightenment all suggest the development of new means of understanding the self.[80]

These alternatives to providentialism developed slowly and often featured the language of the mind but they did not efface a Christian understanding of the world or the belief in providence.[81] While these discussions raised new questions, they coexisted with the narrative of sin as an explanation of the causes of crime.

Both discourses appeared in eighteenth-century accounts by the Ordinary of Newgate which presented sin (in this case drunkenness) along with a psychological explanation for its criminal consequences. When speaking of convicted felons in 1744, James Guthrie pointed to the 'pernicious practice of drinking spiritous liquors which made them seem as if possessed with evil spirits.'[82] The chain of sin remained a common referent, 'for a habit of drinking naturally begets a habit of keeping ill company and this begets all the other ill habits.'[83] However, the Ordinary's accounts also incorporated a language of mental states. Thomas Clements, convicted of the murder of William Warner in 1739, 'lived well and kept a good house, was very honest in his dealings for which he had a good character' until he became 'mightily addicted to drinking.' His violent outbursts ended with the murder of Warner, his employee with whom he was in 'good friendship.' The account explained that Clements 'cared not what he did when he was in liquor, but behaved like a madman, and one out of his senses': his aforementioned 'good character' replaced with a reputation as 'a very irregular man, and unaccountable in many of his actions.' Clements died 'hoping in the mercy of God through Christ.' While he denied 'premeditated design' he was 'sincerely penitent for all the sins of his life.'[84] The concurrence of the two discourses is not surprising given that cultural change is rarely a neat and formulated process by which one mode of explanation immediately and completely replaces another. Instead specific discourses develop to serve distinct purposes and together explicate various aspects of the same phenomenon, in this case crime.[85]

What impact did this introspective, contingent self have on the courtroom and the jury's decision making? Cynthia Herrup's work on law and morality in the seventeenth century provides some insight about the use of legal discretion in the period prior to 1660. Herrup asserts that the religious doctrine of universal human depravity became a lens through which life could be viewed as an endless struggle against vice. In the eyes of the 'godly magistrates' the lawbreaker could be seen as an ill-disciplined sinner rather than a hardened criminal. The search for intent, therefore, became the focus of law enforcers in their assessment of criminal behavior. While all offenders had lost a battle to temptation, real criminals had abandoned even the quest for self-discipline. Neighbors were considered most qualified to evaluate the true nature of the defendant because they could place the offense in the context of the rest of the defendant's life and because they themselves were engaged in a similar struggle against sin.[86]

Although such views continued to be espoused by moral and religious leaders in the eighteenth century, the emphasis within religious discourse incorporated a different set of themes influenced by the age of sensibility and the Methodist movement, both concerned with a search for virtue and the enactment of a Christian vision of morality. These new emphases affected both what offenders said and the application of discretion within the legal system. Defendants appealed to both seventeenth- and eighteenth-century discourses about crime. While they called on ideas about universal human depravity, a common propensity for sin, and the slippery slope from lesser sins to greater crimes, they sought mitigation by portraying their crimes as momentary indiscretions brought on by their mental states rather than signs of a deeper criminal nature that would seriously threaten law and order. The paradigm used to negotiate mitigation shifted during the eighteenth century. A discourse of character and circumstance, influenced by theories of sensational psychology, supplemented that of the universal sinner in search of redemption and forgiveness. The language of excuse created a new landscape of emotion and sensibility that shaped the ways judges and jurors heard and reacted to the language of the mind in 'psychological' pleas.

These discussions of the capacity for responsibility in the courtroom had implications for the larger political narrative. As Britain re-imagined itself, its statehood, and its imperial aspirations in the years between the Glorious Revolution and the French Revolution, public discourse took up questions about the rights and liberties of subjects, the distinctions between estates within the polity, and who exactly should be consulted by the newly circumscribed monarchy and the newly empowered Parliament. Implicitly and explicitly the concept of responsibility was at the center of these discussions which contested definitions of self, gender, race, class, and Britishness. The eighteenth-century criminal court became one of the sites where these debates took place. I show how the cultural exchanges in the criminal trial reconfigured the boundaries between sanity and insanity; masculinity and femininity; aristocracy, middling men, and the working classes to create the modern subject.

Chapter outline

This book demonstrates how participants in England's legal system marshaled definitions of self and sensibility to supplement the narrative of sin with psychological explanations for human behavior. The contingent self constructed in the eighteenth century destabilized the process of determining *mens rea*. By the end of the eighteenth century the legal system responded by consolidating the modern subject whose self might be displaced but whose body could always be held responsible.

Chapter 2 sets out the legal and cultural mechanisms that facilitated the expansion of the language of the mind in the eighteenth-century courtroom and surveys the types of pleas of mental distress that drew most closely on insanity. Several legal developments during the eighteenth century affected the dynamics of the trial, the presentation of evidence, and the trials' possible outcomes. The cases demonstrate the efforts of defendants to fashion pleas of diminished responsibility based on lay perceptions of mental distress. This version of madness differed significantly from exculpatory insanity as defined by the law and in legal commentary. Chapter 2 concludes with a section based on the writings of legal observers who commented on the abundance of the language of mental excuse and speculated on its possible impact on judicial outcomes.

Chapter 3 surveys definitions of the self and sensibility that circulated in the eighteenth century and sets them beside pleas of drunkenness, necessity, passion, and compulsion introduced in court. In these cases defendants and witnesses employed the language of excuse to stretch the boundaries of the insanity defense far beyond any legal definition. Although these excuses were not new to the eighteenth century, they resonated with the vocabulary of sensibility, melancholy, and nervous disorder so common in novels, philosophical tracts, and the popular press.

Chapter 4 correlates the language of the mind that resonated in the English courtroom throughout the eighteenth century with jury verdicts in cases of infanticide to illustrate evolving definitions of the crime and its perpetrator and the changing relationship between crime and the emotions. Unmarried women made up the overwhelming majority of defendants accused of infanticide in early modern England. Although at the start of the eighteenth century their pleas of insanity rarely led to a verdict of not guilty, by 1800 most of the single women accused of infanticide who used pleas of diminished responsibility won an acquittal. These pleas of emotional distress are significant because they were exceptions to the popular, formulaic, and typically successful 'preparation defense' in which women cited the provisions they had made for the child during pregnancy as evidence of their intentions to nurture the baby after its birth. This exceptional testimony shows the growing preoccupation of defendants, prosecutors, judges, and jurors with states of mind and the emotional causes of crime. These trials defined the laboring single woman as temporarily insane, her moral self occluded by the pressures of pregnancy out of wedlock, and accepted infanticide as an almost inevitable, decriminalized response to her situation.

I delve more deeply into the reception of psychological pleas by judges, jurors, and legal reformers in chapter 5. The language of mental excuse complicated the relationship between states of mind and legal responsibility. While legal authorities were interested in the offender's state of mind and may have even encouraged testimony about it as a sorting mechanism of mitigation, they rejected the unbounded emotion that they associated with women and with poor male heads of households. The reception of the language of psychological excuse contributed to a discourse of masculinity that defined the rational man as one who did not deny his feelings but always controlled them and revealed the cultural anxiety surrounding sensibility and justice.

Drawing on a wide range of sources, including pardons, the writings of courtroom observers, treatises by legal reformers, and proposals for solitary confinement, chapter 5 reconstructs reactions to the pleas of mental distress. It is clear that this language of the mind concerned legal commentators and reformers deeply because its admission in court widened the disjuncture between legal prescription and legal practice and led to erratic, unpredictable mitigation. Legal reformers in the late eighteenth century worried about the capricious nature of mitigation in the face of England's 'bloody code'. Some advocated strict enforcement of existing laws while others urged a reduction in the number of capital statutes to make mitigation unnecessary. All reformers on both sides of the issue believed that the solution lay in systematic, standardized, 'certain punishment'.

The case of James Hadfield (1800), the subject of chapter 6, provides a logical conclusion to my study. Eighteenth-century concerns with emotion, sensibility, and states of mind surveyed in chapters 2, 3, 4, and 5 ushered in Hadfield's acquittal and the eventual acceptance of the official insanity defense in 1843 with the M'Naughten Rules. But rather than decriminalizing behavior or creating an easy way for defendants to avoid criminal prosecution, the passage of the 'Act for the Safe Custody of Insane Persons Charged with Offenses' (1800) and the promulgation of the M'Naughten Rules (1843) reduced the number of pleas that defendants could introduce in court, circumscribed the language that could be used to describe mental states, and dictated harsher punishments for those *acquitted* as insane. Historians have associated the anxiety provoked by Hadfield's acquittal for attempted regicide with fears of political instability posed by the popularity of republican ideas in the wake of the French Revolution. This chapter places the arguments made by both the prosecution and the defense in Hadfield's case within the context of the language of excuse so common in the eighteenth-century courtroom and casts the 'Act for the Safe Custody of Insane Persons Charged with Offenses' as a legislative attempt to contain this perceived threat to the definition of *mens rea*.

The thematic outline above parallels a chronological one. The legal mechanisms described in chapter 2 that created space in the legal process for the expansion of pleas of mental excuse date to the 1690s and the first three decades of the eighteenth century. The spread of the culture of sensibility and the rise of Methodism during the 1740s preceded an increase in the frequency of insanity defenses between 1755 and 1769 documented by Nigel Walker. Chapters 2, 3, and 4 connect these two phenomena and explicate the psychological pleas of the mid-eighteenth century. The reception of the language of excuse by legal authorities and reformers in the second half of the eighteenth century is the subject of chapter 5. Although some observers and commentators embraced the language of sensibility and wished to integrate those values into their agenda for legal reform, others favored the restraint of compassion, especially in courts of law. The discussion continued throughout the latter portion of the eighteenth century. Hadfield's trial in 1800, set within the context of these developments as well as *OBSP* trials from the 1780s and the 1790s in which a defendant or lawyer submitted an 'obvious' insanity defense, represents the legal system's attempt to curtail the effects of the language of mental excuse while acknowledging the displaced self.

Along with a limited acceptance of the psychological means of understanding human behavior, the end of the eighteenth century saw a backlash against what was considered its abuse. The Hadfield case and the legislation that followed heralded medicalized and criminalized descriptions of defendants as pathological that could be articulated in court only by lawyers or doctors. The external forces that created the legal subject displaced the permeable language of the eighteenth century that allowed defendants and others who spoke on their behalf to broaden the category of exculpatory mental states and to define these states as temporary and unrelated to the defendant's true self.

2

'Of the Persons Capable of Committing Crimes': Pleas of Mental Distress in the Eighteenth-Century Courtroom

When Lawrence Shirley, Earl Ferrers (1720–1760), stood accused of the brutal murder of his steward, John Johnson, on April 16, 1760, he pleaded his innocence by reason of insanity. At his state trial Ferrers told his peers in the House of Lords that he suffered from occasional insanity, that he had experienced an episode during the murder, and that 'at the time I did not know what I was about.'[1] Writing the summation of his own defense, Ferrers asserted, 'I had no preconceived malice; and was hurried into the perpetration of this fatal deed by the fury of a disordered imagination.'[2] At the time Sir Horace Mann (1701–1786) observed that Ferrers 'had a species of madness in his constitution, which occasionally broke out as his passions were put in motion and entirely depended on them,' while Horace Walpole (1717–1797) commented that 'there was a madness in Ferrers but not the pardonable sort.'[3]

In his plea, at what can only be called an extraordinary legal event, Ferrers harnessed the language of excuse found in ordinary felony cases tried at the Northern Circuit assizes and at London's Old Bailey during the eighteenth century. Before delving into any case studies or the analysis of the words of defendants, however, it is essential to understand the legal mechanisms that made the language of mental excuse more audible in the middle of the eighteenth century. In the first part of this chapter I examine the place of law in eighteenth-century English society, describe the stages of the judicial trial, and give a brief overview of the history of the insanity defense in English law. Part II of the chapter will present a range of mental defenses found in the legal record and the versions of the self they articulated. Though far from qualifying as legitimate insanity defenses in the eyes of the law, the mental excuses cited in these cases make explicit analogy to insanity in their attempts to convince the judge and jury of the offender's diminished responsibility for the crime. The chapter concludes with a survey of the comments of legal authorities who noted the abundance of the language of mental excuse and debated its possible impact on judicial outcomes and on the legal system.

I Legal mechanisms

The law and popular culture

During the seventeenth and eighteenth centuries strict laws, harsh punishments, and flexible enforcement characterized the English criminal process. The lack of an organized police force meant that many defendants had been caught red-handed by their victims; trials often focused on the degree of an offender's accountability rather than strict questions of guilt or innocence. Several legal developments during the eighteenth century affected the dynamics of the trial, the presentation of evidence, and the trial's possible outcome. These developments changed the trial's configuration and shaped the cultural production of the language of mental and emotional excuse during the eighteenth century.

Legal sources and popular pamphlet literature reflect a distinctive characteristic of eighteenth-century English popular culture: its powerful identification with the law.[4] The strength of the ideology of law enabled some and compelled others to recognize England's legal institutions and to participate in the legal process. The administration of the legal system depended on the involvement of local men, drawn from the gentry and the middling ranks, who served as sheriffs, constables, coroners, and justices of the peace; these same men sat on grand juries and on trial juries. The most widespread form of participation had no property or income requirement: the legal system was accusatory and depended on victims and witnesses to initiate judicial action, to provide testimony, and to gather evidence.[5]

Hence the law was not a distant institution with which ordinary folk had little contact. Most English men and women from the ranks of the gentry, the middling sort, and laboring families saw the courts as an effective way to settle disputes, protect their property, remove someone from their community, or reintegrate someone who had transgressed. Conversant with legal practice and legal process, common people in England attended the proceedings at assize courts (which included an assize sermon), watched executions, read or listened to crime pamphlets, and went and were taken to court.[6]

Although the English identification with the law signaled certain values shared by both rulers and ruled, the familiarity of the common people with the legal process and their participation in it did not mean that they interpreted the law in accord with one set of elite values and interests. The law was a site of struggle in which participants from different social backgrounds actively contested vying conceptions of right and custom. Devising their own legal formulations, common people, both men and women, went to law to further their own interests and preserve what they considered any encroachment on their rights.[7]

In the specific topic considered here conversance with the legal process allowed defendants and witnesses on their behalf to appeal to the English legal tradition which had recognized insanity as an exculpatory state of mind since the Middle Ages.[8] In theory the test for insanity sought to determine whether the defendant had the 'will to harm,' and if he or she could distinguish good from evil. The earliest records reveal that juries usually found an insane defendant guilty and then recommended a royal pardon.[9] In the thirteenth century *The Laws and Customs of England* recommended that jurors acquit an insane defendant because 'a crime is not committed unless the intention to injure exists. It is will and purpose which mark malice.'[10] Matthew Hale (1609–1676) described 'ideocy, madness, and lunacy' as mental states that might excuse a person from punishment. If

> totally deprived of the use of reason, they cannot be guilty ordinarily of capital offenses, for they have not the use or understanding, and act not as reasonable creatures, but their actions are in effect in the condition of brutes.[11]

William Blackstone (1723–1780) restated this when he said: 'As a vicious will without a vicious act is no civil crime, so, on the other hand an unwarrantable act without a vicious will is no crime at all.'[12] The question of intent defined insanity as exculpatory.

Generally, the victims of a misdemeanor or a lesser felony perpetrated by a lunatic chose to settle the matter privately with the family or informally in the office of the justice of the peace. In the event of a serious felony that involved the loss of substantial property, a physical assault, or death, the accused would proceed through the official channels of the judicial system. Such cases might make it as far as the grand jury, but they were usually dismissed when the defendant was found *non compos mentis.* In some particularly violent crimes such as patricide, matricide, or infanticide the case went to a trial jury. If found insane, the prisoner was acquitted and remanded to the custody of his family or incarcerated in the county jail.[13]

The place of mitigation

The disjuncture between the 'bloody code' and its constant and irregular mitigation defined the English criminal legal system in the eighteenth century.[14] Men of middling status, in their capacity as sheriffs, constables, and petty jurors, strove to reconcile the importance they placed on the protection of property with an understanding of the mitigating factors that could compel a person to commit a criminal act.[15] In the absence of a standing army or an organized, state-subsidized police force the ideology of the rule of law became the embodiment and the guarantor of English social order. Those among the ranks of the aristocracy, the gentry, and the middling sorts shared a political and religious belief in the authority of the law and abided by its constraints because their own need for the rule of law compelled them to do so.[16]

England's accusatory legal system depended on victims and witnesses to initiate judicial action, and constant negotiation shaped the decision to prosecute, the gathering of evidence, the testimony given, the judge and the jury's reception of the information at trial, and the judge's decision to recommend for or against a royal pardon. Did defendants have any agency in this process? The extent of defendant initiative is a subject of Peter King's comprehensive study of *Crime, Justice and Discretion in England, 1740–1820.* King shows that defendants and their families introduced evidence about extenuating circumstances and details particular to their situation as an appeal for a reduced sentence or an acquittal.

Within the study of the negotiation of mitigation I seek to explore further the scope of defendant agency, trace the cultural forces that shaped it, and assess its impact on the legal system. I argue that during the eighteenth century these traditional excuses were enriched by a vocabulary of mental incapacity that sought mitigation on the grounds that the defendant was not fully responsible when the crime was committed. This language of excuse was predicated on an admission of guilt, and it often attributed the crime to thoughts, emotions, or passions that overwhelmed the offender's capacity for reason and self-control. Placing defendants in the mitigation process demonstrates how they shaped their own fates as best they could within the legal system.

Obviously, claims of defendant initiative are complicated. I do not dispute the fact that English elite values and agendas dominated the legal system or that the assizes were a deliberately formal, intimidating, and effective display of the majesty, authority, and power of the governing classes. But patrician power does not imply plebian passivity. The evidence reflects a complex interplay between popular and elite culture in which each side was shaped by developments in the other and by their contact with each other. The interactions between popular and elite culture must be charted according to the nuances and subtleties that informed the relationship.[17]

The language of diminished responsibility was not new in the eighteenth century, but as the century progressed, its meanings evolved in response to changing attitudes toward the self, emotion, and responsibility. Prompted by the importance of mitigation, authorities may have unintentionally promoted the development of these informal defenses that broke open the narrow definition of legal insanity. At times they may have encouraged the elaboration of claims in the nature of pleas of insanity as one means of excusing or explaining certain crimes as moral aberrations. This implicit collaboration between the accused and some legal authorities did not necessarily render an acquittal or a mitigated verdict. Judge and juror response is impossible to reconstruct and difficult to gauge; nevertheless, a close examination of the structure of the eighteenth-century trial provides glimpses of the inconsistent, unpredictable, and unarticulated alliances that developed in the courtroom.

The dynamics of the legal process

England's accusatory legal system left victims of crime with a range of options about how to respond. They could choose to ignore the crime, deal with it informally by warning the offender privately, or negotiate an unofficial settlement with the perpetrator. The costs of prosecution and the severe penalties inflicted on those convicted of felony discouraged some victims from pressing charges, while others were dissuaded by threats from the accused.[18]

Despite the disincentives, the victim or his other representatives might decide to report the crime to a magistrate. These complaints sometimes served as a warning to offenders by prosecutors who withdrew the complaint when they felt it had served its purpose. In the case of a misdemeanor or a lesser felony, the justice of the peace could mediate an informal settlement between the parties, exercise his power of summary jurisdiction to settle the case out of court, or treat the crime as a lesser offense and send the offender to the quarter sessions rather than the assizes.[19] Although several means of encouraging prosecution in property crimes developed in the eighteenth century, victims retained control over the pre-trial process and could choose the level at which to pursue charges against the accused.[20]

Once alerted to a crime, 2&3 Philip and Mary c. 10 (1555) charged the justice of the peace to take the examination of prisoners suspected of manslaughter or felony, as well as those of witnesses and victims. These investigations, recorded 'in writing, within two days after the said examination,'[21] produced depositions. The statute of 1555 empowered the justices of the peace 'to bind all such by recognizance or obligation, as do declare anything material to prove the said manslaughter or felony, against such prisoner.'[22] The recognizance ordered examinants

> to appear at the next gaol delivery ... where the trial of the said manslaughter or felony shall be, then and there to give evidence against the party.[23]

With the investigation complete, the magistrates sent the depositions to the clerk of the assize who prepared a draft indictment, known as a bill, on behalf of the prosecutor. Although a justice of the peace might grant bail for misdemeanants, those suspected of felony were jailed.[24]

The accused had very few rights at the beginning of our period. The presumption of innocence, so familiar to us today, did not serve as the guiding principle in legal investigations. Barred from attending the magistrate's examination of the victim or other witnesses, suspects had no way of knowing what evidence substantiated the case against them. The trial was supposed to be the first time that the accused would be confronted with the evidence against her; her reaction was to serve as the test of her innocence.[25] Throughout the eighteenth century, however, the rights of the accused expanded. Suspects gained the advice of a lawyer during the deposition process, admission to the examination of their accusers, and the right to cross-examine the victim as she gave her deposition.[26] By the end of the eighteenth century, the magistrate's preliminary enquiry became a public hearing at which each side presented its evidence to the justice of the peace who decided whether or not the case should proceed to trial.[27]

In cases of murder the process of investigation probably proceeded somewhat more systematically than for other felonies with magistrates taking an active role in the inquiry.[28] Cases of felonious, accidental, and sudden deaths involved the coroner and his jury in addition to the justice of the peace. The coroner's jury examined the body and interviewed the person who found it, along with any other witnesses and the relatives of the deceased. The jury's guilty verdict functioned as another indictment on which the accused could be arraigned for homicide.[29]

Accusation, investigation, and indictment characterized the pre-trial phase of the legal process. Those accused of felonies remained in jail awaiting the arrival of judges dispatched from Westminster who rode the assize circuits twice a year presiding over civil and criminal trials and 'delivering the gaols.' The two-day assize session took place at a rapid pace: the large caseload translated into short trials held in quick succession. Business began at seven o'clock in the morning and sometimes continued by candlelight until eleven o'clock at night.[30] The Old Bailey took the place of the assizes in the capital. The central criminal court met eight times a year to handle cases of serious crime in London and the county of Middlesex.[31]

The grand jurors, a group of between 13 and 23 substantial freeholders, assigned the task of 'finding indictments,' heard Crown evidence and decided whether or not the Crown had a case.[32] An indictment, marked 'true' bill, '*billa vera*', indicated that they found probable cause, and the case proceeded to a trial jury. Bills marked '*ignoramus*' or 'not found,' resulted in the prisoner's release.[33]

After the grand jury ruled on the bills, the prisoners were brought into court in chains. One by one they heard their indictments read to them in English and submitted a plea.[34] Those prisoners who 'put themselves on the country' had their chains removed and proceeded to trial.[35] Following the arraignment of a group of prisoners, usually a half dozen, a trial jury was sworn and charged.[36] Although prisoners had the right to challenge individual jurors, they seldom did so. Each juror received a list of the prisoners' names and the charges against them.

The early modern English trial, as described by Sir Thomas Smith in *De Republica Anglorum* (1562) and in the anonymous tract, *Clerk of the Assize* (1682), posed the prosecution's retelling of the crime against the defendant's excuse.[37] The crier introduced the proceedings by asking those present in the courtroom if 'any one can give any evidence, or can saie any thing against the prisoner.'[38] If no one stepped forward, the judge called on the justice of the peace who had examined the prisoner to open the prosecution's case. 'He [the justice of the peace], if he be there, delivereth up the examination which he tooke of him, and underneath the names of those whom he hath bound to give evidence.'[39] The high rate of absenteeism among justices of the peace at the assizes meant that the clerical establishment in consultation with the presiding judge usually presented the prosecution's materials.[40]

Each of the prosecution's witnesses subsequently gave the court sworn oral testimony about the crime:

> Then is heard (if he be there) the man robbed what he can say, being first sworne to say trueth, and after the constable, and as many as

were at the apprehension of the malefactor: and so many as can say anything being sworn after an other to say truth.[41]

The clerk of the assize coordinated the prosecution's case. He kept track of all the depositions as the trial proceeded and:

> he looketh out every examination of every prisoner as his cause is in hearing, and if it be evidence for the king, he readeth it to the jury; and likewise the information, if the evidence for the king falter in his testimony to refresh his memory.[42]

Although oral testimony supposedly superseded written examination, this quotation suggests that the clerk of the assize would 'correct' for any second thoughts or discrepancies in witness testimony. Throughout these proceedings, the judge, the jurors, and the crown counsel might interrupt with questions.

When the prosecution completed its presentation, the accused responded to the charges against him or her with the support of witnesses, who until 1702 gave unsworn testimony. The accused faced intense pressure to construct a convincing defense with very little time to prepare and absolutely no knowledge of the evidence that would be brought against him/her in this intimidating and unfamiliar setting. Until the 1730s defendants could not call on legal representation. A prisoner's unmediated, unsworn response to the charges was considered the strongest defense.[43] To compensate for any disparity in power and knowledge between the prosecution and the defense, the judge was supposed to act as the prisoner's advocate. In complicated cases he could also assign the accused counsel for advice in matters of law.[44] Smith portrayed the trial as an 'altercation' between the two sides until the judge 'hath heard them say inough.'[45] In this format, dubbed by John Langbein the 'accused speaks' trial, the proceedings generally lasted between twenty and thirty minutes. The structure of the 'accused speaks' trial required the defendant to respond to the evidence against him, in person, without the aid of a lawyer. It compelled the accused to 'serve as an informational resource at trial.'[46] Given the structure of the altercation trial, it should not surprise us that defendants developed a language of mental excuse.

In the 'accused speaks' trial the judge constituted an important presence, intervening and questioning the victim, the accused, and any other witnesses and often interjecting comments and thinly veiled opinions. The judge directed every aspect of the trial: he controlled the flow of evidence, advised the jurors on how to weigh it, pointed out its strengths and weaknesses, and shaped the way the jury interpreted it.[47] The conversational nature of the trial and the exchange of questions and observations between the judge and jury gave the judge an informed sense of the jury's opinion of the evidence.[48] While some judges dispensed with summation or any detailed instructions to the jury, others charged the jury very specifically. In his journal, François de la Rochefoucauld (1765–1848) described the end of a trial at the Suffolk assizes in 1784:

> When the judge finds that the evidence is sufficient, or that he has extracted everything that the witnesses and the accused can say, he rises and reads aloud to the petty jurymen his notes on the trial, expounds the law, indicates the most serious points, and gives the reasons for his opinion.[49]

Although the legal scholarship has rendered varying interpretations of the role of the judge, the dynamic of the early eighteenth-century trial, staffed so predominantly by amateurs, must have weighed heavily the opinion of the paid, professional, and learned judge.[50]

The jury's deliberation followed this 'brief contest of stories.'[51] Prior to the eighteenth century the jurors did not necessarily sit together in the courtroom; they adjourned to consider all the verdicts from a group of arraigned prisoners with no written aids except a list of defendants.[52] By the beginning of the eighteenth century juries began to pronounce their verdicts at the end of each case; this new practice eliminated the need for the jury to leave the courtroom for its deliberation. Instead, the jurors huddled together and conferred in their seats. For the first time the jury sat together; its deliberations took place in the noisy crowded courtroom, in close proximity to the prisoner, the victim, and the spectators.[53] With the large number of cases heard by each jury (sometimes up to 12) and the fast pace of the trials, the jurors who served at the assizes quickly became well versed in their duties; those lacking experience deferred to the judge and the foreman. As the eighteenth century progressed, it became more difficult to find trial jurors and many served on more than one jury at an assize session; these jurors quickly gained experience and confidence.[54]

Jurors used their discretionary powers to mitigate the harshness of the law and to apply it with selective rigor or leniency.[55] Property offenses constituted the majority of the cases that filled the assize calendar: the theft of goods valued at a shilling or more was grand larceny and a capital felony, while thefts under a shilling were petty larceny and non-capital.[56] Through 'pious perjury' juries often undervalued the goods stolen and reduced the offense from a capital to a non-capital offense.[57] In addition to the under-valuation of goods, jurors could bring in a 'partial verdict' that acquitted the prisoner of the indicted offense but convicted him of a less serious crime. Jurors often reached such partial verdicts in cases of violent physical assault such as murder. By reducing a charge of homicide to manslaughter, a non-capital offense, juries avoided the imposition of the death penalty.[58] Finally, jurors mitigated on the basis of an assessment of a myriad of characteristics specific to each defendant, such as age, sex, rank, standing in the community, good neighborliness, and respectability. Among these mitigating factors, the nature of the offense played an especially important role in the jurors' decisions about the excusable nature of the crime.[59]

During their brief deliberations jurors offset their allegiance to the political elite, the protectors of property who legislated the 'bloody code,' and their membership in their local community with its particular notions of acceptable or forgivable behavior. Jurors applied a flexible standard of proof which allowed them to assess the defendant's crime in the context of his or her general character.[60] They might raise the standard of proof to justify an acquittal on the grounds of insufficient evidence instead of on merciful grounds alone. Under the guise of the standard of proof, jurors could balance competing ideas about the enforcement of the law, the death penalty, and the specific character of each defendant.[61]

Peter King's work has demonstrated a consistent pattern of verdicts between 1740 and 1820. According to King at least a third and sometimes nearly half the accused in Essex and elsewhere were discharged either by the grand jury or the petty jury and 10 percent of cases ended with a partial verdict.[62] After the pronouncement of the verdicts, jurors often explained their decisions either voluntarily or at the behest of the judge.[63]

Eighteenth-century jurors were of middling status, middle-aged, and literate. Many had experience as parish office holders and many served as jurors repeatedly or even regularly. Their familiarity with the trial and the process of deliberation may have decreased their reliance on the judge's opinion, but it did not increase the tension between judges and jurors. King concludes that juries exercised a degree of independence from judges and that their verdicts often leaned toward a more merciful outcome for the accused. While some judges left a record of their disputes with juries and their insistence on a reassessment of the evidence, the vast majority of cases does not reveal any discussion, let alone disagreement.[64] King concludes that 'judicial authorities may have had to accept the jurors' standards and attitudes, including their more merciful approach to capital cases involving theft without violence.'[65] In most trials the verdict reflected a compromise between the different classes, values, and interests of those who observed and participated and attempted to affect the trial's outcome.

Despite the scholarship that has attempted to quantify and elucidate the factors that a jury considered in its deliberations and how those related to the verdicts rendered, it is important to remember that 'it is impossible to be certain why some accused were acquitted, others convicted of the charge in the indictment, still others of a lesser charge and then either clergied or whipped.'[66] With this caveat in mind, this study will shift the focus away from a purely quantitative methodology that emphasizes verdicts to bring into focus other interactions in the courtroom.

Allocutus, the next phase of the trial, allowed the convicted prisoners a chance to declare anything that could prevent their punishment.[67] During the sentencing that followed, the judge could exercise his discretionary power to grant a reprieve to a convicted felon and to recommend him for a royal pardon.[68] A judge might reprieve a prisoner if he

> is not satisfied with the verdict, or the evidence is suspicious, or the indictment is insufficient, or he is doubtful whether the offense be within clergy, or sometimes if it be a small felony, or any favourable circumstances appear in the criminal's character, in order to give room to apply to the crown for either an absolute or a conditional pardon.[69]

If a judge did not grant an immediate reprieve, a prisoner could petition the king for an individual pardon or for inclusion in the judge's general pardon, called a 'circuit pardon' or 'circuit letter.' Once reprieved, the prisoner remained in jail and returned to court at a later session to plead to the pardon when it had been issued under the Great Seal.[70]

A free pardon was absolute and comparable to an acquittal, but most pardons issued after 1660 were granted on condition that the prisoner suffered an alternative, non-capital punishment such as detention in a house of correction, payment of a fine, or transportation to the American colonies for a term of 7 or 14 years.[71] Judges often cited extenuating circumstances to justify pardons; these mitigating factors could pertain to the crime (i.e. that the offense was unattended by violence, that the prisoner had not used a weapon, that the defendant was unarmed, that he had returned the stolen object to its owner) or to the criminal (i.e. the prisoner's age, virtuous character, or good reputation).[72] The specific nature of pardons and their relation to the pleas of mental distress is the subject of chapter 5.

Throughout the eighteenth century the 'accused speaks' trial, reconstructed in this somewhat static description, underwent important changes that altered the momentum of events in the courtroom and the power dynamics among the participants. Although remnants of the 'accused speaks' trial remained, by the end of the century the adversarial trial had emerged.[73] These innovations in the administration of law included the regularization of the pardon process, the sworn testimony of witnesses for the defense, the Transportation Acts, the emergence of strong counsel for the prosecution and, more importantly, the existence of counsel for the defense. These procedural changes created spaces for the language of excuse and its permeation of the legal system.

After the Glorious Revolution of 1688–1689, concern about the rising rate of property crime, especially in London, prompted the clarification and regularization of the pardon process. In 1693 the Privy Council took control of the administration of capital punishment in London by deciding which prisoners convicted at the Old Bailey would hang and which would receive a pardon. This system evolved out of a temporary measure designed to spare Queen Mary the work of deciding whom to pardon in the absence of William III, but it became a permanent arrangement by which the Privy Council appropriated judicial authority over pardon decisions. After each session of the Old Bailey, the Recorder of London delivered an oral report on each of London's criminal cases to the members of the Council who then decided whether or not to grant the prisoner's request for a pardon.[74] The systematization of the pardon process in London may have encouraged those prisoners who lacked a judge's recommendation to apply for a pardon independently. In their petitions for pardon and the supporting materials they submitted prisoners and their advocates had a forum in which to elaborate on the offender's mental state without denying guilt.

Beyond changes in the pardoning process, several pieces of legislation altered the trial itself. 1 Anne s.2. c.9 (1702) affected the presentation and reception of all pleas including those of mental excuse by mandating that

> every person or persons who shall be produced or appear as a witness or witnesses on behalf of the prisoner ... shall first take an oath to

depose the truth the whole truth and nothing but the truth in such manner as the witnesses for the queen are by law obliged to do.[75]

This statute eliminated a discrepancy between witnesses for the prosecution, who had testified under oath before 1702, and those for the defense, who had not. William Blackstone described the earlier practice as 'unreasonable and oppressive.' He summarized Edward Coke's (1552–1634) opinion of the incongruity in the status of witnesses as a 'tyrannical practice' because as Blackstone concluded, 'the jury gave less credit to the prisoner's evidence, than to that produced by the crown.'[76]

Whether, as Blackstone argued, 'the courts grew so heartily ashamed' of the denial of sworn testimony by defense witnesses, and whether that shame eventually yielded the 1702 statute, does not concern us here.[77] However, the wording of 4 Jac. I, c. 1 (1606) allowing for sworn defense testimony at the trials of English subjects accused of crimes in Scotland, implied that sworn testimony would result in 'better informacion of the conscience of the jurie and justice' because sworn testimony 'produced for his [the accused's] better clearinge and justification.'[78] These phrases suggest the prejudice met by unsworn testimony and its dismissal by jurors and judges prior to the statute of 1702. Although a more trusting reception of defense witnesses could not have been immediate, it is safe to assume that the statute of 1702 increased the credibility of defense testimony if only because those who lied under oath would now face prosecution for perjury.

With more credible witnesses on board, the stakes for devising more nuanced pleas rose again in the early eighteenth century. The Transportation Act (4 Geo. I, c. 11), introduced into the House of Commons by the solicitor-general in December 1717 and passed into law in 1718, created a serious, non-capital punishment for convicted felons. The statute allowed the courts to sentence a prisoner to a term of transportation in the American colonies for seven years; those pardoned for capital crimes received a term of 14 years.[79] Although transportation had been available as an alternative to the death penalty for the century preceding the act of 1718, this legislation and 6 Geo. I, c. 23 (1720) systematized and regularized its use by providing public money to cover the costs.[80]

As John Beattie has shown, evidence from the first few years after the passage of the Transportation Act illustrates the swift and significant effect it had on the English legal system. Between 1718 and 1720 transportation completely replaced whipping, branding, the pillory, and imprisonment; moreover, the availability of transportation led trial juries to increase the use of partial verdicts, verdicts that convicted prisoners of less serious charges than those stated in the indictment. In some of these cases a partial verdict replaced an acquittal. As a whole, transportation increased the severity of non-capital punishment.[81] Although transportation did not replace capital punishment for more serious crimes like rape, murder, burglary, or horse theft, evidence of extenuating circumstances in capital cases often convinced judges and jurors to sentence the prisoner to a term of transportation rather than hanging. The severity of transportation provided legal authorities a punishment that they believed did not compromise or undermine the power of the law.[82]

For defendants who might previously have been branded, whipped, and dismissed, the impact of this new punishment must have been quite dramatic. Most prisoners probably felt an overwhelming fear and anxiety at the prospect of having to leave their homes and travel on a treacherous sea voyage to an unknown destination and a life of indentured servitude. The slim prospect of ever again seeing their families, friends, and homes provided little consolation. In response to this new punishment, far more widely applied than the death penalty, defendants may have elaborated on more conventional defenses in an attempt to escape this new fate.

For those who faced the death penalty, transportation offered an alternative that also encouraged them to elaborate on their defenses at trial in an attempt to convince the judge and jury to bring in a reduced sentence or to support a convict's petition for pardon. King's research shows that judges responded to exactly this sort of information when they decided whether to mitigate or pardon.[83] The new punishment widened the discretionary powers of the judge and jury in the face of the increasing number of capital statutes. A plea that drew on the insanity defense to make an argument for mental delusion and distress distinguished the defendant from gang members, old offenders, and vagrants. However problematic the pleas of mental excuse, their references to a history of erratic behavior and their reliance on the corroboration of family and neighbors made it difficult for the perpetrators of organized, premeditated crime to use them.[84]

In addition to the changes in criminal process recounted so far, the increased presence of counsel for the prosecution and, soon after, for the defense changed the dynamics in the courtroom and led to what John Langbein has called the 'lawyerization' of the criminal trial.[85] Langbein has identified the rise of defense counsel as the major development in the eighteenth-century courtroom that ended the altercation of the 'accused speaks' trial and precipitated the emergence of an adversarial trial.[86] As mentioned above, prior to the eighteenth century legal commentators advised that the defendant's own words, unmediated by counsel, spoke best for the honesty and sincerity of the accused as the most effective test of the accused's innocence or guilt. With the judge as their advocate, defendants conducted their own defense.

The altercation that had characterized the 'accused speaks' trial of the sixteenth and seventeenth centuries was first eroded by the appearance at the beginning of the eighteenth century of a prosecuting solicitor responsible for the investigation of criminal cases on behalf of institutions such as the Bank of England, the Royal Mint, and the Post Office for crimes that lacked an individual victim. Responding to the absence of a police force, these institutions employed solicitors to ensure the prosecution of criminal cases; they collected evidence, prepared witnesses, and guided the cases through the pre-trial process and the trial itself.[87] To compensate for the advantages provided to the prosecution by these lawyers and to offset the evidentiary problems that came to light in scandals surrounding the rewards system and the crown witness system, judges allowed defense lawyers to appear at trial starting in the 1730s.[88]

Unlike prosecutors who might comment on evidence as they presented the 'examination-in-chief,' lawyers for the defense were barred from 'addressing the court' and could only advise the defendant on points of law or help examine or cross-examine witnesses. Although these restrictions were supposed to preserve the voice of the accused, so prominent in the 'accused speaks' trial,[89] counsel, in fact, enabled the accused to remain silent without losing the ability to defend himself. The existence of counsel reconfigured all stages of the trial: it increased the number of witnesses as well as the quantity and quality of evidence and by the 1750s divided the presentation of the evidence into the prosecution's accusation followed by the defendant's denial.[90] These changes shifted the burden of proof toward the prosecution and affected the rules governing the permissibility of evidence.[91] The structured timing of arguments may have replaced some of the conversational, spontaneous questioning typical of trials in the seventeenth and early eighteenth centuries. Yet we should resist the temptation to portray these changes as a complete overhaul of the trial; as late as 1771, William Eden (1745–1814) described the trial as 'rather in the nature of a discussion between the parties.'[92]

The change in the structure of the trial did not mean that a majority of defendants was represented by counsel. Langbein points out that the number of cases at the Old Bailey in which defendants had the benefit of counsel was 'only a relative trickle until the last decades of the eighteenth century.'[93] Beattie asserts that not more than 10 percent of defendants at the Old Bailey had counsel in the middle decades of the eighteenth century.[94] By the 1780s only a quarter to a third of defendants were represented by counsel; this remained the case into the first third of the nineteenth century.[95] Provincial assizes may have seen a higher rate of counsel as barristers sometimes worked for little or no money in order to gain experience at trial.[96]

Regardless of whether a specific defendant retained counsel, the presence of lawyers in the courtroom affected the dynamics of all trials.[97] Langbein ascribes to counsel the receding role of the judge and the silencing of the jury's questions during the trial.[98] Defense counsel expanded the prisoner's right to know what evidence the prosecution planned to present, it increased the scrutiny of the indictment and all the evidence presented in court, and it improved the likelihood of cross-examination.[99] One can only speculate, but it seems logical to conclude that the demystification of the process of litigation contributed to the elaboration of pleas, especially the pleas of mental excuse. If a defendant knew the prosecution had incriminating evidence against her, she or her lawyer could 'exploit other avenues of defense'[100] such as elaborating on extenuating circumstances, including mental states, to argue for mitigation.

Langbein asserts that one of the most significant results of the 'lawyerization' of the trial was the silencing of the accused.[101] For the cases that featured a language of mental excuse, discerning the effects of defense counsel is not easy. As products of the 'accused speaks' trial, these cases featured the language of the mind in pre-trial depositions or at trial as initiated by the defendant, witnesses on his or her behalf, the victim, or witnesses for the prosecution. For the most part, these defendants did not retain counsel. As Nigel Walker has shown, the percentage of 'obvious' insanity excuses peaked between 1755 and 1769, when the presence of defense lawyers is estimated at only 10 percent of all criminal trials.

The slow introduction of defense counsel coincided almost exactly with the culture of sensibility and the amplification of the language of excuse. Were these developments related? Not directly. Despite their middling status and their familiarity with the culture of sensibility, defense lawyers generally did not initiate the language of mental excuse in the courtroom. The constraints on defense lawyers not to address the jury barred them from recounting the story of the crime from the point of view of the accused. Lawyers may have been hesitant to introduce the language of mental states because of the admission of guilt built into these excuses. The uncontrolled nature of the excuses and their reach beyond the bounds of legal exculpation made their effects unpredictable and would have complicated the management of the case and distracted counsel from their primary objective, which was to challenge the prosecution's case.[102] For the reasons explained in chapter 3, lawyers may have also considered the arguments of emotion and sensibility inappropriate for or detrimental to the defenses of common people, especially men. Considering all the reasons to refrain from using the language of mental excuse, lawyers probably did not initiate such pleas. However, what we will see in chapter 5 is that when questions of mental states were raised, especially by the victim or his or her witnesses, counsel for the defense pursued the line of questioning and emphasized the effects of this evidence.

Langbein's contention that the principles of the lawyerized trials were exported to trials where counsel played no role supports my speculation that defendants may have drawn inspiration and models for imitation from watching lawyers for both the prosecution and the defense. They may have felt empowered to deploy their own strategies and enact their knowledge of the law as they saw counsel doing in other trials. Ironically, it was on the eve of the emergence of the adversarial trial that Langbein's 'trial of citizen equals' developed some of its most sophisticated excuses.[103] These excuses may very well have driven judges to hand over the management of the trials to lawyers.[104] Although the admission of counsel for the defense diminished the role of the judge at trial, this trade-off may have been a deliberate means to silence defendants and the proliferation of uncontrolled excuses introduced by or for them.

The structure of the 'accused speaks' trial required the defendant to respond, unaided, to the evidence against him or her. In the face of the intimidating and unfamiliar role into which the accused were cast in the altercation trial, some defendants developed a language of mental excuse to explain their criminal behavior. The changes in the trial that took place throughout the eighteenth century affected legal procedure before, during, and after the trial. Together they influenced the texture of these excuses and amplified their effect. Whether influenced by the jury's new practice of sitting together in the courtroom, or the attention and success of the crime pamphlet, the coaching of counsel present at the magistrate's initial investigation of the crime or later at the trial, or the fear or prospect of transportation, the accused and others who participated in legal dramas knew that they had only a brief court appearance at which to influence the trial's outcome and look ahead to the post-trial pardon process. In this setting it is not difficult to imagine that witnesses and defendants harnessed the tradition of the 'accused speaks' trial, peppering their testimony with the dramatic language of the mind to try to catch the attention of their listeners: the judge and jury, as well as the wider audience who observed the drama and spectacle of the assize proceedings.

Legal opinions of insanity

At least as far back as Justinian's *Digest*, legal codes and commentary accepted insanity as both an explanation and an excuse for criminal behavior. Early English legal sources, echoed by Christian teachings, exempted the insane from legal liability, citing their condition as their punishment.[105] Edward Coke declared the punishment of someone who did not understand its implications useless:

> The execution of an offender is for example ... but so it is not when a madman is executed, but should be a miserable spectacle, both against law, and of extreme inhumanity and cruelty, and can be no example to others.[106]

All legal handbooks published in the sixteenth and seventeenth centuries included sections on those who were *non compos mentis*. They reiterated Coke's opinion, and in their advice to local law officials they urged lenient treatment of criminals found to be insane.[107]

In *The History of the Pleas of the Crown*, published posthumously in 1734, Matthew Hale delved more deeply than previous judicial commentators into the causes and legal implications of different states of mental incapacity. Hale classified idiocy as a congenital defect: its victims were easily identified and excused from trial.[108] Dementia or madness resulted from

> the distemper of the humours of the body, as deep melancholy or adult choler; sometimes the violence of a disease, [such] as a fever or palsy; sometimes from a concussion or hurt of the brain, or its membranes or organs.[109]

This disease manifested itself either as 'partial insanity of mind' or 'a total insanity.' 'Perfect madness' or 'a total alienation of the mind' excused the guilt of felony and treason, while a less menacing, less predictable form of the illness, partial insanity, affected 'some persons, that have a competent use of reason in respect of some subjects, [who] are yet under a particular *dementia* in respect [to others].' Those who suffered partial insanity did not necessarily avoid responsibility for crime. For example, although melancholy caused 'excessive fears and griefs,' it did not render its victims 'wholly destitute of the use of reason' and so left them accountable for their offenses.[110]

Lunacy could manifest itself as a permanent state or one interspersed with lucid intervals. Hale restated the popular notion that the phases of the moon exerted 'great influence in all diseases of the brain ... especially about the equinoxes and summer solstice.'[111] During a period of lunacy 'the person that is absolutely mad for a day, killing a man in that distemper is equally not guilty, as if he were mad without intermission.' But the exemption from guilt was limited. A person who committed a crime during a lucid interval, 'which ordinarily happen between the full and change of the moon,' was fully responsible for the offense because 'in such intervals [they] have usually at least a competent use of reason, and crimes committed by them in these intervals are of the same nature and subject to the same punishment, as if they had no such deficiency.'[112] Hale's analysis of lunacy suggested that it could displace the offender's 'true' self. His legal inventory of psychological states traced the contours of mental disease and revealed an underlying tension between understanding mental illness and limiting its exculpatory nature.

John Brydall (b. 1635) took a different approach to the topic when he promised to provide a comprehensive guide to lunacy and the law.[113] His 'collection (methodically digested) of such laws, with the cases, opinion, and resolutions ... as do properly concern the rights of all such, as are wholly destitute of reason' published in 1700 addressed some of the issues that other legal commentators overlooked such as the 'hard and difficult' question of proving insanity. Brydall warned that 'it is not sufficient for the witnesses to depose, that the testator was mad, or besides his wits.' Their testimony must 'yield a sufficient reason to prove' that 'they did see him to do such things, or heard speak such words, as a man having wit, or reason, would not have done, or spoken.' Brydall gave very specific examples of such behavior (which we will see rehearsed in the courtroom):

> Namely, they did see him throw stones against the windows; or see him usually to spit in men's faces; or being asked a question, they did see him hiss like a goose, or bark like a dog, or play such other parts as mad-folks use to do.[114]

Unlike Hale's catalogue of mental states, Brydall emphasized the offender's history of mental incapacity and the witness' experience of it. This evidence alone satisfied a common concern of judicial authorities: counterfeit. Brydall stipulated that the testimony of a single witness could prove insanity, but if witnesses disagreed about the defendant's insanity, 'their testimony is to be preferred, which depose he was of sound memory' because 'the same is more agreeable to the disposition of nature, for every man is a creature reasonable.'[115] Brydall's analysis consolidated the 'true' self assumed and demanded by the law.

Published in 1769, William Blackstone's survey 'Of the Persons Capable of Committing Crimes' reviewed previous opinions on the topic of exculpatory mental states. The insanity defense came under the rubric of a defect of understanding:

> For where there is no discernment, there is no choice; and where there is no choice; there can be no act of the will, which is nothing else but a determination of one's choice to do or to abstain from a particular action: he therefore, that has no understanding, can have no will to guide his conduct.[116]

Blackstone's discussion included a revealing reference to the statute of 1744. The Justices' Commitment Act (17 Geo. II, c. 5) empowered justices of the peace to apprehend offenders whom they considered dangerous. Blackstone endorsed the statute and warned against allowing 'absolute madmen' to 'go loose, to the terror of the king's subjects.'[117] Blackstone's comments echoed the concerns of witnesses who spoke of the threat of violence posed by defendants whose insanity they did not question.

The association of mental illness with danger, unpredictability, and violence led to the legal comparison of the insane with wild animals. In this context the word 'brute' first appeared in *Laws and Customs of England*. In a discussion of responsibility for suicide the author asked 'what shall we say of a madman bereft of reason? ... It is asked whether such a one commits felony against himself.' The author concluded that the insane could not commit a felony 'since they are without sense and reason and can no more commit a wrong or a felony than a brute animal, since they are not far removed from brutes.'[118] In the context of civil law the *Laws and Customs of England* cautioned against contracting with the insane because 'such men are not far removed from brute beasts which lack reason.'[119] Unfortunately, the words brute and beast impressed legal scholarship with an image of the mentally ill as raging wild animals that persisted in seventeenth- and eighteenth-century discussions of insanity.[120]

The bestial image of the insane sometimes made an appearance in court as the 'wild beast test' or the 'right–wrong test.' The formality of this nomenclature belies the vague meanings assigned to these terms and their inconsistent application. Judges and juries did not equate insanity only with wildly frenzied behavior, and they often queried the defendant's will to harm and ability to distinguish good from evil without mention of any such test.[121] Although the scholarship on the subject has overemphasized its importance, the 'wild beast test' encapsulates the two anxieties about the insanity plea that emerge from a review of the legal literature: counterfeit and dangerousness. The first concerned authenticity and the challenge of proving a person's displaced state of mind. The second accepted the defendant's genuine mental incapacity and spoke to the terrifying and real danger it posed.

II Mental excuses in court

The insanity defense

The history of the insanity plea documents a tension between a belief in the just exculpation of crimes committed by the insane and the fear of unpunished dissemblers and dangerous lunatics. The complicated distinctions between various manifestations of mental impairment reflect this tension, as do the difficult and unreliable tests for madness and the attempts in the legal literature to distinguish between exculpatory frenzy and accountable melancholy.

Previous research on the insanity defense has asserted the uniformity of the practical application of these legal opinions. Studies of the insanity defense have found that in an ordinary criminal trial in the eighteenth century charges against an offender considered to be lunatic, distempered, frenzied, or dangerous were generally dismissed by the grand jury. The defendant was usually released to the custody of his or her family or committed to a house of correction.[122] When a case did come to trial, the defendant found *non compos mentis* was acquitted. Medieval and early modern precedent substantiates this general pattern.[123]

The problem that remained unresolved until our period was the prevention of the lunatic's future criminal behavior. Family members who took custody of the insane could not guarantee that their relatives would not engage in further acts of violence. Some families chose to allow the lunatic's indefinite detention as an alternative to caring for the individual themselves.[124]

During our period, legal authorities assumed the pre-trial application of the *non compos mentis* exemption. The defendant's insanity probably determined the informal resolution of many crimes in ways that left no written records. These cases were settled in the office of the justice of the peace who assigned custody of the offender to members of his or her family or confined the offender in the local gaol or in a madhouse without a formal trial.[125] By the end of the eighteenth century, crimes perpetrated by obviously insane persons were resolved with even fewer legal formalities. When Margaret Nicholson tried to stab George III on August 2, 1786, she was promptly diagnosed as insane by a physician and incarcerated in Bethlem Hospital until her death 40 years later.[126] In a case from 1796, a coroner's warrant sent Mary Lamb directly to a madhouse in Hoxton after she stabbed her mother.[127] Neither of these two cases resulted in a trial.

Despite this seemingly neat trend toward immediate detention and exemption from trial, some cases of obvious insanity made it to the Old Bailey. The descriptions of these trials leave the impression of their quick dispatch without much jury deliberation or hesitation. Henry Clifford came to trial in 1688, indicted for stealing a brown gelding. He was 'sent back [to gaol] and ordered to be discharged as a lunatick' because he appeared to be 'a distracted person, both in prison and at the bar.'[128] When Elizabeth Bennit was charged with stealing various linens valued at 20 shillings in 1711, 'the fact was plainly proved upon the prisoner; But it appearing upon the tryal that she was *non compos mentis*, the jury found her as such, and acquitted her for felony.'[129] In 1734 the *Gentleman's Magazine* reported that a defendant, one Maddocks, faced charges at the Glamorganshire assizes at Cardiff for the 'murder of his parents whom he'd cut to pieces with an axe.' The special jury impaneled to judge his sanity found him lunatic and ordered him held in custody until the next assizes.[130] In another case from 1762 a young man appeared at the Old Bailey for shooting his father's maid in the side. According to the *Gentlemen's Magazine*, his acquittal followed the jury's conclusion that 'at the time the fact was committed he was of insane mind.'[131] In the summary of William Hall's trial for assault and attempted robbery in October 1772, the *OBSP* reported that 'it appearing on the evidence that the prisoner was insane, he was acquitted, and the court gave directions that proper care should be taken of him.'[132]

In all of these cases the prisoner's personal appearance, demeanor, and history of peculiar behavior served as evidence of his or her mental state. Members of the offender's community made most of their judgments about the accused before word of the crime ever reached the magistrate. In these cases of obvious insanity, no one insisted on holding the offender responsible for his or her crime. Instead, both the legal discourse and the popular understanding of the crime focused on the prevention of further violence and crime. The community and the legal establishment did not believe that the insane possessed the rational capacity to understand punitive measures. The detention of the offender before trial, in place of a trial, or after trial was represented not as a sentence or a punishment but as a preventive measure undertaken to protect both the offender and the community from future harm. Newspaper accounts warned people to take action to prevent tragic crimes involving the insane. The report of a 1759 murder of a little girl outside of Birmingham ended with a 'caution against suffering persons disordered in their senses to wander at large without a keeper.'[133]

For the most part these obvious cases of insanity did not present many legal questions for judges and jurors. The problem of defining exculpatory mental states arose when the insanity of the accused was not clear. And in the eighteenth century, as interest in emotional distress and the psychological motives for crime rose, the number of problematic cases increased. Blackstone instructed that doubts about the offender's insanity, 'shall be tried by a jury.' These juries ruled only on the defendant's sanity, and they ruled before legal proceedings began against the accused.[134] In 1756 Robert Ogle was indicted for the murder of Francis Martin. 'His appearance at the bar seeming to discover he was not right in his senses,' a jury was empanelled to 'determine whether he was or was not of sound mind and memory, fit to take his trial.'[135] The proceedings at Ogle's trial illustrate how witnesses made a case for 'legal insanity' and convey the court's concern about authenticity.

The interrogation of Ogle's sanity reveals varied and textured descriptions of insane behavior. Asked 'How has he appeared as to his understanding,' James Arlington, Ogle's jailer, replied that the prisoner 'sometimes ... has appeared as a madman, and sometimes not quite so bad.' Arlington elaborated: 'his mind changes several times every day, he does not at all seem settled in his mind. In the morning he was a little flurried in his head.' When asked for a general statement about Ogle's behavior since his imprisonment, Arlington answered that 'he has very odd actions.'[136] William Nichols, with whom Ogle had lodged for two and half years before the murder, told the court that Ogle was 'not in his senses.' Ogle's lawyer, William Cane, reported that in his first interview with the prisoner 'he behaved very decent to me, but rambling in his mind from one thing to another, asking me what became of the French at Minorca.' Cane concluded that Ogle was incapable 'of attending or minding the evidence, or remembering it when he heard it.'[137]

In response to these statements, the prosecutor questioned the genuine nature of Ogle's state of mind. He asked Arlington if the prisoner's 'odd actions' 'seem to be real.' Arlington replied, 'indeed they are real. He looks out at the window to people in the yard, talks several languages that I do not understand, and points to people, and makes many mad motions.' When queried about Ogle's capacity for 'taking his trial,' Nichols answered in the negative and cited Ogle's indifference to the trial as corroboration. Like his questions to Arlington, the prosecutor again probed the authenticity of Ogle's condition asking if Nichols believed it to be 'counterfeit or real?' When Nichols replied, 'really, my lord, it is real,' the judge stepped in to say, 'people that counterfeit are very often off their guard, did you see any thing that could induce you to believe that it was put on?' The judge's question summarized the prosecution's quandary: how to establish the prisoner's true state of mind.

The testimony about Ogle's exculpatory madness closely followed the guidelines articulated by Brydall. For these witnesses evidence of an exculpatory mental state included an ever-changing disposition, rambling speech, and odd gestures. Two of the witnesses presented Ogle's indifference to the horrific nature of his crime and to his trial as evidence of his insanity. Nichols referred to the prisoner's lack of concern about his trial, noting that 'he said, *never mind it, never mind it*, and seemed to take no notice of it at all,' as evidence of his inability to stand trial. Cane spoke of Ogle's dismissal of the consequences of his crime. 'I do not think he behaved like a rational man; a rational man would have been concerned for this person he had killed; but he seemed to have no concern at all.' Cane's moral equation linked rationality, compassion, and responsibility. Ogle's lack of compassion for his victim was part of the proof of his insanity.[138]

In their concern to determine whether Ogle's insanity was counterfeit, judger and jury may have been guided by Hale's words:

> For doubtless most persons that are felons of themselves [i.e. suicides], and others are under a degree of partial insanity, when they commit these offenses: it is very difficult to define the indivisible line that divides perfect and partial insanity, but it must rest upon circumstances duly to be weighed and considered both by the judge and jury, lest on the one side there be a kind of inhumanity towards the defects of human nature, or on the other side too great an indulgence given to great crimes.[139]

Hale crystallized the dilemma that legal authorities faced when they decided whether to admit insanity as a legitimate excuse for criminal behavior. In this case the court revisited the question of authenticity several times during the investigation before concluding that Ogle was 'not of sound mind and memory.'

When the prisoner's insanity went undetected before trial, the trial jury embarked on the delicate task of decoding the complex language used by defendants, witnesses, and victims to describe the prisoner's mental incapacity and of applying the general guidelines reiterated by Coke, Hale, Brydall, and Blackstone to decide who qualified as *non compos mentis*. Discussions of lunacy and its manifestations in pre-trial records and trial accounts reveal the struggle of witnesses, judges, and jurors to determine the limits of exculpatory madness. The same contradictory themes expressed in legal commentary emerged in testimony about madness. Arguments about the prisoner's dangerousness and the need for his or her imprisonment to prevent future violence stood opposed to descriptions of the offender's honesty and upstanding character, a good self obscured or displaced by mental distress.

Arguments for insanity rested on two kinds of evidence: the offender's history of peculiar behavior and the inexplicable nature of the crime itself. In many cases members of the community articulated the perpetrator's excuse for her or him. Neighbors used a wide array of words and phrases to describe the defendant's mental incompetence. The states of mind to which they referred ranged from melancholy to frenzy with many of the descriptions combining symptoms of these contrasting conditions. Melancholy referred to seemingly passive or trance-like states. Witnesses represented crimes committed by a melancholic person as a shock to the community. They often admitted that they knew about the defendant's melancholy, but that he or she had not previously behaved criminally. Witnesses used words such as 'confused' 'despondent,' and 'dejected' to describe the melancholic state. Frenzy, on the other hand, was necessarily erratic, dangerous, and potentially violent. Frenzied behavior could be described as 'lunatic,' 'insensible,' 'passionate,' 'insane,' 'crazy,' 'distempered,' and 'dangerous.'[140]

Claims about the frenzied state of mind often found expression in an uncontrolled rage, anger, or passion that fit exactly with the image of Bracton's brute. While many of the criminal offenses took place during a frenzied episode, accounts of the events surrounding the crime often mentioned the offender's previous melancholy. In 1708 Elizabeth Cole confessed to throwing her child off of a bridge into the icy Thames. Several witnesses, among them the defendant's brother, testified that:

> it appear'd plain that she had for a considerable time been under a great trouble of mind, and in a desponding condition.

While this sounds like a description of melancholy, witnesses also said that

> she would commit many extravagant actions, and particularly when she lay in three months ago, would rise out of her bed and dance about the room; which disorders of mind continu'd upon her ever since.[141]

Cole protested that she was in her right senses and explained 'I sent my dear child to heaven, and am resolv'd to go after her.' She presented the murder of her child as an act of love, born of a maternal instinct that she promised to follow with her own death, by suicide or as a consequence of her prosecution and conviction.

In April 1719 Hannah Gill appeared at the Old Bailey charged with stealing 18 pounds of tobacco worth 14 shillings. Like Elizabeth Cole, Gill's guilt was irrefutable: the prosecutor, Thomas Winfield, testified that he caught her red-handed as she stuffed tobacco into her coat. Gill made no statement as to her guilt or innocence. Instead 'she looked very wildly, and did several mad actions while she was at the bar.' Several witnesses appeared on Gill's behalf. One testified that

> he had known her 19 years, and that she ran mad when she lay in with her first child and had not been sound since, though she had intervals of sense; that she was sometimes raving and at other time melancholy.

Another woman told the court that the night before the crime Gill came to her house and 'appeared very bad.' A third witness who lived nearby 'confirmed that she was lunatick and that she had seen her dance naked in the middle of the court.' The woman who took care of Hannah's children said that on a recent visit Gill 'was so bad she did not know her.' This same woman reported that Gill 'said they were going to hang her for killing her two children.'[142] The references to 'outrageous,' 'raving,' behavior, dancing, and imagined infanticide convey the wildness, uncontrollable impulses, and unpredictability identified with madness especially among women who had recently given birth.[143]

The association of both Cole and Gill's insanity with childbearing and infanticide certainly gender their frenzy as female although descriptions of agitation, emotional outbursts, and wildness occur in the trials of men as well. At Stephen Swate's murder trial in 1708 a witness told the court that he was 'walking to and fro about the shop.'[144] At Samuel Prigg's trial for murder in May 1746 a witness for the defense testified that Prigg 'sometimes ... has talked wildly, and I have taken him to task as he has been rambling backwards and forwards.' The witness continued with a succinct history of Prigg's mental condition: 'he always seemed a good sort of a man and a sensible man before his illness seized his head: I saw him about three weeks ago, he said he believed he should drown himself.'[145] Another witness told the jury that she had known Prigg for many years, but in the month before the murder she said 'I looked upon him to be very wild with his eyes, and very melancholy, and like a person out of his senses.'[146] In May 1751 when Philip Gibson was tried at the Old Bailey for assault and robbery, a witness for the defense called Gibson 'a right lunatic' because he

> used to get up out of bed, and sing, *tol de rol*, I shall be hanged, I shall be hanged. All the people used to say he was not in his right senses, and that certainly he would not be hanged. He'd talk to himself, plead guilty, and sing.[147]

In both of these cases the man's frenzied demeanor included rambling speech and allusions to suicide. Although only the women are described dancing, the men also suffered from an inability to control both their physical and mental capacities. Although men and women exhibited similar behavior during their frenzied episodes, the potential for insanity identified with women's reproductive capacity and the vulnerability to madness during pregnancy and both immediately and long after giving birth linked women to insanity in a fundamental, universal way, quite distinct from male madness.[148]

Images of violence, agitation, and danger recur in many descriptions of frenzy, especially those of male prisoners. On April 14, 1743 at eight in the evening William Cowper stabbed his mother in her home in Burton in West Riding, Yorkshire. His sister Ellinor deposed that on the night in question William 'began to discourse in scripture, and fell into great distractions, by which she was feared he would doe some mischiefe.' His brother, Thomas, found William 'standing in the same room, and in great distraction.' He described his brother as 'violently mad' and 'in great disorder ever since.'[149]

On August 23, 1749 Robert Bower, esquire, deposed that as he rode home the previous evening 'Robert Barber came running towards this informant in a furious manner with a stick in his hand and abused this informant.'[150] Bower said that Barber 'insulted, abused, and violently threatened' him for six months prior to this attack and that Barber had promised that 'if he had then a sword in his hand [he] would run it into this informant's guts.' Bower called Barber 'a very dangerous person ... at times rather inclined and subject to fits of lunacy ... disordered in his senses and ... very unfit to be suffered to go at large.'[151] Bower requested that Barber be 'secured in some proper place of safety or prison' because 'he apprehends himself in danger of his life.'[152] Christopher Harland corroborated Bower's story and added that 'Barber has often threatened and particularly within these two months last past to pull down part of the outhousing of Mrs. Ann Burdett ... and to peel the bark from off the trees before her house.'[153] Harland also considered Barber 'to be a very mischievous and dangerous person ... and to be a very unfitt person to be suffered to go at large.'[154]

When James Shackleton was found guilty of arson in December 1758, the verdict on the indictment read 'did it but not by felony not being in his right mind.'[155] Three months later, in March 1759, Thomas Lane and Joseph Hey petitioned for Shackleton's continued detention calling him 'a very dangerous man' who 'had not the right use of his senses but [is] subject to fits of frenzy and lunacy and has been so for several years last past.' The petitioners warned that 'it would be dangerous to let the prisoner be at liberty.'[156]

Many descriptions of frenzy cited melancholy as one of the symptoms of mental distress. Typical cases mention melancholy only briefly. At Richard Cooper's trial for the murder of Margaret Harle in 1731 Jane Saunders and Mary Ray testified that for two months before the crime they 'thought he looked melancholy.'[157] In the same year a witness at Edward Stafford's murder trial said 'he did believe by his behavior that he was affected with a deep melancholy, or something of that kind' while another said that 'the prisoner of late was always in some melancholy posture.'[158] At 2 o'clock on 8 August 1755, the day that George Taylor slit his son's throat, his daughter asked a neighbor, Ann Bewick, to 'bear her company' because 'her father had not eaten any thing that day and was very melancholy.'[159] In these examples witnesses represented melancholy as an ongoing condition and the crime as the result of an unexpected, frenzied outburst.

Melancholy rarely appeared as the primary evidence of an offender's insanity. The representation of John Swift found in the depositions describing his brutal murder of his three-year-old daughter Mary in 1783 is a dramatic exception. Ann Hawksworth said that she had known Swift for two years and that she 'had often observed him as low and dejected.' Ruben Lindley testified that he had known Swift for 'upwards of twenty years, and he had frequently known him to be insane, and in a low, dejected way ... and several times since he had known him [Swift had been] out of his senses.'[160] Hawksworth, who asserted that she 'never knew him [Swift] offer any violence to any other person,'[161] walked into Swift's home and saw 'Mary Swift, an infant, lying on her mother's knees, with her throat cut, and discharging a quantity of blood.' When she asked John if he was guilty, he answered that 'he had no thoughts of hurting the child, and imagined he had been rubbing the back of a penknife across the infant's throat, and was very sorry the thing had happened.' Swift explained to Joseph Ingham that 'he wanted hanging out of the way,' that 'he had no intention of hurting the infant,' and that he rubbed the knife across her throat 'to frighten her.'[162] These representations seek to portray Swift's brutal crime as the result of a trance rather than a violent impulse.[163]

The language in these depositions demonstrates how participants in England's legal system broadened the definition of mental illness. According to Hale, melancholy caused partial insanity which usually manifested itself in 'excessive fears and griefs' without rendering its victim 'wholly destitute of the use of reason.'[164] This sort of partial insanity was not considered a legitimate excuse for capital crime because 'a person labouring under melancholy distempers hath yet ordinarily as great understanding, as ordinarily a child of fourteen years.'[165] The testimony about the mental states described above contested the legal opinion that those who suffered from melancholia retained their reason. Neighbors presented these murders as the results of melancholy, not malice. The evidence suggests that witnesses believed that melancholy displaced the offender's true self and that if the defendants had been well, they would never have committed their crimes.

Between the two extremes of melancholy and frenzy, defendants speaking in their own defense used a rich and varied language of mental excuse to frame their claims for diminished responsibility. In June 1720 John Newman offered to return the linens he had stolen and explained that 'he was crasy sometimes and had been lunatick this twelve-month.'[166] James Codner told the court that he had been 'indisposed in his head for some time' before his indictment for the theft of three books in December 1720[167] while Richard Cooper, mentioned earlier for his shooting of Margaret Harle in 1731, pleaded that he 'had been out of order at times in his head and mind.'[168] At his trial for seditious words in 1756 Charles Ferrel explained, 'I had been out of my senses.'[169] Claiming he was 'certainly insensible, or he should not have done it,' William Ward explained the theft of four Books of Common Prayer in 1772.[170]

Often the witnesses who spoke for the accused emphasized the offender's honesty and good character, arguing implicitly that the defendant's true, virtuous self was displaced by mental distress. When accused of stealing ten yards of ferreting and a dozen yards of laces in 1716, Jane Bartwick denied the charges and brought witnesses who 'deposed she was a very honest woman: but that sometimes she was crazy and behaved herself like a mad woman.'[171] Witnesses for Joel Farringdon, indicted for arson in 1731, described him as a 'mad man ever and anon for three years' who was 'often out of order in his head, and sometimes so bad, as to be bound in his bed.' In addition to these stories of his erratic behavior 'a great number of his neighbours gave the prisoner a very honest, and inoffensive character.'[172] Seven character witnesses appeared for Ann Burger when she claimed she was wrongly accused of the theft of linens in 1756. Mary Bucknell told the court that

> I have had her often in my house, and would have trusted her with any thing, and would now. She bears a very good character, but sometimes I have thought her not right in her senses. Sometimes her understanding has been very good, and sometimes very bad.[173]

Mary Swainstone testified that she had known Burger for seven years, that 'her character is that of an honest woman,' but that she had 'observed [Burger] to be a good deal uneasy in her mind sometimes, she having met with great misfortunes.' Elizabeth Owen explained that after Burger's husband died she 'was extreme poor and threw herself into the channel.'[174]

These cases mixed a claim of true legal insanity with descriptions of mental states considered exculpatory by the neighbors and friends of the accused. In contrast to the association of wildness and violence found in more typical accounts of insanity, some of these narratives lack evidence of patent lunacy before or during the crime. The broader conceptions of mental illness introduced into the legal discourse challenged juridical guidelines by including 'melancholy fitts,' 'something like madness,' 'disordered' and 'indisposed' minds in the category of excusable insanity. These assumptions about mental illness went beyond legal definitions of exculpatory states of mind and opened the possibility of widening the category to include many kinds of mental confusion enacted by inexplicable physical, environmental, or social circumstances.

Emotion and excuse: the place of pity

How often was the language of mental excuse mentioned and what impact did these pleas of mental distress have in the courtroom? A very rough estimate of the language of mental excuse reveals that it was brought consistently into 5–9 percent of all the cases recorded in the *OBSP*.[175] The language of mental excuse is not easy to quantify. Although the trial in the eighteenth century was transitioning toward a more formal set of arguments, the spontaneity and conversational style so typical of the 'accused speaks' trial was still evident. Language of mental excuse was introduced by participants unsystematically and inconsistently at every stage of the criminal process from the deposition to the trial, and even for the first time in the post-trial process. After Susanne Winton's conviction for theft and arson in 1786, the chaplain of the gaol, a Mr. Underwood, told the judge that 'the prisoner had not so good an understanding as most girls her own age.' In his rejection of the petition, the judge referred to the case made at Winton's trial by her defense counsel. 'For tho' counsel were employed for her, they never ventured to put a question to any of the witnesses called on her behalf respecting her intellect.'[176]

Cataloguing and quantifying the evidence is especially difficult when the language was mentioned by the victim or the prosecution's witnesses without any comment from the accused. Sometimes deponents with obvious sympathy for the defendant brought an excuse of mental confusion which the defendant adamantly denied. When Elizabeth Cole, mentioned earlier, threw her five-year-old daughter into the Thames in 1708, 'her friends would have insinuated as if she were lunatick; But she said, no, she was as right in her sences as any of them, and that she knew very well what she had done.'[177]

As asserted earlier, this language of mental excuse was a product of the 'accused speaks' trial which certainly pre-dated the eighteenth century. This language was not created in the eighteenth century, but it was amplified by several overlapping phenomena. This language was heard very differently within the culture of sensibility and in light of the concern with the self that so distinguished the eighteenth century. The extent of the record itself tells us about its resonance within eighteenth-century English culture, and the changes in the criminal trial outlined above featured this language more prominently. The sources themselves speak to the perception among commentators that this language was destabilizing to the criminal justice system.

The language of mental excuse in the courtroom did not go unnoticed. Despite our difficulty quantifying this phenomenon, contemporaries thought it widespread. From the mid-century sources reveal a preoccupation of legal authorities, commentators, and observers with the emotion this language might arouse in listeners and with the compassion it

could elicit in prosecutors, judges, and jurors who considered themselves 'men of sense.' Within the context of legal reform many debated
the possible impact of the language of mental excuse on judicial outcomes and on the legal system.[178]

A judge's charge to a jury in King's Bench recorded by Pierre Jean
Grosley (1718–1785) during his tour of London in 1765 illuminates the
place of pity in the criminal trial. The judge began his 'long discourse'
by observing that 'the law which called them to sit in judgment upon
their peers, had its origin in ages, when frankness, integrity, and simplicity, reigned in conjunction with ignorance.' He explained that the
jury endured 'from a presumption that the passions would respect the
most august use that men could make of their understanding, in becoming arbiters of the life and death of their fellow-creatures.' The judge
concluded his speech by urging the jury to

> join, in discharging their present duty, the simplicity, frankness, and
> integrity of their ancestors to the knowledge which had been
> obtained in the following ages; in a word, by means of these great
> helps to suppress all undue pity, and the several emotions which the
> passions are capable of exciting.[179]

The judge's opening remarks connected the language of excuse and
the ethos of sensibility. He advised the jurors to repress their emotions
during their deliberations and to 'suppress all undue pity.' In order to
'respect the most august use that men could make of their understanding,' he cautioned them about the 'emotions which the passions are
capable of exciting.' This advice urged jurors to ignore the feelings
elicited by the psychological excuses defendants presented as grounds
for acquittal or mitigation of punishment.

Observers of England's courts wrote extensively about the divergence
of legal prescription from legal practice effected by the introduction of
language that threatened to broaden conceptions of mental illness and
diminished responsibility. For legal reformers concerned to redesign
England's legal system based on standardized, certain punishment, the
perception of the influence of mental excuses within the context of the
'era of sensibility' intensified their larger concerns about the existing
trend to widespread, unsystematic mitigation.[180]

A vociferous debate swirled around the issue of sensibility and whether
the admirable susceptibility to one's own feelings and the feelings of
others belonged in the legal setting. Recurrent use of the word compassion conveyed widespread anxiety about restraining the judgment and

sensibilities of prosecutors, jurors, and judges. The definition of compassion used by legal reformers refers to 'the feeling or emotion, when a person is moved by the suffering or distress of another, and by the desire to relieve it; pity that inclines one to spare or to succor' (OED). While another sense of the word implies suffering together with another who is an equal or fellow-sufferer, in this particular context the sense of the word refers to compassion that is shown 'towards a person in distress by one who is free from it, who is, in this respect, his superior.'

In *An Enquiry into the Causes of the late Increase of Robbers* (1751) Henry Fielding (1707–1754) worried that the 'tender hearted ... cannot take away the life of a man.'[181] He explained that this 'error springing out of a good principle in the mind' deterred victims from pressing charges. Fielding elaborated:

> It is certain, that a tender-hearted and compassionate disposition which inclines men to pity and feel the misfortunes of others ... is of all tempers of mind the most amiable.

Although Fielding acknowledged that 'the passion of love or benevolence whence this admirable disposition arises, seems to be the only human passion that is in itself simply and absolutely good,' he cautioned his readers that 'knaves ... are ever lying in wait to destroy and ensnare the honest part of mankind.' Fielding advised the 'good-natured and tender-hearted man to be watchful over his own temper; to restrain the impetuosity of his benevolence, carefully to select the objects of this passion.'[182] He warned that the failure to prosecute spread crime and undermined the law because 'notorious robbers ... perpetrate future acts of violence, through the ill-judging tenderness and compassion of those who could and ought to have prosecuted them.'[183] In this passage Fielding struggled to reconcile the ethics of sensibility with his concern to raise prosecution rates. He acknowledged the value and importance of benevolence, but betrayed his frustration with the over-identification of victims with malefactors. While he praised compassion and pity in the abstract, he urged his readers not to let these praiseworthy attributes interfere with any stage of the prosecution of crime.

In the same year Samuel Johnson (1709–1784) remarked that 'they who rejoice at the correction of a thief, are yet shocked at the thought of destroying him. His crime shrinks to nothing, as compared with his misery; and severity defeats itself by exciting pity.'[184] In contrast to Fielding, Johnson spoke against the 'frequency of capital punishments,' but he echoed Fielding's conclusion that rather than deterring crime, this punishment 'prevents its detection.' Johnson urged restricting the penalty of death 'as the last resort of authority,' warning that 'he who knows not how often rigorous laws produce total impunity, and how many crimes are concealed and forgotten for fear of hurrying the offender to that state in which there is no repentance, has conversed very little with mankind.'[185] As if responding to Fielding's admonition to the 'tender-hearted,' Johnson warned that 'whatever epithets of reproach or contempt this compassion may incur from those who confound cruelty with firmness, I know not whether any wise man would wish it less powerful, or less extensive.'[186] For Fielding, compassion threatened to undermine legal process while Johnson credited its tempering effect. Both men described compassion as a powerful influence on the workings of the law.

In the fourth volume of his *Commentaries on the Laws of England* (1769), William Blackstone echoed these themes in his survey of criminal procedure. His 'muted and deferential plea'[187] for reform praised English law 'supposed to be more nearly advanced to perfection' but suggested that 'even here we shall occasionally find room to remark some particulars, that seem to want revision and amendment.'[188] Although he did not advocate abolishing capital punishment, Blackstone cautioned that the 'multitude of sanguinary laws' undermined the legal system. England's 'bloody code' and its inconsistent enforcement contradicted the ideal of law as 'permanent, uniform, and universal'[189] because

> the injured, through compassion, will often forbear to prosecute: juries, through compassion, will sometimes forget their oaths, and either acquit the guilty or mitigate the nature of the offence: and judges, through compassion, will respite one half of the convicts, and recommend them to the royal mercy.[190]

Blackstone's warning echoed Henry Fielding: uncontained compassion eradicated the concept of *mens rea*, criminal intent.

Unlike Blackstone, William Paley (1743–1805) staunchly defended the death penalty as the most powerful tool for the prevention of crime. However, he too expressed concern about the impact of harsh penalties on the sensibilities of onlookers and their relationship with legal institutions and practice. Paley agreed with Blackstone that

> barbarous spectacles of human agony are justly found fault with, as tending to harden and deprave the public feelings, and to destroy

that sympathy with which the sufferings of our fellow creatures ought always to be seen.[191]

Paley found the alternative to this destruction of sympathy, an intense identification with the suffering of the condemned, completely unacceptable because 'they counteract in some measure their own design, by sinking men's abhorrence of the crime in their commiseration of the criminal.'[192] In other words, sympathy increased mitigation and the number of acquittals. Paley suggested 'a mode of execution ... which would augment the horror of the punishment, without offending or impairing the public sensibility by cruel or unseemly exhibitions of death.'[193] Paley's analysis acknowledged the hold that sensibility had on English culture; with the adoption of private execution in 1868 the English government heeded the call to end 'unseemly exhibitions of death.'[194]

In his comments on the English legal system Martin Madan (1726–1790) elaborated on Paley's warnings. Madan complained about judicial officials who 'preferring their own feelings as men, to the duty which they owe the public as magistrates ... have been making so wanton and indiscriminate an use, or rather abuse, of certain discretionary powers with which they are invested.'[195] Madan admonished juries who 'frequently acquit the prisoner, against all fact and truth.'[196] He asserted that the verdict ought to reflect an evaluation of the facts of the crime alone and that juries ought to avoid giving 'a verdict *according* to their *feelings*, but *against* their *oath*.'[197] Madan listed liquor, youth, good character, and the influence of others as circumstances that struck 'the minds of the jury' when they gave 'verdicts diametrically opposite to the evidence which has been delivered.'[198] Madan appealed to the cult of sensibility by asserting that those who observed '*twelve* people *perjure* themselves, and not be affected by it, must one would think, be void of all feeling, of all *proper* feeling.'[199] Madan blamed judges as the jurors' accomplices who took 'little notice of the matter' and ended the trial by congratulating the prisoner on a 'narrow escape' and a 'very *merciful* jury.'[200] In cases where a jury brought in a conviction, Madan took aim at judges who 'exercise this power of reprieve wantonly, and indiscriminately.' He insinuated that a judge who pardoned did so 'to gratify his feelings as a man.'[201] According to Madan the problem with English justice was its susceptibility to emotion and feeling, the very humanity of those charged to enforce it.

In contrast to Fielding, Madan, and Paley, some reformers encouraged the convergence of sensibility and justice. William Eden (1745–1814) argued in 1771 for reform based on his concern that the 'bloody code' undermined the ethos of sensibility. He contended that 'sanguinary laws are the probable consequence of national prosperity. Sensibility sleeps in the lap of luxury.'[202] As an antidote, Eden entreated legislators to consider the offender when drafting new laws. He spoke for a sort of empathy: 'In the promulgation of every new offence, let the lawgiver expose himself to feel what wretches feel; and let him not seem to bear hardest on those crimes, which, in his elevated station, he is least likely to commit.'[203] Instead of distinguishing this legislation from one's dormant sensibility, Eden explained that 'penal laws are to check the arm of wickedness; but not to wage war with the natural sentiments of the heart.'[204] Rather than arguing for their separation, Eden normalized the coexistence of sensibility and justice.

According to Eden, the 'unnatural' division of sensibility from law resulted in the dynamic between judges and defendants about which Madan also complained. Eden observed that 'when the penalty prescribed bears an evident and excessive disproportion to the offence, the humanity of the judges will be interested in the evasion of it.'[205] At trial, the harsh penalties for theft 'admitted' the jury's 'mercy under the shield of interpretation; the impulses of benevolence are opposed to the obligations of religion and jurors are taught to trifle with their oaths, and to call such trifling "a kind of pious perjury." '[206] This identification continued after conviction when the condemned, once 'a valuable member of society' who 'erred only from some momentary impulse of our imperfect nature; one, who in the recollection of reason hath found repentance,' elicited the 'tears of his fellow citizens' who urged the authorities 'Yes, I do think, that you might pardon him.'[207] Although Eden advocated legal reform to eradicate the need for such practices and to ensure the certainty of proportional punishment, he understood this routine mitigation as an inevitable, human response.

Many of these reformers accepted explanations for crime that pointed to psychological or social forces beyond the offender's control. Eden hypothesized that some criminals, previously 'valuable member[s] of society ... erred only from some momentary impulse of our imperfect nature' and that regret followed their 'recollection of reason.'[208] Manasseh Dawes (d. 1829) commented in 1782 that 'criminals do not offend so much from choice as from misery and want of sentiment.'[209] According to Dawes, 'our actions [are] the inevitable effect of some cause in the mind, which determines our will to commit them.'[210] Those with 'vulgar minds ... are the least sensible of social right and wrong, have no sentiment, no taste, and are incapable of knowing their own good, or the good of others.'[211] They

> can neither conceive, nor acknowledge those palpable truths, which almost always escape them. They are accustomed to receive impressions without distinction ... incapable of analyzing objects.[212]

These psychological states 'may lead the human mind to adopt pernicious maxims, and render the passions disorderly, so as to corrupt the understanding, the source of all good.'[213] Dawes drew a straight line from mental distress to crime when he opined that:

> viewing things differently at different times, according to our good or bad logic, the violence of our passions, and all those circumstances which change the appearance of objects in our fluctuating minds, overrule and control us as mental causes that direct our volitions, making whatever happens in consequence their certain effect.

Dawes identified the offender's scarcity of sentiment and unrestrained passion as the sources of crime. Only the admission of sensibility into the legal process could correct this imbalance.

Like Fielding, Blackstone, Eden, and Paley, Dawes spoke of the opposition between strict laws and compassion. Rephrasing Voltaire, Dawes explained the working of compassion on legal process. Prosecutors

> being exposed to the attempts of violence or perfidy, detest the crimes of which they may possibly be the victims; yet there is a compassion in the human heart, which makes them at the same time detest the cruelty of punishment.

According to Dawes, the universality of compassion deterred the victim from pursuing his attacker

> because sensible of the possibility, from the infirmity of human nature, that they may offend, and form a part of the guilty, they feel for themselves in feeling for others, and regret that as they may be influenced by a like determination of mind to commit criminal actions, they will be punished for effects not in their power to restrain.[214]

In this discussion Dawes related the displaced self to sensibility. The victim's awareness of 'the infirmity of human nature' and his identification with the ubiquitous vulnerability to mental distress created doubts about the fairness of prosecuting the criminal.

In order to understand the full dimensions of crime, Dawes embraced the affinity of sensibility and justice. In the courtroom

> men of sense will compassionate all human and social offenders, lament their offences, and sigh over the unhappy cause of them; – they will look upon the wretched prisoner ... and grieve over his condition.[215]

Dawes did not deny or discourage the effects of compassion on a jury. Instead he saw it as the beginning of a process of dispensing mercy.

> They will not be contented that he has offended, but they will examine why; and tracing the cause, be disposed to forgive an effect, which it was impossible to avoid; and thus feeling the force and power of the mind, they will sparingly punish the man.[216]

Dawes urged legal reforms that would incorporate this perspective on human psychology and behavior.

Although these reformers disagreed about whether sensibility should play a role in the assessment of legal responsibility, none contested its potency. Even those who sought to separate sensibility from justice, like Fielding, Paley, and Madan, acknowledged its commanding presence in every courtroom and at every stage of the legal process. Those who endorsed the coexistence of sensibility and justice, in particular Eden and Dawes, traced crime to a moment of mental weakness, the result of psychological and social forces beyond an individual's control.

Conclusion

The changes in the criminal trial that unfolded during the eighteenth century converged with the examination of self and the culture of sensibility in the courtroom. These developments amplified the vocabulary of excuse and may have encouraged defendants to embellish their stories in ways that expanded the boundaries of the insanity defense. Defendants argued for their lives by elaborating their psychological circumstances, producing stories that jurors were willing to hear. The press exaggerated and circulated these stories in pamphlets and newspapers read by the middling sort including jurors and other judicial authorities. Although they did not always recognize these explanations as exculpatory, many legal observers expressed concern about the effect of emotion on the criminal process.

The representation of mental distress as the cause of crime contrasts with explanations proposed in seventeenth-century crime pamphlets that began with sin that led to crime and only then described mental disturbance as the result of guilt. Both explanations existed in the eighteenth century, but the former appeared more frequently in the legal record. As we shall see in the next chapter, the mental excuses surveyed above and the ideas about the self that circulated in the eighteenth century inspired excuses that fell farther and farther outside the legal parameters of the insanity plea. Drawing on stereotypes about women and the poor and their inability to control their emotions, defendants attributed crime to mental disorientation caused by drunkenness, necessity, passion, and compulsion.

3

Old Excuses, New Meanings: 'Temporary Phrenzy,' Necessity, Passion, and Compulsion

So far our discussion has been limited to informal pleas that made a more or less direct comparison with insanity even though they did not meet the vague and often inconsistently applied 'standard of proof' for such a defense. This chapter will take us farther afield to explore the variety of mental excuses used by defendants and witnesses on their behalf who made a more distant analogy to insanity by referring to drunkenness, necessity, passion, and compulsion as forces that clouded their mental capacity and caused them to commit a range of crimes. But defendants were not the only participants in the legal process who made reference to these mental states. Prosecutors and their witnesses and lawyers often mentioned evidence about mental distress, and defense counsel, judges, and jurors queried states of mind.

The language of excuse drew upon a traditional equation of the self with morality that can be traced back to Aristotle and Augustine. With their testimony defendants inverted the identification of the self with moral understanding. They attempted to argue that the very fact that they had done something immoral proved that they were not at that moment themselves.

What cultural and intellectual trends informed those who spoke, heard, and responded to this language of the mind? From John Locke and David Hume (1711–1776) to Adam Smith (1723–1790), British philosophers contributed to the Enlightenment's attention to psychology and preoccupation with the self.[1] Like defendants, these writers imagined a permeable self easily displaced by passions and emotions. These definitions of the self, deeply influenced by theories of sensational psychology developed by Locke and Isaac Newton (1642–1727), were inflected by the culture of sensibility and changing ideas about masculinity and emotion.

While women had long been criticized for being more emotional, less rational, and less able to control their feelings, the relationship between gender, reason, and emotion shifted during the eighteenth century. The culture of sensibility urged both men and women to value the emotional component of identity and the self. However, a tension remained between the importance of emotion and self-mastery: unrestrained emotion threatened masculinity, the political order, and the dispensing of justice. Another important tension revealed itself even more prominently when the language of the mind was introduced in a court of law: the search for authenticity, so essential to the culture of sensibility, clashed with the performance of emotion and sensibility in a public space. Many observers and critics charged that the very attempt to display one's inner, 'true' self implied artifice and design. This tension within the culture of sensibility heightened longstanding concerns with counterfeit in insanity pleas and was even more prominent in pleas that made only the most tenuous claims of mental distress.

The culture of sensibility was rich with allusions to melancholy, delicacy, and nervous disorders expounded in the medical literature by George Cheyne (1671–1743) in *The English Malady* (1733) and by others who followed him.[2] The heart and mind were inextricably linked in the theory of sensibility which read every physical frailty as a sign of a virtuous character. Eighteenth-century physicians described hypochondria and melancholy as both signals of a susceptibility to feeling and symptoms of disease and disturbance. This discussion of 'refined,' 'delicate,' and 'sensible' nerves no doubt informed the vocabulary of mental excuse common to the pleas of insanity examined in chapter 2 and spilled over into the claims of mental distress made in the cases of drunkenness, necessity, passion, and compulsion we will examine here.

This chapter places an array of eighteenth-century conceptions of responsibility and the self that circulated in philosophical tracts, literature, and the popular press alongside several different mental and emotional excuses common to the legal record. These pleas and their somewhat precarious connection to the insanity defense took on new meanings in this cultural context and were heard in ways that troubled courtroom observers and challenged a legal system on the eve of reform.

I Theories of self and sensibility

Unstable selves and the quest for self-government

In order to explicate the eighteenth-century meanings of drunkenness, necessity, passion, and compulsion, and identify their relationship to the vocabulary of mental excuse and the insanity plea, we must examine the cultural context in which ideas about identity, self, and responsibility circulated. The *Oxford English Dictionary* defines the self as 'that which in a person is really and intrinsically *he* (in contradistinction to what is adventitious); the ego (often identified with the soul or mind as opposed to the body); a permanent subject of successive and varying states of consciousness.'[3] The self refers to one's sense of a cohesive, continuing, singular identity.

According to Raymond Martin and John Barresi, the eighteenth century saw the transformation of the self from a soul, a spiritual element, ministered to by religious ideas, into a physical entity, the mind, an object of psychological study.[4] In light of this transformation, driven by both Christian and secular concerns, the aspect of the self that most preoccupied eighteenth-century people, including British philosophers, social commentators, and novelists, was its coherence, stability, and consistency, often discussed in terms of the nature and existence of a true self.[5]

In An Essay *Concerning Human Understanding* John Locke defined the self as

> that conscious thinking thing, (whatever substance, made up of whether spiritual, or material, simple, or compounded, it matters not) which is sensible, or conscious of pleasure and pain, capable of happiness or misery, and so is concern'd for it self, as far as that consciousness extends.[6]

Locke's rejection of the idea that identity emerged fully formed at birth led him to question the immortality, indivisibility, and immateriality of the soul posited by the Cartesians and the Neo-Platonists in the seventeenth century.[7] Instead of the soul, Locke proposed consciousness as the element that united a person's experience through memory. The exact extent of a person's consciousness troubled Locke. Although he acknowledged that one could have 'distinct incommunicable consciousness at different times' in which case 'the same man would at different times make different persons,'[8] Locke's theory never dispensed with a continuity of consciousness; instead his work associated the unity of consciousness and memory, a coherent self, with responsibility, accountability, ethical behavior, and political rights.

Locke's ambiguity about the extent of consciousness allowed other theorists, namely the skeptics, to posit the self as a fiction that did not exist. According to David Hume, 'what we call a mind, is nothing but a heap or collection of different perceptions, united together by certain relations, and supposed though falsely, to be endowed with a perfect simplicity and identity.'[9] Hume described a displaced self, at times replaced by a coherent one: 'the same continued and uninterrupted being may ... be sometimes present to the mind and sometimes absent from it without any real or essential change in the being itself.'[10] Like Locke, Hume's theory of the self was not free of contradiction: he posited a coherent self elsewhere in his work, most notably in his auto-biography.[11] Hume's writings, the attention they received, and the con-troversy they stirred reflected the intense scrutiny and debate that surrounded subjects such as the self, the soul, identity, and person, these 'dangerous and disputed formations,' during the eighteenth century.[12]

Contemporary literature, especially the novel, reflected a similar con-cern with questions of identity and responsibility.[13] This is especially apparent in Daniel Defoe, who focused on the relationship between character, morality, and circumstance with a 'casuistical emphasis on intention and qualifying circumstance.'[14] In *Moll Flanders* (1722) Defoe discussed the distress of poverty and the emotional turmoil thought to result from indigence or even the threat of poverty.[15] When justifying her descent into a life a crime, Moll explained self-servingly that 'vice came in always at the door of necessity, not at the door of inclination'.[16] Although Defoe cast doubt on Moll's true intentions, he also described the apprehension of poverty which 'doubled the misery' she felt and had an almost physical effect on her: she remarked that 'the terror of approaching poverty lay hard upon my spirits.'[17] The relationship between poverty and insanity haunted Moll. She described her state of mind as she contemplated her impending penury:

> I sat and cried and tormented my self night and day, wringing my hands and sometimes raving like a distracted woman; and indeed I have often wondered it had not affected my reason, for I had the vapours to such a degree that my understanding was sometimes quite lost in fancies and imaginations.[18]

She prayed 'give me not poverty, lest I steal.'[19]

Moll recounted the psychological impact of poverty: 'a time of distress is a time of dreadful temptation, and all the strength to resist is taken away; poverty presses, the soul is made desperate by distress, and what can be done?'[20] As she committed her first crime, she explained:

> I am very sure I had no manner of design in my head, when I went out, I neither knew or considered where to go, or on what business, but as the devil carried me out and laid his bait for me, so he brought me to be sure to the place, for I knew not whither I was going or what I did.[21]

Moll refused responsibility for the crimes she committed in a state of 'distress.' She disowned any malevolent intent and pointed to the devil as the perpetrator. She described herself as a passive victim, her mind distracted and her body at the mercy of outside forces beyond her control. Defoe's narrative alerted the reader of his skepticism about Moll's true motivation, even as he expressed sympathy for the plight of the poor.

Anthony Ashley Cooper, the third Earl of Shaftesbury (1671–1713) responded to the anxiety elicited by the permeability, divisibility, and incoherence of the self by positing the existence of an innate moral sense that could differentiate good from evil.[22] Shaftesbury claimed that the

> sense of right and wrong ... being as natural to us as natural affection itself, and being a first principle in our constitution and make, there is no speculative opinion, persuasion, or belief, which is capable immediately or directly to exclude or destroy it.[23]

The existence of a self implied a conscience, 'an inward eye [that] distinguishes and sees the fair and shapely, the amiable and admirable, apart from the deformed, the foul, the odious, or the despicable.'[24] For Shaftesbury, the true self could only be a good self that embraced individual responsibility.[25]

The expression of the good self relied on self-mastery. Shaftesbury described a self permeated by 'appetites, and sense, the fancys of all kinds.' The difference between madness and sanity rested in the 'controuler or manager' of fancy. 'Tis by means therefore of a countrouler or corrector of fancy, that I am sav'd from being mad ... the CORRECTRICE, by whose means I am in my wits, and without whom I am no longer *my-self.'*[26] Shaftesbury continued:

> every man indeed who is not absolutely beside himself, must of necessity hold his fancys under some kind of discipline and management. The *stricter* this discipline is, the more the man is rational and in his wits. The *looser* it is, the more fantastical he must be, and the nearer to the madman's state.[27]

The self described by Locke universalized the potential for instability and incoherence, and in the new psychology of the eighteenth century that incoherence became associated with insanity.

As Shaftesbury pointed out, 'if the fancys are left to themselves, the government must of course be of theirs. And then, what difference between such a state and madness?'[28] The association of 'fancies' with madness made the achievement of self-mastery even more important. The rational man – and in this case the gendered language is quite precise – responded to 'appetites' and 'fancies' with self-control.[29] In the face of displacement by passion and the possibility of insanity, Shaftesbury defined the true self as the one in full control of itself and those characteristics that could displace it. 'If I vote with FANCY, resign my *opinion* to her command, and judge of happiness and misery as *she* judges; how am I *my-self?'*[30] The undisciplined emotions are gendered feminine while the mastered, true self retains masculinity, reason, and control.[31]

The command of self did not make one impervious to external influence. In fact, the passions and affections defined humanity and individual identity. 'A man is by nothing so much *himself*, as by his *temper*, and *the character of his passions and affections*. If he loses what is manly and worthy in these, he is as much lost to himself as when he loses his memory and understanding.'[32] Nor did the male capacity for self-command nullify the influence of passions and other forces that might displace the self.

> A DISTEMPER in my eye may make me see the strangest kind of figures ... But let my senses err ever so widely; I am not on this account beside my-self: nor am I out of my own possession, whilst there is a person left within; who has power to dispute the appearances, and redress the imagination.[33]

The battle for self-control shaped a person's character and carved out the true self. 'I am accosted by ideas and striking apprehensions: but I take nothing on their report. I hear their story, and return 'em answer, as they deserve. FANCY and I are not all one. The disagreement makes me my own.'[34] Shaftesbury and other eighteenth-century writers could not bear to give up on the true self even in the face of their own decon-struction of it. Despite the discontinuity and displacement they described, they reconstituted the true self in order to accommodate their belief in personal accountability and free will as well as the conceptions of leadership and morality that they understood as residing in rational, well-born masculinity.[35]

The Scottish Enlightenment took up the theme of an innate moral sense in the latter half of the eighteenth century.[36] Adam Smith wrote that

> to feel much for others and little for ourselves, that to restrain our selfish, and to indulge our benevolent affections, constitutes the per-fection of human nature; and can alone produce among mankind that harmony of sentiments and passions in which consists their whole grace and propriety.[37]

The goodness in a person enabled him or her to feel for others and cre-ated compassion. Smith defined 'pity or compassion' as 'the emotion which we feel for the misery of others, when we either see it, or are made to conceive it in a very lively manner.' For Smith, pity was a universal quality, 'by no means confined to the virtuous and humane ... [and] the most hardened violator of the laws of society, is not altogether without it.'[38] Smith's analysis made an asset of the permeability and instability of the self. The very volatile and porous nature of the self made it susceptible to the feelings elicited by the experiences of others and these sympathetic feelings created opportunities for benevolence and virtue.

The sensitivity and responsiveness to feeling did not exclude a con-cern with what Samuel Johnson called the 'management of the mind.'[39] Those who expounded on sensibility, emotion, and passion shared Shaftesbury's opinion of self-command as the most admirable quality of a virtuous person. Adam Smith touted sympathy as essential to virtue because it enabled a man to control his feelings.

> The man who feels the most for the joys and sorrows of others, is best fitted for acquiring the most complete control of his own joys and sorrows. The man of the most exquisite humanity, is naturally the most capable of acquiring the highest degree of self-command.[40]

In times of crisis Smith recommended a composed response:

> A fretful temper, which feels, with too much sensibility, every little cross accident, renders a man miserable in himself and offensive to other people. A calm one, which does not allow its tranquillity to be disturbed … is a blessing to the man himself, and gives ease and security to all his companions.[41]

But Smith also warned against too extreme an interpretation of self-command. Too calculated an equilibrium and a complete lack of affect could lead to insensitivity: 'the man who feels little for his own misfortunes must always feel less for those of other people, and be less disposed to relieve them.'[42] In his somewhat fraught discussion of the subject of self-command Smith drew a sharp distinction between 'insensibility' and 'that noble firmness, that exalted self-command, which is founded in the sense of dignity and propriety.'[43]

Smith's preoccupation with the 'firmness' of self-command suggests his concern to define a sensibility that accommodated feeling and emotion without compromising masculinity. 'Our sensibility to the feelings of others, so far from being inconsistent with the manhood of self-command, is the very principle upon which that manhood is founded.'[44] Indeed, manhood depended on just such an intuition and response to emotion. However, the command and mastery of emotion's effects was essential to its experience. 'We esteem the man who supports pain and even torture with manhood and firmness; and we can have little regard for him who sinks under them, and abandons himself to useless outcries and womanish lamentations.'[45] Smith associated unrestrained emotion with femininity and questioned the sincerity of a man who expressed his feelings or his sympathy for others in an uncontrolled, 'womanish' fashion.

In his analysis, Smith drew a sharply gendered distinction between emotion and sensibility. 'Humanity is the virtue of a woman, generosity of a man. The fair sex, who have commonly much more tenderness than ours, have seldom so much generosity.'[46] Emotion, and particularly sympathy, remained qualities associated with women and marked by their undisciplined, impulsive character.

> Humanity consists merely in the exquisite fellow-feeling which the spectator entertains with the sentiments of the persons principally concerned, so as to grieve for their sufferings, to resent their injuries, and to rejoice at their good fortune. The most humane actions

require no self-denial, no self-command, no great exertion of the sense of propriety. They consist only in doing what this exquisite sympathy would of its own accord prompt us to do.[47]

Sensibility, or what Smith called 'generosity,' was marked by its masculine traits. It is exercised, measured, and not without reason: 'We are never generous except when in some respect we prefer some other person to ourselves, and sacrifice some great and important interest of our own to an equal interest of a friend or of a superior.'[48] While Smith acknowledged that women felt in a deeper and more immediate way than men, he asserted that they were unable to achieve the reasoned sacrifice entailed by true sensibility.

The object of sensibility also had a responsibility to display his or her sorrow with the appropriate constraint. 'We reverence that reserved, that silent and majestic sorrow, which discovers itself only in the swelling of the eyes, in the quivering of the lips and cheeks, and in the distant, but affecting, coldness of the whole behaviour.'[49] Unbounded emotion called its own sincerity into question. 'We are disgusted with that clamorous grief, which, without any delicacy, calls upon our compassion with signs and tears and importunate lamentations.'[50] For both the observer and the observed, undisciplined feeling represented danger to masculinity and the social order.

Johnson frequently commented about the forces that displaced the self from virtue. 'We are in danger from whatever can get possession of our thoughts; all that can excite in us either pain or pleasure has a tendency to obstruct the way that leads to happiness, and either to turn us aside or retard our progress.'[51] The constant threat from 'our senses, our appetites, and our passions' resulted in 'the descent to life merely sensual.'[52] Only religion, piety, and solitude could retrain the mind toward virtuous thoughts and deeds.

The capacity for self-command had the power to turn humanity from sensual pleasure to reason and from depravity to virtue. 'Nature will indeed always operate, human desires will be always ranging; but these motions, though very powerful, are not resistless; nature may be regulated, and desires governed.'[53] In order to maintain and enhance morality, Johnson urged daily self-examination and emphasized the aspect of choice in the translation of thought to behavior: 'we may govern our thoughts, restrain them from irregular motions, or confine them from boundless speculation.'[54] Johnson echoed Shaftesbury when he created the coherent self: the person who 'regulated his thoughts by those of reason'[55] and inhabited the true self that aspired to command and virtue.

These texts reveal their writers' gendered interpretation of moral capacity; Johnson will serve as an example in his explication of women's weaker capacity for self-control. According to him, women were especially vulnerable to the 'incursions of appetite.' Johnson warned that 'female goodness seldom keeps its ground against laughter, flattery, or fashion.' Observing that 'neither education nor reason gives them much security,' Johnson concluded that women fell prey to the 'influence of example' more often than men. Although he had no explanation for this phenomenon, Johnson speculated that women might 'have less courage to stand against opposition, or that their desire of admiration makes them sacrifice their principles for the pleasure of worthless praise.'[56] These passages indicate Johnson's belief in the precarious state of women's virtue, perpetually threatened by female vulnerability, permeability, and inconstancy.

Along with the assumption that women had a weaker capacity to withstand the force of passions and affections, the capacity for self-control had basis in class as well. According to Johnson, 'the common classes of mankind ... seldom range beyond those entertainments and vexations, which solicit their attention by pressing on their senses.'[57] Thus the good, true, and coherent self, while a potential possession of all humanity, resided more easily in men. Among men, the true and reasoned self belonged to those of good breeding and intelligence. These theories of the self implied the inherent inferiority of impoverished men and all women and fortified the gender and status hierarchies of the early modern world by equating elite selves with a coherence that endowed them with more power, responsibility, and authority.

Despite men's greater capacity for self-control, their mastery was never beyond challenge. While

> the man who acts according to the rules of perfect prudence, of strict justice, and of proper benevolence, may be said to be perfectly virtuous ... his own passions are very apt to mislead him; sometimes to drive him and sometimes to seduce him to violate all the rules which he himself, in all his sober and cool hours, approves of.[58]

Smith warned that without self-command 'the most perfect knowledge ... will not always enable him to do his duty.' Like Shaftesbury, Smith reminded his readers that no amount of self-control would make a man able to ignore all 'human weakness' and 'the violence of passions.'

> There are some situations which bear so hard upon human nature, that the greatest degree of self-government, which can belong to so

imperfect a creature as man, is not able to stifle, altogether, the voice of human weakness, or reduce the violence of the passions to that pitch of moderation, in which the impartial spectator can entirely enter into them.[59]

Smith, however, did not condone a man's resignation to his passions. He believed that experience, especially war and death, shaped and strengthened one's self-command. 'Self-command is not only itself a great virtue, but from it all the other virtues seem to derive their principal lustre.' The well-born masculine self, endowed with reason, practiced self-command and perfected it. The admirable qualities emerged as 'a certain intrepidity, a certain firmness of nerves and hardiness of consti- tution.'[60] He who mastered himself behaved with virtue and deserved positions of power, leadership, respect, and prestige.

Sympathy, virtue, and authenticity

As the ethics of the cult of sensibility were applied to conceptions of responsibility and the self, they constituted a new cultural domain con- cerned to draw on intellectual trends to create a new set of moral stan- dards. As Adela Pinch has remarked, this period was marked by its 'fascination with trying to account for where feelings come from and what they are.'[61] The culture of sensibility valued a 'delicacy of senti- ment' that would direct behavior away from 'riches or pleasure ... the gratifications of passion, and the delights of sense' and toward virtue.[62] The relationship between emotion and morality preoccupied the litera- ture of sensibility that was at its most influential and widespread from the 1740s to the 1770s.[63] Although novels are the best-known expres- sion of the culture of sensibility, philosophical essays, newspapers, sermons, and crime pamphlets also provided forums in which to ponder the place of emotion and sympathy, compassion and morality.

According to Pinch, 'the era of sensibility defined relations between middle-class British men and women and their social others: Indians, slaves, the poor, and the mad.'[64] The literature of sensibility modeled these relations by showing 'people how to behave, how to express them- selves in friendship and how to respond decently to life's experiences.'[65] Henry Mackenzie's tremendously popular *The Man of Feeling* (1771) nar- rated the search for virtue through emotional expression. Harley, the protagonist, literally embodied sensibility, enacting its values as he encountered a beggar, a lunatic, and a prostitute. He sought out the places where those on the margins of society gathered, playing cards with two vagrants, visiting an insane asylum, and expressing concern for the natives of India as he questioned the morality of empire.[66]

Through direct contact with the suffering of others, Harley performed compassion, the highest emotional state, and implicitly affirmed his own superior sensibility and virtue. Mackenzie summarized this sentiment when he wrote 'to the humane, I know there is a pleasure in goodness for its own sake.'[67]

The dynamic between the viewers of suffering and those they viewed necessitated some acknowledgment of the interiority of the observed.[68] In terms of the culture of sensibility a recognition of the existence and value of the sufferer's self and the capacity for sensibility among the lower orders evolved over the course of the eighteenth century. Although some writers insisted that sensibility was a characteristic unique to the higher orders, others described it as a shared, equalizing characteristic that crossed the lines of class.[69] The individual self may not have been defined as part of the identities of the lower orders at the beginning of the century. However, by the latter half of the eighteenth century, having a sense of oneself meant recognizing the subjectivity of the other. This acceptance of a working-class subjectivity by middle-class observers was not an act of beneficence. The acknowledgement of the feelings and the suffering of the poor affirmed the superiority of middle-class sensibility attained though contact with these suffering others.[70]

Scholars have traced the origins of the culture of sensibility to the Cambridge Platonists and Latitudinarians who posited an innate, virtuous moral sense. Sensibility developed into a movement through the writings of theologians and moralists who wished to dismiss the theories of stoics that experienced a resurgence of popularity in the late sixteenth century and the early decades of the seventeenth. The stoics defined all passions as destructive, unnatural obstacles to virtue. They urged the extermination of passions and the exaltation of reason. Humanity's anti-rationalism and unrestrainable depravity rendered reason impotent in the face of selfish passions.[71]

In their anti-stoical, anti-Puritan, and anti-Hobbesian writings, English moralists and theologians, including Isaac Barrow (1630–1677), John Tillotson (1630–1694), Robert South (1634–1716), Samuel Parker (1640–1688), Gilbert Burnet (1643–1715), Richard Bentley (1662–1742), and Samuel Clarke (1675–1729), imagined their religious ideas liberating the English Church from its past errors. They emphasized the moral ends of Christianity and the realization of justice, humanity, and mercy through charity. Their themes of 'good nature,' and 'universal benevolence' taught that human beings reflected their humanity through their desire to relieve suffering.[72]

The belief in the power of benevolence and feeling led to a consideration of 'the tender passions and affections.' In their sermons, these clerics argued against the stoic condemnation and distrust of emotion. Instead, Platonist and Latitudinarian teachings maintained the neutrality of the passions which they believed could be 'ordered to virtue.' They credited the emotions as the source of energy and power that invigorated men and motivated their good deeds. Pity and compassion led to effective benevolence and revealed a person's genuine goodness. The argument for the organic nature of benevolent feelings contradicted the belief in innate depravity postulated by the Puritans. It also provided a rebuttal to Thomas Hobbes (1588–1678) and his contention that without a strong government, the natural passions led to a state of war. In the place of the arbitrary morality postulated by Hobbes, these writers argued that the capacity for pity, tenderness, and benevolence distinguished men from other creatures and compelled them to fulfill their duty by living in conformity with their nature.[73]

Other literary genres took up similar themes to those expressed by Latitudinarian clerics as the scholarly interest in sensational psychology merged with the discussion of an innate moral sense. In *The Christian Hero* (1701) Richard Steele (1672–1729) defended both the passions and Christianity as the true paths to virtue.[74] While he conceded the depravity and irrationality of human beings, Steele believed that Christianity and reason could redirect the passions toward benevolence and virtue. The argument rested on the belief in the innate tendency to good in human nature and the assertion that pity, a passion, was the source of benevolence and essential to virtue. According to Steele, God 'has impress'd upon us all one nature, which ... presses us by natural society to a close union with each other; which is, methinks, a sort of enlargement of our very selves when we run into the ideas, sensations and concerns of our brethren.'[75] Through the capacity for compassion, 'men are insensibly hurried into each other and by a secret charm we lament with the unfortunate, and rejoice with the glad.'[76] The eyes provided the pathway to compassion 'for one man's eyes are spectacles to another to read his heart.'[77] Feeling the joy and grief of another 'seen and felt at a look' created the 'coelestial fire, we call charity or compassion', which 'opens our bosoms, and extends our arms to embrace all mankind.'[78] According to Steele sensibility revealed the true nature of humans, 'fram'd for mutual kindness, good will and service.' This kind of sensibility and the virtue it promised were achievable only within an innately and essentially religious, specifically Christian, view of the world.

Steele used *The Christian Hero* and his other publications, most prominently *The Tatler* (1709–1710) and *The Spectator* (1711–1712, 1714), to intervene in what he called a 'universal and destructive torrent of error and pleasure.'[79] This 'general insurrection against virtue' caused 'men [to be] hurry'd away in the prosecution of mean and sensual desire and instead of employing their passions in the service of life, they spend their life in the service of their passions.'[80] Steele's writing fits into the campaign to improve the general moral tone which began in the late seventeenth century. These efforts to eliminate vice led to the formation of Societies for the Reformation of Manners (SRM) that attempted to curb drunkenness, Sabbath-breaking, swearing, and other offenses.[81] Steele and other proponents of sensibility sought a much broader reformation of manners that would reform many of the values and behaviors associated with secular, Restoration masculinity. These included both activities such as gambling, drinking, dueling, and sports and sites of vice such coffeehouses, taverns, alehouses, and playhouses.[82]

In *The Tatler* and *The Spectator* Steele and Joseph Addison (1672–1719) popularized the sensational psychology developed by Locke and Newton and attempted to act as the arbiters of taste and the refinement of manners. These publications promoted emotion (within social limits), moderation over excess, reflection over impulse, and education in Christian and social duty over instinct.[83] Steele and Addison hoped to guide the tastes of the new consumers of household furnishings, clothing, groceries, literature, and art by espousing the values of Christian morality and self-discipline. Their efforts to shape tastes and sensibilities relied on and were inspired by the rise in literacy in the eighteenth century. Addison and Steele believed that the higher rates of literacy among servant women and the lower middle classes necessitated such an intervention because they increased the threat of unmediated, undirected consumption.[84]

In the middle of the eighteenth century Methodism, which spread quickly at exactly the height of the culture of sensibility, set out to continue the reformation of manners, often calling on emotion and sensations in an effort to revive religion, reform the Church, and redirect morals. In the service of this goal John Wesley (1703–1791) often edited and republished novels that elicited 'pleasurable pain.'[85] The authors of novels claimed their work took up the mission defined by Addison and Steele.

In his works, Samuel Richardson (1689–1761), the most prominent of the sentimental novelists, brought together the discussion of self, sensational psychology, the culture of sensibility, and the realization of virtue. For Richardson, sensibility embodied the search for and the expression of the authentic, real self. In his novels and his extensive commentaries on them Richardson struggled to depict sensibility as the locus of virtue. According to Richardson the capacity to feel and display sentiment, defined as feelings, judgments, instincts, and opinions, allowed one to realize moral rectitude.[86] Through the literary convention of the epistolary novel, Richardson's protagonists, most notably Pamela and Clarissa, engaged in self-examination and self-revelation using the language of sensibility. This language did not rely solely on the spoken word; instead its vocabulary (summarized succinctly by John Mullan as 'of gestures and palpitations, sighs and tears') was formed by those disruptions or interruptions of speech.[87] While the authenticity of speech was perpetually undermined by possible 'conflict and deceit' contained within it, the heart served as the conduit of truth, revealing the real self.[88] Richardson's aim was to present an unmediated, authentic inner self. This performance of sensibility attempted to erase the line between the interior self and exterior appearance.[89]

The process of self-expression and revelation met the criticism of some contemporary readers who believed that Pamela's performance of her inner self impugned its own authenticity. Her self-knowledge seemed to promote design and imply power, thus weakening its claim to innocence, immediacy, spontaneity, and virtue.[90] In *Clarissa* Richardson tried to shore up his claims of authenticity by disconnecting sensibility from agency and virtue from power.[91] Although this is true throughout the novel, the most dramatic example occurred when Clarissa was raped. When urged by Anne Howe and her mother to prosecute a case against Lovelace, she refused, saying, 'I would sooner suffer every evil (the repetition of the capital one excepted), than appear publicly in a court to do myself justice.'[92] Christine Roulston speculates that Clarissa feared bringing her case to court because a legal representation of the events would distort the story and perhaps cast doubt on her claim to authenticity. In the process of shaping the story to the rules of the legal process, Clarissa would lose control of her self-representation and the articulation of her virtue.[93] As Roulston points out, it was not making the story public that Clarissa avoided, but rather the loss of control and authenticity that would result from a legal presentation in a court of justice.

In making her case to the Reverend Lewen against a public prosecution, Clarissa speculated that the circumstances surrounding her rape, her clandestine meeting with Lovelace as well as her stay at his house, would be held against her in court. She asserted that these 'pleas in my favour' would render 'little advantage *in a court* (perhaps bandied about, and jested profligately with) ... which *out of court*, and to a *private* and *serious* audience, would have carried the greatest weight.'[94] On a more pragmatic level, Clarissa pointed out that most rape cases in the eighteenth century did not end with a conviction.[95] Clarissa concluded that 'the warning that may be given from those papers to all such young creatures as may have known or heard of me, may be more efficacious, as I humbly presume to think, to the end wished for, than my appearance could have been in a court of justice.'[96] Clarissa implied that the performance of her case in court would undermine its authenticity and her credibility while the publicity of the crime of which she was a victim through her letters would preserve her privacy, her self-representation, and her authenticity. Clarissa's argument reiterated Richardson's suspicion of and disappointment in aural speech as compared to the more direct and effective communication achieved by the experience of reading or by bodily gestures such as 'palpitations, sighs and tears.' This discussion encapsulates many of the tensions within the culture of sensibility between public display and private experience, authenticity and artifice, the possibility of merging the inner self with exterior affect, and the definition of the authentic as opposed to the superficial self. These questions followed the language of sensibility into the courtroom in the form of pleas of mental distress and the critiques of those who heard them.

II Representing selves in the courtroom

The question of self-mastery took on even more urgency in moments of discontinuity that resulted in or coincided with a crime. Short of a formal defense of insanity that claimed a complete lack of comprehension, the legal system made no provisions for missteps resulting from the self's momentary displacement. As Patricia Meyer Spacks succinctly put it, 'moral responsibility depends on consistent identity' and so did English law.[97]

Johnson wrote on just this question in the *Rambler* in 1750 when he discussed the unrealistic 'expectation of uniformity of character' in the face of 'the power of desire, the cogency of distress, the complications of affairs or the force of partial influence.'[98] In terms similar to those used by defendants speaking a language of excuse Johnson explained that

> the wisest and best men deviate from known and acknowledged duties, by inadvertency or surprise; and most are good no longer than while temptation is away, than while their passions are without

excitements, and their opinions are free from the counteraction of any other motive.

For Johnson, the consistently virtuous and the thoroughly abandoned numbered a minority. For most, virtuous behavior always hung in the balance between 'riches or pleasure ... the gratifications of passion, and the delights of sense' and 'laws of which they own the obligation, and rewards of which they believe the reality.' According to Johnson, human beings existed 'in a kind of equipoise between good and ill' and struggled to accommodate the immediate enjoyment of wealth, passion, or sensual pleasure and moral rectitude.[99]

Echoing the moral sentiments implied in the testimony of defendants and others who introduced the language of the mind in court, Johnson opined that 'such is the state of all mortal virtue, that it is always uncertain and variable.' As if speaking to a jury assessing the merits of a defendant's case, Johnson advised that rather than judging a person 'by too short an acquaintance, and too slight inspection,' one must weigh carefully the good and the bad that exist in an offender.

> Let none too hastily conclude that all goodness is lost, though it may for a time be clouded and overwhelmed; for most minds are the slaves of external circumstances, and conform to any hand that undertakes to mould them, roll down any torrent of custom in which they happen to be caught, or bend to any importunity that bears hard against them.[100]

Johnson's essay presented each crime as an individual act motivated by specific weaknesses rather than a sign of greater, irreparable depravity. He cautioned against drawing too great a distinction between the virtuous and the depraved and expressed confidence in an inherent good self that would manifest itself with sufficient coaxing and tutelage.

Ideas about the self and sensibility circulated more easily and quickly starting at the end of the seventeenth century due to the increase in literacy and reading which crossed lines of gender and status. The dramatic rise in literacy rates in both men and women resulted in a 60 percent literacy rate for men and 40 percent in women by 1750. This rise in literacy rates is attributed to the centrality of biblical texts in Protestantism, the spread of charity schools and boarding schools, and the profit motive of the publishing business. Circulating libraries, chapbooks, serialization, cheap editions, and the market in secondhand books all made reading materials more accessible to a wider reading audience. By the century's end most men and the majority of women could read. This majority obviously included artisans, shopkeepers, yeomen, husbandmen, and servants who read newspaper articles, crime pamphlets, and novels that probed questions of human psychology, motivation, feeling, and morality.[101]

The men and women who introduced pleas of mental excuse in court translated the 'gestures and palpitations, sighs and tears,' that 'puncture and interrupt speech,' the displays of sentiment, the capacity to feel, into a vocabulary of excuse to try to save their lives.[102] As we saw at the end of chapter 2, the concerns of legal authorities about the effects that this language might have on the legal process indicates that this language aroused sympathy in its listeners, but it also introduced the same questions about authenticity so familiar to contemporaries who criticized the culture of sensibility. The problem of performing one's emotions in public immediately raised the specter of counterfeit, already so familiar to legal authorities from discussions of the insanity defense.

Drunkenness: a 'temporary phrenzy'

Many defendants used the language of mental incapacity to explain crimes committed while they were drunk. Hale called drunkenness a vice which resulted in *dementia affectata*. He admitted that liquor 'deprives men of the use of reason, and puts many men into a perfect, but temporary phrenzy,' but he argued that the drunken defendant 'shall have no privilege by his voluntary contracted madness, but shall have the same judgement as if he were in his right senses.'[103] Blackstone accepted the connection between intoxication and insanity, but he maintained the legal principle of culpability when he called drunkenness 'artificial, voluntary contracted madness.'[104] For Blackstone drunkenness never diminished the gravity of an offense. Instead, he asserted: 'our law looks upon this as an aggravation of the offense, rather than as an excuse.'[105] Even more than the mental pleas that stretched the limits of the insanity defense, drunkenness clearly diverged from a legitimate and acceptable excuse. However, on the spectrum of mental excuses intoxication also sat closest to insanity because legal commentators used a language that stressed the characteristics it shared with insanity to debunk the acceptability of a plea of drunkenness.

Along with the most common crime – theft – defendants introduced intoxication as an excuse when charged with attempted rape, sedition, and arson. They used the drunkenness plea to explain accidental deaths resulting from quarrels as well as domestic disturbances and other erratic, violent behavior. Defendants blamed the mental state induced by drink for relatively harmless effects such as memory loss and for more serious conditions in which a defendant's intoxication made him or her susceptible to persuasion to commit a crime. Two kinds of excuses emerge: in the first, a simple drunkenness plea, offenders argued generally for diminished responsibility. The second kind of plea linked the effects of intoxication with insanity.

The excuse of simple drunkenness was gendered male and in an overwhelming majority of cases it was a man who presented the plea of alcohol. While women often ran alehouses and drank at taverns and inns, the defense of alcohol, associated with hard drinking and physical aggression, fits well with contemporary conceptions of honor and masculinity, which often celebrated the heavy drinker.[106] The image of a drunk man, while not always attractive or appealing, was not unfamiliar to jurors and judges who drank to drunkenness themselves and knew the effects of alcohol. An excuse of drunkenness from a man was more exculpatory than the image of a drunk woman, which might incur only more disapproval.

Deponents used a diverse and nuanced language to describe intoxication. When charged with stealing a double-breasted coat in May of 1740, Christopher Thwaites said that 'when in liquor he knows not what he does ... he being so stupidly drunk.'[107] Hannah Hore, accused of stealing in 1750, told the court she was 'fuddled,' while in 1752 John McDaniel explained that his act of breaking and entering was a result of his being 'incapacitated if he had ever intended to do hurt, through liquor.'[108] Charged with treasonable words in 1756, Thomas Richardson described himself as 'insensible with the effects of liquor,' while in 1768 Robert Johnson mentioned that he intended to return the horse he had taken when he 'came to his senses.'[109] James Cartwright, indicted for attempted assault and robbery in 1772, explained, 'I was so intoxicated that I did not know any thing I did.'[110]

The deposition given by Thomas Heavysides on August 10, 1728 allows us to analyze the components of the simple drunkenness plea and their significance. Heavysides confessed that:

> he took up the said purse [belonging to Jonathan Armstrong] in which was about five pounds in gold and silver ... This examinant upon farther examination confessed that it was drink and the devil's temptation made him pick the said Armstrong's pocket.[111]

Heavysides tried to distance himself from his act by blaming the effects of alcohol and diabolical temptation for his moral lapse. He implied that stealing was not a part of his normal ethical code and that had he been sober, the crime would not have been committed. As in other routine cases of theft, the defense followed a definite, formulaic pattern. The confession depicted the crime as the result of an accidental opportunity which arose in a state of drunkenness. We see here just how far defendants stretched the excuse of drunkenness; they used it to explain their moral weakness even while their manual dexterity (in this case the ability to pickpocket) remained intact.[112]

Offenders admitted their guilt as a part of their defense, but this leaves us with the question of what exactly they thought about their level of responsibility for the crime. Henry Wharton, indicted for riot in 1756, explained that 'he was encouraged to join by a great number of inhabitants of Keswick and was made drunk or else he would not have done it.'[113] George Wardle admitted that he stole 16 rabbit skins in 1796, but he added 'that he was in liquor or that he would not have done so.'[114] These defendants blamed intoxication for their crimes rather than blaming themselves; their depositions represent the drunk offender and the sober deponent as two different people.

William Foster's case from 1742 is in many ways typical of the simple drunkenness defense. Our defendant admitted that:

> last night or early this morning he went into the said Thomas Turnell's lodging room and took a pair of breeches out from under the said Mr. Turnell's pillow and thereout feloniously took the net purse now produced.[115]

Despite his confession, Foster qualified his accountability for the crime by adding: 'at that time he this examinant was much in liquor or should not have been guilty of the offense aforesaid.' While he admitted his guilt, Foster explicitly asserted that he would not have committed the crime in a sober state of mind.[116]

Defendants distanced themselves from their crimes when they related the effect of drunkenness on their mental capacity and their ability to act ethically. Most commonly they described an impaired memory. Robert Heron's examination in 1768 is typical:

> But this examinant being then very much intoxicated by liquor cannot now recollect any thing further that happened ... or whether ... [he] took any money ... or not.[117]

The loss of memory was not restricted to cases of theft. When charged with the murder of Isaac Tully in 1750, James Clark deposed that:

> to the best of this examinant's remembrance the last time he saw the said Isaac Tully was upon a marsh ... and that being so much in

liquor he does not remember whether the said Isaac Tully got into the boat with him, or how he came by his death.[118]

All of these examples point to a common conclusion drawn by defendants entering a plea of simple drunkenness: their testimony asserted that the crime was out of their usual, sober character, that it would never have happened but for the influence of alcohol, and that they had no malicious intent. When John Moer was tried for horse theft in January 1716, the author of the *OBSP* summarized the verdict by saying, 'the prisoner, it seems, was a very honest man, a trooper (cavalryman), and being in drink thought what he did was a very harmless frolick.'[119] The plea of simple drunkenness rested on the declaration by defendants that their crimes were anomalous and unpremeditated acts committed without wicked intent.

Witnesses for both the prosecution and for the defense often included attitudes about drunkenness in their depositions and courtroom testimony. In Richard Harwood's case from 1743 the defendant's deposition does not survive (if it was ever taken), but the words of his victims, Elizabeth and William Roberts, expressed their opinions about Harwood's crime. Elizabeth deposed that 'there was a scaffold reared up against the said William Roberts' house' in June 1742. At one in the morning as she lay in her bed, she saw that 'a man came on to the said scaffold and was getting in at the frame of a window.' As soon as she heard him, Elizabeth 'got up and alarmed the family.' When confronted with his crime of unlawful entry, the defendant, Richard Harwood, apparently said that 'he was drunk and came to lay in that bed.'[120]

William Roberts confirmed that 'he saw the said Harwood soon after the said attempt,' but 'that he did not the next day suspect that the said Harwood had any evil or wicked intent.' William dismissed the incident as 'a drunken fit,' and testified that he 'has been with the said Harwood several times since and sold him upon credit a piece of Russia drab for a frock which he would not have done if he had thought the said Harwood had any ill design at the time of the attempt.'[121]

This case illustrates the important role played by the offender's perceived intent in the community's assessment of guilt. William Roberts, the supposed victim, addressed the question of the defendant's intent directly. He stated quite emphatically that he did not think Harwood had an 'evil or wicked intent' when he broke into the house. Roberts felt so strongly about Harwood's lack of sinister design that he considered Harwood credit worthy and did business with him after the incident. The prosecutor himself dismissed the crime as 'a drunken fit.'[122]

William Roberts' deposition suggests that communities tolerated certain misbehavior that they considered harmless; those acquainted with the accused measured the damage of a given crime by assessing the nature of the offender's intent based on a broader knowledge and opinion of his or her personality and character. Neighbors often gave drunk defendants the benefit of the doubt; a generally good reputation and a usually sober character served as proof that the offender lacked evil design and provided collateral against future mischief.[123]

No offense illustrates this localized relationship between intention, responsibility, and guilt better than deaths resulting from fights that broke out in taverns or alehouses.[124] Testimony of deep friendship without conflict between the killer and his victim recurs predictably in the depositions. The descriptions of camaraderie accompany the defendant's expression of deep regret and sorrow. During the investigation of John Parr's murder by John Coultherd in 1758, Parr's widow deposed that 'they were good friends before this discourse happened.' Coultherd's wife said that when her husband heard that Parr was dead he said, 'God forbid, I hope not.'[125] In the depositions about Latus Ricarby's assault of Edward Purchas in 1758, the victim deposed from his sickbed 'that he does not believe the said wound was given through any quarrel, malice, or evil intent whatsoever.'[126] Purchas was convinced that Ricarby stabbed him with no evil intent because the accused was a friend who was drunk.

Thus far all of the cases discussed share a fundamental similarity: all the defendants blamed their crimes on their weakened will. Each offender entreated the magistrate to see his or her crime as an aberration. Defendants wove together strands of the religious discourse of the seventeenth century that appealed to a universal propensity for sin with eighteenth-century discussions of displaced selves; they sought forgiveness or a less severe punishment for crimes they portrayed as momentary indiscretions to whom all were equally susceptible rather than serious threats to law and order or signs of a deeper criminal nature.[127]

Of course, not every mention of drunkenness was intended to exculpate the defendant. Some witnesses linked drunkenness, dangerousness, and violence to mark the accused as a threat to the community. These negative images of drunkenness usually accompanied a recommendation for the continued detention of the accused. In 1737 prominent members of the Ripley community filed an affidavit calling Robert Stephenson 'very profane swearing drunken quarrelsome and dangerous' and urging his imprisonment. In another dramatic case, Alice Downham cited her husband Joseph's 'carnal and inhumane' abuse 'especially when he was in liquor' when she petitioned for his continued confinement in 1763. She feared that he would 'kill or destroy her,' and described two past instances when he attempted to do just that. This testimony corroborated the image of laboring people as less responsible and less able to control themselves and in no way aided the defendant's cause.[128]

Some defendants elided drunkenness and insanity more explicitly, perhaps with the hope that they would receive an automatic acquittal or pardon. Women are more visible in this set of cases. This is consistent with ideas about insanity in the early modern period: the high consumption of alcohol by a woman would have been considered one more sign of the outlandish, antisocial behavior of the insane or a symptom of emerging understandings of alcohol addiction. Alcohol was considered especially harmful to laboring women, perceived as especially vulnerable to addiction, and the women's families, who would suffer as a consequence of their inability to fulfill their duties as wives and mothers.[129]

When Elizabeth Lawler stole the carcass of a lamb in May 1718, the prosecutor and the defendant competed to name the mental condition associated with the crime. Thomas Kotum testified that he pursued Lawler and 'apprehended [her] with the lamb under her arm.' The accused 'pleaded that she was disordered in her head and crazy, and did not know what she did nor how she came by it.' In response, Kotum 'owned indeed that she was drunk.' The prosecutor and the defendant accounted for the same deviant behavior in different ways. The defendant claimed that she was not culpable because of her mental impairment; the prosecutor responded to this defense by maintaining that Lawler was intoxicated. Kotum re-inscribed Lawler's responsibility for her crime by asserting that she was drunk rather than insane.[130]

Other testimony from the *OBSP* combined insanity and intoxication by citing the effects of drink on someone with a history of 'lunatic' behavior. At three in the morning on March 3, 1715, Nathaniel Parkhurst, esquire, burst into the room belonging to Lewis Pleura on board a ship where they were both held prisoner. Parkhurst, described as 'having been up all night drinking,' cried 'damn ye, Sir Lewis, pay me the four guineas you owe me' and stabbed Pleura to death. At his trial the prisoner 'did [not] deny it any otherwise than by saying he knew nothing of it and that he had been an imperfect man as to his senses, for two years and a half past.' While several witnesses corroborated Parkhurst's story and 'swore to a great many lunatic and whimsical things that he had been guilty of within that space of time,' others testified that 'he was in a capacity of distinguishing what he did, having lately transacted some business relating to his liberty, in which he appeared to be in his right senses.'[131] This disagreement echoed the concerns of legal commentators about substantiating the offender's real state of mind.

In another set of insanity-drunkenness pleas defendants linked the combination of drunkenness and physical impairment with the onset of temporary insanity. At Sarah Hatchet's trial for the murder of Thomas Watson in 1726, a witness deposed that while Hatchet was 'very drunk' she cried out to him in reference to the murdered man: 'I hit his head while his throat was cut.'[132] Hatchet denied knowing the victim or being anywhere near the scene of the crime; a watchman and several witnesses corroborated her testimony. In addition:

> several witnesses deposed that the prisoner was quite beside her senses and would say anything when she got drunk, that her head had been so disordered by some unlucky blows that she received from her husband, who used to beat her unmercifully, that a half-pennyworth of geneva would make her speak all the extravagancies of a person in Bedlam.[133]

Without implying a universal effect of alcohol, the witnesses ascribed this particular prisoner's false confession to a mind 'disordered' by physical abuse and alcohol. They attributed her pattern of unrestrained, inappropriate speech to gin and the infirmity wrought by her injuries.

William Smithson's Old Bailey trial for the theft of a trunk full of clothes in December 1778 saw a detailed interrogation of the notion that physical injuries exacerbated by alcohol could render a person insane. When granted the opportunity to speak in his defense, he said, 'I know nothing of the matter; I was very much in liquor; when I am in liquor I am out of my mind; I don't know what I say or do. I had a fracture in my head some years ago.' The court asked the victim if 'he, when he fetched the trunk, appear[ed] to stagger, or seem unable to carry the trunk?' The prosecutor replied that 'he did not appear to me to be drunk; if he had been drunk he could not have carried it.' Another witness said, 'when we took him in bed, he appeared exceedingly stupid, whether it was real or affected, I cannot take upon me to say; he never stirred a limb, nor got out of bed till he was dragged out.'[134] This testimony reiterated the concerns expressed by Hale, Brydall, and Blackstone about counterfeit and the impossibility of authenticating another person's state of mind or true intent.

Several witnesses assessed Smithson's mental capacity. Elizabeth Dennis said she had known Smithson for two and a half years and that 'he is a very honest man as far as I know; only when he is in liquor he is just as if he was out of his senses almost.' The court responded by asking, 'Do you think he is capable of knowing then what he does?' To this question Dennis replied, 'I don't think he is some times.' Margaret Smith testified that:

> I have known the prisoner two years; he is a very honest, sober, industrious, good husband; only when he gets a little liquor in his head, he does not know what he does.[135]

Margaret illustrated her point by telling the court that Smithson came to her drunk in September of that year and falsely reported his daughter's death. The unusual detail of this testimony and the court's interest in it provide a glimpse of contemporary understandings of the effects of alcohol, the presentation of this evidence in court, and the court's struggle to assign responsibility in these cases.

Smithson had a clear idea of the effect that alcohol had on his thought process, and he articulated it clearly; furthermore, his friends and neighbors knew about his fears about intoxication. Theirs was not the formulaic testimony repeated so often in the *OBSP*. The witnesses for Smithson qualified the standard character description ('he always bore an excellent character,' 'he is a very honest, sober, industrious, good husband') with very specific references to Smithson's behavior while intoxicated. The witnesses made an explicit connection between the effects of alcohol and a more lasting, serious mental impairment. Samuel Smith said that when Smithson was drunk, he was 'like a mad man' and that 'he is quite out of his mind,' while Elizabeth Dennis testified that when in liquor he was 'quite out of his senses.'[136]

These insanity-drunkenness cases demonstrate a clear knowledge of the law among defendants and witnesses who understood the scope of the insanity defense. Defendants and their supporters tried to associate crimes committed by those experiencing the effects of alcohol with the uncontrollable behavior expected of those deemed *non compos mentis*. Sometimes they called on a history of mental illness or physical injury to support their contention that drunkenness had more profound effects than mere stumbling or slurred speech. They hoped that if they convinced the judge and jury of a real link between the two states, the court would accept the drunkenness-insanity defense as a legitimate plea that would serve as grounds for dismissal, acquittal, or pardon. Even if they failed to associate their state of mind with exculpatory insanity, they hoped to make a case for mitigation.

Necessity

In the insanity defenses examined in chapter 2 and in the drunkenness defenses surveyed above, defendants explained their states of mind during a crime by analogy. They compared their disoriented mental states to legal insanity and distanced what they claimed to be their true selves from their offenses. Thus defendants and others who spoke about them expanded the meaning of exculpatory madness. While the defense of insanity existed in the law and commentators often compared drunkenness and insanity (even to disqualify drunkenness as a legitimate excuse before the law), the definition of legal insanity specifically excluded necessity, passion, and other compulsions from an insanity defense. Despite these restrictions, defendants and their neighbors, justices of the peace conducting an investigation and clerks recording it, introduced speculation about compulsion in depositions and trial records. These explanations represented crime as the result of a self displaced by financial distress, love, anger or 'passion,' and 'the instigation of the devil.'[137]

Defendants referred to their poverty as a force that overwhelmed their powers of self-restraint and compelled them to commit crimes. Here defendants appealed to an explanation for crime whose lengthy history documents a struggle between the desire for a limited acceptance of this excuse and the establishment of boundaries for its use. As early as the seventh century the *Penitential of Theodore* admonished legal authorities to care for the poor.[138] This opinion was reiterated in ecclesiastical and secular legal codes throughout the Middle Ages which advised leniency in the judgment of the poor.[139]

According to Common Law, the value of the goods stolen determined the seriousness of the offense. The theft of goods valued at a shilling or more was grand larceny and a capital felony, while thefts of under a shilling were petty larceny and non-capital. Britton's thirteenth-century opinion used the distinction between grand larceny and petty larceny to set the most important precedent regarding the reception of the plea of poverty by legal authorities. Britton defined burglary as a felony punishable by death, however, 'poor people, who through hunger enter the house of another for victuals under the value of twelve pence, are excepted; as are also idiots and madmen, and others, who are incapable of felony.'[140] By excluding from punishment burglary and petty larceny by the poor, Britton seems to have accepted poverty as an excuse for theft.[141] He did, however, distinguish between the intent of the insane and that of the poor. The language of the law made a practical distinction by defining the poor as rational. The twelve pence rule implied that the poor offender was considered rational in so far as he or she was able to contain the theft to this amount of money. This understanding of poverty and the law is ambiguous. On the one hand, the hungry were regarded as rational and responsible by the twelve pence rule; on the other hand, the mention of the poor with madmen and idiots seems to acknowledge that the desperation of poverty may result in actions for which one should not be held accountable.

In the sixteenth century Edmund Plowden's (1518–1585) discussion of poverty focused the language of the age on the word necessity. In his report on *Reniger v Fogossa* he stated that 'we may see also ... that necessity shall be a good excuse in all laws, and that all laws give place to necessity.'[142] Plowden claimed that 'the law of God gives place to necessity: so that the words of the law of God may be broken for necessity without offense to God.'[143] Like legal commentators before him, Plowden defined the exemption of poverty only in terms of the theft of food to satisfy hunger. He did not redefine such theft as a non-crime; he claimed only that in cases of necessity such criminal behavior ought to be tolerated. Francis Bacon (1561–1626) also favored the exemption of the hungry from responsibility for the theft of food and this opinion was echoed in manuals for justices of the peace that advised legal authorities to impose only a mild punishment for those who explained petty larceny as the result of hunger.[144]

Matthew Hale's opinion about the plea of poverty reversed the legal scholarship of the previous millennium. Hale adamantly rejected poverty as a justification for breaking the law because 'men's properties would be under a strange insecurity, being laid open to other men's necessities.' For Hale the issue was clear: the acceptance of the excuse of poverty would 'let loose ... all the ligaments of property and civil society' which the legal system served to protect.[145] Despite his definition of such crimes as the results of 'a sixth species of defect of will ... arising from *compulsion* and inevitable *necessity*,' Blackstone echoed Hale's opinion that poverty was not an acceptable excuse for crime.[146] Both Hale and Blackstone protested that a legal excuse of poverty was unnecessary in England where, by virtue of the Poor Law, 'charity is reduced to a system, interwoven in our very constitution.'[147]

This abbreviated history of the plea of poverty suggests that rational necessity was losing its cultural meaning in the eighteenth century and was slowly replaced by a plea of poverty predicated on insanity. This new plea claimed that the defendant lacked a felonious intent because the crime resulted from the psychological effects of the 'pressure of poverty.' The result was a new correlation between necessity, insanity, and crime.

Pleas of poverty elided necessity and compulsion. When he offered his defense for stealing two pairs of worsted stockings in 1746, Thomas Welsh told the court that 'necessity obliged me.'[148] After he pleaded guilty to forgery in 1750, William Smith said that 'a case of necessity urged me to commit the fact I am charged with.'[149] Valentine Dudden told the court that he stole two saws in 1772 because 'I was really in want, and had been ill a great while; I did it through necessity; I am a carpenter.'[150] While this language did not make a direct reference to mental incapacity, it suggested that the duress of poverty prevented restraint and promoted the crime.[151]

Other offenders described a murderous state of mind brought on by their inability to provide for their families. When three-year-old John Atkinson was found dead in 1749, his mother, Mary, was indicted for his murder. Mary admitted that 'she did cut the throat of ... her infant son with a razor, that she had no other inducement or reason for so doing but the fear of the said child wanting bread.'[152] In a similar case from 1756 George Taylor, a schoolmaster mentioned in chapter 2, admitted to killing his five-year-old son 'by cutting his throat with a penknife.' When asked 'what induced him to commit so barbarous a crime,' he answered that:

> he had no premeditated design of murdering the child but it coming into the said house ... and crying for bread it immediately occurred to this examinant's mind that he would not long have bread to give it.[153]

These defenses addressed the question of motive by stating a lack of rational intent: Mary Atkinson said she had 'no other inducement or reason for so doing,' while George Taylor, perhaps in a phrase constructed by the clerk or the justice of the peace, denied a 'premeditated design.' Each case suggests that the mental state created by the inability to provide for a child drove a parent to murder.[154]

These pleas imply that the perpetrator had to resort to crime in order to fulfill or void a role as parent and provider. Husbands made similar arguments about their wives. When Richard Sweetman assaulted Mary Whitmarsh with the intent to steal her money in 1750, he told the court, 'I had a pistol in my hand, and was going to make away with myself, being in extremity and want, having a wife in a starving condition.' Sweetman claimed that 'thinking about [his] soul' he reneged on his suicidal intentions and decided to rob Mary Whitmarsh instead. In 1751 Edward Meredith confessed to the theft of a large sum of money at his Old Bailey trial.[155] Meredith told the court, 'I am a young man that has had a great deal of trouble with a young woman which I lately married ... I had no money to support her and my brains were turned, and between whiles I am not in my senses.[156] Meredith denied any choice in the matter alleging that his crime resulted from mental distress working on honorable intentions. The intimate, domestic contexts in which these claims occur combine passion and poverty, bolstering the argument that those accused were driven to a desperate act by their best intentions to provide for their loved ones.

These pleas of poverty defined criminal intent as an issue of character in which the defendant or the witnesses who appeared on his or her behalf tried to convince that jury that the accused was an upstanding member of the community and that the crime had been an aberration and an isolated incident. The implicit message was that the perpetrator had to resort to crime in order to fulfill a role as provider – for self or for family – that he or she, but in most cases he, had no other choice, and that even though the law had been broken, the crime was a part of an honorable identity. Deponents and witnesses attempted to persuade the justices, jurors, and judges who listened to their testimony to separate a generally innocent character from a specific criminal act, based on extenuating circumstances such as financial hardship or the compulsion of necessity. The language in which defendants protested that they 'lacked felonious intent' for crimes committed 'from mere necessity' emphasized an understanding that poverty caused despair and despair proved not only a lack of felonious intent but also a kind of insanity. Poverty, which once was accepted as the cause of crime, now became the source of a modified, temporary insanity which propelled its victims toward crime.

While theft for provision was never considered the result of felonious intent, it had been understood as a rational, logical choice of action, the consequence of poverty. In the eighteenth century crimes of poverty were regarded as the effects of insanity caused by despair. By portraying this kind of crime as the result of social conditions over which they had no control, poor defendants and their supporters explained their infractions by associating their behavior with uncontrollable duress. These defenses reveal a subtle and sophisticated understanding of English law which linked necessity with compulsion and the lack of criminal intent typical of an insanity defense.

Passion and compulsion

When defendants expanded mental excuses to speak of passion and compulsion as the causes of their crimes, their language of the mind became a language of emotion and made a direct appeal to the ethos of sensibility. These informal defenses bore only the faintest resemblance to an insanity defense. They too were not unique to the eighteenth century and legal commentators explicitly forbade them as legitimate pleas, but the era of sensibility altered their significance.

Some male defendants blamed love for their crimes, indicating that their feelings for another person impaired their ability to think clearly and to act ethically. When Francis Pratt stole 18 sheep in 1758, he explained that 'he was crossed in love, which turned his brains, that he did not know what he was doing when he took them.' Pratt argued for the temporary nature of his mental displacement when he added that he had 'served a great many good masters and never wronged them of anything.'[157] In the eighteenth century's most famous case of 'love and madness' James Hackman shot his former lover, Martha Reay, as she left a theater in Covent Garden on April 7, 1779. At his trial he claimed that 'the will to destroy her who was ever dearer to me than life, was never mine' and that he planned to kill himself 'until a momentary phrenzy overcame me and induced me to commit the deed I deplore.'[158] As evidence of his mental state and his suicidal rather than homicidal intentions, Hackman presented a letter he wrote to his brother-in-law before the crime stating that his loss of Miss Reay 'has driven me to madness.'[159] Although he never mentioned love, uncontrolled jealousy seems to have motivated Arthur Hagan to kill his wife Ann in 1764. Arthur told the two justices of the peace investigating the case that he suspected his wife of 'carrying on a criminal correspondence' with another man. The couple 'fell to words and scolded for some time' before Arthur reached 'the height of his passion took a knife out of his pocket, and stabbed her in several parts of her body.'[160]

In the murder of one man by another discussion of passion and the temper of both the victim and the accused inflected much of the testimony. In July 1721 Richard Grantham killed Norton Fitzgerald in a 'sudden heat of passion.' Witnesses represented this passion as both temporary and unusual. They described the two men as 'intimate friends' and 'a great many gentlemen' testified to the prisoner's 'quiet and peaceable behavior.'[161] Similarly in a case from the following year several of John Garton's fellow officers 'gave the prisoner the character of being very humane, hardly ever known to be in a passion, and abuse men; but was remarkable for his lenity and even temper.'[162] William Platten's temper and emotional control were the subject of discussion at his trial for the murder of Richard Snow in 1761. Platten hit Snow with a heavy piece of wood that he threw off a barge claiming, 'I was hauling in the ropes, and threw that piece of wood out of my way, without seeing where it would go.' Joseph Hurry, the master of the ship, appeared on Platten's behalf. Asked about Platten's 'temper and disposition of mind' he responded that Platten 'is of a very humane, good-natured disposition, not apt to be passionate, quite the contrary.'[163]

Just as a placid and calm temperament might exonerate or mitigate, a defendant's reputation for unprovoked violence, uncontrolled emotional outbursts, and indifference to the consequences of his or her actions bolstered an argument for harsher punishment or prolonged imprisonment. Two constables sent to arrest John Platton in 1729 described him as 'so dangerous and desperate a man that he cares not what he does.'[164] A petition from 1737 urging the continued detention of Robert Stephenson, mentioned earlier, called him 'a very prophane swearing drunken quarrelsom and dangerous man.' The petitioners cited Stephenson's 'threatening words, barbarous and cruel treatment' of his neighbors, and unprovoked violent behavior in the past and expressed their fear of physical harm in the future. Robert Foster declared that 'Stephenson regards neither what he says or does when he is in his passion' while Thomas Rodwell asserted that 'he does not regard what mischief he does to any person in his anger.'[165]

Another kind of compulsion was the influence of acquaintances, friends, lovers, and husbands. The language in these cases did not explicitly mention mental incapacity or displacement, but the defendants suggested that they were under the powerful sway of those around them who demanded that they engage in unlawful behavior.[166] Accused of stealing 76 pounds of brass metal in 1731, Timothy Young said 'his brother had drawn him into commission of the crime,'[167] while in 1740 Elizabeth Jordan claimed that 'she was drawn into' breaking into Thomas Welburne's house and stealing money and linen 'by the persuasions of Jane Bryan.'[168]

Some wives mentioned their husbands in a bid to portray the real criminal as a man and their involvement as passive and innocent. Ann Jones, caught stealing window dressing and a blanket in 1721 with her husband Humphrey, told the court 'that she was obliged to carry them by her husband.'[169] At her trial for knowingly receiving stolen goods in 1750, Ann Dunkerton said, 'what I did was by my husband's direction,' while a year later Catherine Butler denied any knowledge of forgery and told the court 'my husband compelled me to do it.'[170] Although women claimed the influence of men far more often, some men were portrayed as the victims of the undue influence of disreputable women. When John Turner was indicted for stealing in 1736, he denied the fact and a witness told the court that 'the man was a very honest fellow, 'till he was seduced by this vile slut.'[171]

The devil appears in the trial transcripts as a powerful, unpredictable source of compulsion. By attributing their offenses to the devil, the accused gave the impression that their crimes resulted from an external, inexplicable force and that they were not in control of their behavior. When Jeremy Pearson killed John Murgatroyd by 'cutting his throat with a knife' in 1733, Pearson said that 'he never had any quarrel' with the victim 'but that he was moved thereto by the instigation of the devil.'[172] After he set fire to his brother's stack of 'pease' in 1765, William Tunstill explained that he did so 'being overcome by the instigation of the devil owing to human failings.'[173] Although their formal defense might not refer to the devil, defendants at the Old Bailey often mentioned the devil to their apprehenders. Mary Pollard told the shopkeeper's wife who caught her stealing in 1749 that 'the devil was in her when she did it'[174] and Robert Sparrow told James Fitzhenry in 1756 that 'the devil tempted him to do it.'[175]

None of the excuses reviewed here originated in the eighteenth century. In response to accusations of crime, defendants had long mentioned the 'privilege of necessity,' the compulsion of a husband, and the instigation of the devil to explain their misbehavior. However, given the general interest in psychology and self during the eighteenth century, and considering the language of excuse prevalent in the courtroom and rooted in the legally sanctioned insanity defense, these old excuses started to resemble pleas of mental distress.

Like the cases of insanity, drunkenness, and poverty, these defendants referred to the circumstances that propelled them into crime as temporary states during which they could not control themselves. Their testimony contained an assumption that when not obscured by external forces, their moral instincts were good and their behavior within the law. In this context character shaped representations of intent. Defendants and witnesses represented the accused as an upstanding member of the community and the crime as an isolated incident. Implicitly, they argued that their emotions had disoriented them and caused them to act unlawfully. This representation of the chain of events leading to a crime contrasts with earlier scenarios: while in the seventeenth century, mental distress was the result of sin and crime, these cases from the eighteenth century presented an incoherent mental state as the cause of and explanation for the crime. If heard by a seventeenth-century audience, these admissions would sound like the first step to graver crimes, but an eighteenth-century audience could sympathize with an explanation of crime as 'an act of the mind,' an aberration, caused by a temporarily displaced self.

Conclusions

This chapter demonstrates how defendants used the language of excuse in the eighteenth-century courtroom to broaden the limits of exculpatory insanity by introducing a wide spectrum of mental states as explanations for crime. These excuses, spoken in the language of the mind, illustrate the familiarity of English defendants with the process of law and suggest the influence of sensibility on people of all social ranks in eighteenth-century England. Furthermore, the vocabulary of mental excuse brought to court reveals part of a dynamic that existed between the defendants and those who heard their stories.

By proclaiming its impartiality and transparency, the English ideology of law encouraged popular conversance with legal process. The City of London attested to this interest in public justice when it began officially to supervise and subsidize the publication of the *OBSP* as a 'true, fair, and perfect narrative' in 1778.[176] For the City of London, the *OBSP* proved the existence of English justice and served to remind potential lawbreakers of the consequences of crime. But as authorities knew, this educational tool and its competitors, the Ordinary's accounts, broadsides, crime pamphlets, and newspapers, could also serve as instructional manuals in the arts of evasion.[177] Their familiarity with legal process and the exculpatory nature of certain states of mind allowed defendants, their families, and even their prosecutors to inflect their testimony with allusions to mental incapacity and to distance themselves from responsibility for their crimes.

Although defendants had long mentioned drunkenness, 'necessity,' and 'passion' to explain their crimes, the vocabulary of the mind was amplified as the century progressed. In the face of a legal system that demanded a coherent and cohesive self 'fit to take his trial' and allowed only a single narrowly defined exception, defendants used the language of mental states to re-inscribe the legal definition of self and to plead for their lives. To account for their criminal behavior and to excuse it, they claimed a space between the coherent self and the insane self that we might call the 'displaced self.'

The concept of sensibility had a powerful effect on how states of mind were negotiated in court. Their use of the language of mental excuse suggests that offenders were caught up in this new understanding of self and sensibility along with judges and jurors. When confronted with a crime, they had to find a way to explain the accusations and their guilt to themselves and to their community. Alternate explanations rested on the reconstruction and narration of experience and emotion and involved some admission of guilt. This admission focused attention away from the details of the crime and onto the prisoner's psychological state at the time of the crime.

Given the culture of sensibility and the interest in psychology during the eighteenth century, these pleas, based on a displaced self, appealed to legal authorities struggling to define the essence of self and the relationship between emotion, responsibility, and justice. Justices of the peace who presided over the deposition process and judges and jurors who listened to these pleas in court must also have been influenced by the 'era of sensibility.'

Domestic servants played a crucial role in the spread of the culture of sensibility beyond the aristocracy and those of middling status.[178] Their increased literacy combined with their exposure to reading as part of the daily life of the household. They bought and read novels, observed their mistresses reading privately, were present at public readings of the latest books, and overheard and engaged in discussions of 'the domestic life and the private experience of the characters who belong to it.'[179] This gave them intimate knowledge of the privacy of reading, the innermost thoughts and feelings of the characters who peopled these novels, and the values espoused in sentimental literature.[180] The vocabulary of feeling, pain, and compassion, with its repeated allusions to melancholia, was in no way restricted to the elite audiences whom the authors first envisioned as their readership. Not surprisingly, however, these women identified far more with Pamela, a fellow servant, and the agency and power she exercised than they did with Clarissa's reticence about a legal representation of her story. Given far fewer choices than Clarissa, with their lives at stake, they represented themselves and their mental states by infusing their testimony with the language of mental excuse. The language used in court by exactly these servant women when they faced charges of infanticide, the subject of chapter 4, suggests just how influential the culture of sensibility was.

4

Bodies of Evidence, States of Mind: Infanticide, Emotion, and Sensibility

Recent research has shown fairly conclusively that during the eighteenth century 'juries became increasingly reluctant to find against the defendant' in cases of infanticide.[1] Scholars have suggested that the jury's sympathy with the plight of unwed mothers and the discomfort of legal authorities with the harsh statute of 1624 accounted for this phenomenon.[2] This chapter seeks to deepen these arguments by outlining the legal and cultural context in which leniency and dissatisfaction with the 1624 statute, known as the 'Concealment of Birth of Bastards Act,' emerged.[3] Here I will explore the relationship between the language of the mind that resonated in the courtroom throughout the eighteenth century and jury verdicts in cases of infanticide within the context of the culture of sensibility. This analysis will reveal evolving definitions of the crime and its perpetrators.

Poor working women, many of them unmarried domestic servants, made up the overwhelming majority of defendants accused of infanticide in early modern England.[4] Although at the start of the eighteenth century single women's pleas of insanity rarely led to a verdict of not guilty, by 1800 most of those accused of infanticide using pleas of diminished responsibility gained an acquittal. The distinctive place of infanticide in English law allows us to highlight the changing relationship between crime and mental states during the eighteenth century. I focus on trial accounts in which defendants or witnesses on their behalf submitted a defense for infanticide that referred to the emotional or psychological state of the accused in their explanations of the crime. These defenses described the defendant as 'insensible,' 'agitated in mind,' or 'confused.' They are significant because they were exceptions to the popular, formulaic, and typically successful 'preparation defense' in which women cited the provisions they had made for the child during pregnancy as evidence of their intentions to nurture the baby after its birth. This exceptional testimony demonstrates the growing preoccupation of defendants, prosecutors, judges, and jurors with states of mind. How did states of mind relate to the understanding of the body? During the latter part of the eighteenth century in testimony about infanticide, the state of the defendant's mind became so privileged by defendants, jurors, and other legal authorities that the evidence about the body no longer determined the outcome of the trial. This is especially intriguing in light of the copious evidence presented about the body by expert witnesses such as male and female midwives, surgeons, and coroners.[5] Attention to the language of emotion in these infanticide cases, often more vague than the physical evidence, recast the crime and the criminal. Inside the courtroom psychological pleas redefined the motives for infanticide and contributed to the decline of its association with concealment and secrecy. Outside the courtroom these pleas reflected society's new attitudes about emotion and responsibility.

As the 'most specifically female crime,'[6] infanticide serves as a telling case study, allowing us to examine the changing relationship between the emotions, crime, and the state as revealed in the courtroom dialogue among defendants, witnesses, victims, judges, and jurors during the eighteenth century. The interest in feelings and emotions characteristic of the era of sensibility promised to provide middle-class men and women with a means to negotiate their relationships with their social others, including infanticidal mothers, poor working women, many of whom worked as domestic servants in middle-class homes.[7] The culture of sensibility impressed its followers with the moral obligation to engage in 'a process of sympathetic identification with the pain and pleasure' of those they encountered.[8] The culture of sensibility affected both the poor working women accused of infanticide and the middling men who served as jurors.

The development of the vocabulary of mental excuse revealed important shifts in conceptions of the self, and gender played a crucial role in this process. Although perceptions of women as more emotional, less rational, and less able to control their feelings persisted, during the era of sensibility both men and women regarded the emotions as essential to every sensible person.[9] On the other hand, as we have seen in our examination of Adam Smith's discussion of gender and sensibility, unbounded emotion could jeopardize masculinity and the political order. Self-command, therefore, became as important as sensation and sympathy. The developments discussed here reveal that with their use of the language of the mind defendants may have forced judges and jurors to acknowledge the female self (and by extension the poor, male self) during the eighteenth century, but by the end of the century the mental excuses employed by women had the unintended effect of eroding female agency.

Infanticide, marital status, and insanity

Marital status determined the attitude of legal authorities toward women who committed infanticide. As we saw in the cases discussed in chapter 2, married women who committed infanticide faced murder charges, and they were often acquitted when they claimed they had suffered temporary insanity brought on by pregnancy and childbirth.[10] Single women accused of infanticide in the seventeenth century were tried under the statute of 1624. The statute presumed that any mother of a bastard child who concealed its death was guilty of murder unless she could establish by the oath of at least one witness that the child had been stillborn. The statute claimed to address the problem of 'lewd women' asserting that they committed these crimes 'to avoid their shame' and 'to escape punishment.' The statute suggests that in the eyes of the law infanticide by an unmarried woman was viewed as a reasoned, premeditated (though immoral and criminal) act undertaken to preserve her reputation and status.[11] Such motives were not considered in the trial of a married woman accused of killing her baby because married women ordinarily seemed to lack any incentive to conceal the birth of a child.[12]

Hale treated the crime of infanticide as a special case within the category of insanity. He cited a 1668 trial at the Old Bailey in which a married woman 'having not slept many nights fell into a temporary phrenzy, and killed her infant in the absence of any company.'[13] After a good night's sleep, the woman 'recovered her understanding,' and had no recollection of her act. The judge instructed the jury that:

> if it did appear, that she had any use of reason when she did it, they were to find her guilty; but if they found her under a phrenzy, tho' by reason of her late delivery and want of sleep, they should acquit her.[14]

He cautioned them further that:

> had there been any occasion to move her to this fact, as to hide her shame, which is ordinarily the case with such as are delivered of bastard children and destroy them; or if there had been jealousy in her husband, that the child had been none of his; or if she had hid the

infant, or denied the fact, these had been evidences that the phrenzy was counterfeit.[15]

Based on her 'honesty and virtuous deportment' and 'many circumstances of insanity appearing to the jury,' the defendant was found not guilty.[16]

Hale specifically included the category of married mothers who committed infanticide among his examples of exculpatory mental states. In his analysis Hale considered married women who killed their newborn babies *a priori* different from mothers of illegitimate children who committed the same crime. The law assumed that married mothers were not driven to their crimes by the same desperate or criminal motives as unmarried women. Infanticide by married women was considered so shocking and so unlikely that the only motive assigned to it was insanity.[17]

Mary Dixon's trial at the Old Bailey in 1735 confirmed the widespread application of Hale's recommendation. Dixon, a married woman, threw her infant son into the house of office. The testimony that followed the description of the crime included language about Dixon's state of mind during the crime. Dixon testified that 'my senses went from me and I did not recover my self, nor know what I did or said.'[18] Several witnesses corroborated Dixon's claim that she suffered some sort of mental haze immediately after the discovery of the crime. Phoebe Webster described Dixon as 'weak and faint' on the morning that the baby was found. When Webster asked 'how she could be so barbarous, and why she did not call for help,' Dixon answered only 'because I was wicked.' Mrs. Morgan reported that Dixon 'made no answer' to her questions and that she was 'seemingly very weak.' Mrs. Bousset said that she 'could find no sense in her' and that when she called the midwife, both women 'thought she was dead.'[19] Despite Mrs. Morgan's proviso that she could not say 'whether she [Dixon] was out of her senses or not,' the consensus affirmed Dixon's insanity, and she was acquitted.

Dixon's testimony addressed the question of intention directly. She told the court, 'I was under no temptation of being so barbarous, for I had a good husband who was able to maintain the child; and I had at the same time one child living of four years old.'[20] Unlike more typical cases involving insanity described in chapter 2, none of the witnesses mentioned that Dixon had a history of peculiar behavior and the prisoner took the stand and spoke at length about her crime and her state of mind. These two variations on the usual, successful insanity defense reveal the special status of infanticidal insanity and the assumptions about its temporary character, caused, in Hale's words, by 'a phrenzy' associated with childbirth.[21]

Unmarried women accused of infanticide seldom used the insanity defense before 1730. A plea of insanity entailed at least an implicit admission of guilt, and if unsuccessful, led to immediate conviction and possible execution. Instead, these women used 'loopholes' in the statute of 1624 to make their defense. Single women accused of infanticide testified that the baby was born dead, that the baby died immediately after birth because they were delivered alone, that they had not concealed the pregnancy, and that they had prepared for the delivery and the birth of the child. Women in the community often confirmed these stories by telling the court that they knew about the pregnancy and that the mother had made some arrangements for the lying in and had prepared necessary provisions for the child such as clothing.[22] By 1715 the uniform and formulaic testimony in these cases usually resulted in the mother's acquittal.[23] Elizabeth Turner, indicted for murdering her child in June 1734, told no one she was pregnant and at first denied the crime when an infant's body was found in a box in her employer's cellar. Although Turner said nothing in her own defense, a witness on her behalf testified that when Turner's coat was stolen 'for garnish money,' the thieves found 'baby things' sewn in it. These included a shirt, a cap, a stay, a forehead cloth, and a biggin. These preparations led to Turner's acquittal.[24]

The drop in convictions for infanticide by 1715 signaled that the preparation defense had become the legal mechanism by which the courts negotiated the crime. Of the women tried for infanticide at the Old Bailey during the eighteenth century, 86 percent were acquitted and there were no convictions for infanticide from 1775 until the repeal of the 1624 statute in 1803. Historians have explained the drop in convictions by citing the jury's implicit sympathy for the accused, mostly young working women with few means to support a child.[25] Judges and jurors may have rejected the presumption of guilt written into the statute of 1624, as William Blackstone did when he wrote that the law 'savours pretty strongly of severity.'[26] Nevertheless, the legal fiction by which the crime was negotiated, the preparation defense, affirmed the statute of 1624 and the legal system that produced it.[27] This legal mechanism accepted the statute's definition of infanticide as a crime and mounted a defense that refuted concealment, the issue around which the statute revolved.

What about the exceptions to the preparation defense? Why in the face of such an effective explanation would single women accused of infanticide argue anything else? Here I wish to examine those cases in which defendants presented evidence of emotional turmoil to explain their behavior. Unlike women who brought a preparation defense, they acknowledged the crime and sometimes even admitted their role in the murder. In their pleas, they drew upon new epistemologies of emotion that reveal the preoccupation with self and sensibility in the second half of the eighteenth century. This testimony played on the implicit sympathy evident in most trials for infanticide. By demanding that the court's sympathy be made explicit, however, this testimony called into question the statute of 1624: it redefined the accused as insane and the act of infanticide as *prima facie* proof of this insanity.

This change in attitudes toward women accused of infanticide manifested itself in a cultural shift that realigned the association of sanity and marital status. The medical literature articulated new attitudes toward single women accused of infanticide by questioning both the assumption of their guilt and of their criminal intent. By the end of the eighteenth century the crime itself became evidence of madness that required little or no supporting testimony about marital status or mental alienation.

William Hunter's lecture to the members of the Medical Society on July 14, 1783 (published posthumously in 1784) reflected this change of opinion. Dr. Hunter (1718–1783) was a renowned physician, anatomist, surgeon, and man-midwife trained in Edinburgh and London. He specialized in surgery, later becoming the leading obstetrician in England. His patients included Queen Charlotte, to whom he was appointed physician extraordinary in 1764. In his lecture 'On the uncertainty of the signs of murder in the case of bastard children,' Hunter warned his colleagues against 'early prejudice' in cases that looked like infanticide and reminded them that the act could not be considered a murder unless it was

> executed with some degree of cool judgement, and wicked intention. When committed under a phrenzy from despair, can it be more offensive in the sight of God, than under a phrenzy from a fever, or in lunacy?[28]

Hunter pointed to the diagnosis of temporary insanity when he reminded his audience that:

> in making up a just estimate of any human action, much will depend on the state of the agent's mind at the time; and therefore the laws of all countries make ample allowance for insanity. The insane are not held to be responsible for their actions.[29]

Hunter suggested instead that single women 'with an unconquerable sense of shame' who found themselves pregnant out of wedlock, 'overwhelmed with terror and despair,' suffered 'distress of body and mind [that] deprives them of all judgement and rational conduct.'[30] He speculated that these women, driven by a 'violently agitated' mind, experienced 'a conflict of passions and terror,' and that in this state 'an irrational conduct may appear very natural.'[31] The shame of such a pregnancy drove one of his patients, 'struck with panic,' to suicide when she 'lost her judgement and senses.'[32] Hunter explained the deaths of seemingly healthy babies born to women delivered alone 'distracted in ... mind, and exhausted in ... body, [who] will not have strength or recollection enough to fly instantly to the relief of the child.'[33] In Hunter's evaluation the most virtuous women were more likely to respond to the psychological distress of a pregnancy out-of-wedlock by committing the crime of infanticide.[34]

Hunter's speech signaled a change in the attitude of the medical community with regard to the effects of pregnancy out of wedlock on the mind of the mother. He argued that the very motives cited in the statute of 1624, shame and fear, produced mental distress leading to 'phrenzy.' Hunter's analysis complicated the clear connection between concealment, murder, and reason which formed the basis for the assumption of guilt by introducing another factor – an 'agitated' mind – to which he attributed the crime. He expressed the belief that the accused bore no responsibility for crimes committed in such a psychological state. Hunter concluded that

> every humane heart will forget the indiscretion or crime, and bleed for the sufferings which a woman must have gone through; who but for having listened to the perfidious protestations and vows of our sex, might have been an affectionate and faithful wife, a virtuous and honoured mother, through a long and happy life.[35]

In Hunter's narrative, the infanticidal mother, 'weak, credulous, and deluded,' played the victim to the villainous male seducer, the father of the child who was, in Hunter's words, 'really criminal.'[36]

Hunter's interpretation of the crime of infanticide and its causes is an excellent example of the 'humanitarian narrative' defined and deconstructed by Thomas Laqueur.[37] Hunter's lecture stripped the women accused of infanticide of all agency granted to them, however peremptorily, by the statue of 1624. He remade them into the passive victims of their male seducers and redefined them as insane. This redefinition nullified their intention and their criminal and moral responsibility. The humanitarian narrative effectively furthered the cause of medical professionalization, as reflected in Hunter's frequent references to his vast clinical experience which conferred his unique authority and ability to diagnose and to treat these women.

'She had not the government of her understanding': trial outcomes and the language of the mind

How do we account for this dramatic shift in the discourse of infanticide during the eighteenth century? Although William Hunter articulated the change, the medical community did not direct the drop in the conviction rate of single women accused of infanticide, nor did physicians first redefine the relationship between infanticide, single women, and insanity. I want to suggest that one reason for this new association of infanticide by unmarried women with insanity rests in the development of the language of mental excuse. Saying they were 'not sensible,' 'agitated in mind,' 'almost distracted,' 'stupefied,' 'confused,' and 'delirious,' witnesses and defendants explained a wide range of psychological states. This language and the larger interest in sensibility convinced those participating in the courtroom dialogue – from defendants and witnesses to judges and prosecutors – that the women accused of infanticide had no criminal intention of murdering or hurting their children and that they should not be held responsible for the crime. This new conception of women as passive agents of crime contrasts sharply with the seventeenth-century image of women as treacherous, threatening, active criminals reflected in the statute of 1624.[38]

We can trace the trend toward a language of mental excuse by using infanticide as a quantified case study. Although a statistical analysis of verdicts has been absent from most parts of this study and the lack of evidence of jury deliberations makes the conclusions to be drawn necessarily speculative, a focused examination of just one crime and its trials' outcomes can reveal a cultural shift. Infanticide is particularly interesting because the language of the mind emerged alongside the preparation defense, already so effective for single women by the second decade of the eighteenth century, when the conviction rate dropped.[39] The insanity defense, generally the reserve of married women, simply did not serve the purposes of single women whose crime was considered evidence of their sanity, reason, and malicious intent. Single women, almost assured an acquittal using the formulaic preparation defense, did not need the discourse of mental excuse to help their case and to save their lives.

A set of 123 trials for infanticide at the Old Bailey in London between 1714 and 1803 forms the basis of this chapter.[40] Most of the women in this sample faced charges under the 1624 statute. The trials resulted in 111 acquittals and 20 convictions.[41] The language of emotion and excuse appeared in 22 cases, of which 13 resulted in an acquittal and nine in a conviction. At almost 20 percent of infanticide cases, these women drew on the association between women's reproductive capacity and an inherent vulnerability to insanity and introduced the language of mental excuse at a much higher rate in infanticide cases than men and women did in other criminal trials, but women did not adopt it as their most common line of defense, and it succeeded less often than other pleas.

What can this small sample tell us? The exceptions to the commonly used preparation defense shed light on changing perceptions of the crime, the criminal, and the self during the eighteenth century. In 22 cases from the sample, single women attributed their behavior immediately before, during, or after a birth to a form of insanity or mental turmoil.[42] In the first part of the century these pleas met with the jury's skepticism, but as the century wore on, the language of emotion became more successful.

Mary Radford's trial for infanticide in 1723 saw the first introduction of the language of emotion.[43] The presence of such language increased in the 1720s and 1730s with eight of the cases that included language of emotion taking place in those two decades. Of the nine pleas of emotion brought to the Old Bailey before 1745, six resulted in a conviction.[44] Two of the acquitted women were married. After 1745, the success – but not the incidence – of the insanity plea increased. Between 1745 and 1774, nine women presented evidence of insanity resulting in six acquittals. Of those six, none was married. There were no convictions for infanticide after 1774.[45] Between 1775 and 1803 four women introduced the insanity plea, and like all the other women tried for infanticide, their juries brought in acquittals.

As a group, an examination of the cases in which defendants or witnesses introduced the language of mental excuse leaves few hints as to why these women explained their actions this way. Aside from references to mental distress, the 22 cases do not share any commonalities that distinguish them from the other cases of infanticide tried at the Old Bailey during the eighteenth century. Seven of the newborn infants were found in the vault, or privy, while another suffocated in a close-stool-pan (a chamber utensil enclosed in a box), seven women were accused of inflicting wounds with a knife or another sharp object, three infants were thrown out of a window, two died by drowning, one was strangled, and one mother admitted to choking her child by putting her finger down its throat. Aside from the cases of throwing a baby from the

	The Language of Emotion and Conviction Rates, 1714–1775		
Dates	*Convictions*	*Acquittals*	*Married women acquitted*
1714–1745	6	3	2
1746–1775	3	6	0

window, none of the other methods of killing was unique to women who claimed that they suffered mental distress. As recounted by witnesses, several of the women admitted to some part of the crime before their trial. This could have made a plea of mental distress more likely or more necessary, but admissions of this sort were also found in cases that made no mention of mental states.

Bodies of evidence, states of mind

How did defendants portray their state of mind during the crime? Two different sorts of testimony about mental states emerge in infanticide trials. The first excuse explained the crime as a consequence of the mother's idiocy, presented in legal terms as a permanent mental deficiency originating at birth.[46] In the second category, witnesses or defendants associated the crime of infanticide with the mother's experience of childbirth, specifically the pain of labor. They likened this state of mind to a 'phrenzy' or temporary insanity.

Although Mary Radford made no reference to her mental state at her Old Bailey trial in 1723, her mistress and several other witnesses 'gave the prisoner the character of a very silly creature; that she was a half natural, and that her mother was so before her.'[47] Sarah Allen claimed that she was out of her senses when she committed the crime in 1737, while an unnamed witness in her defense told the court that 'the prisoner always was a silly, giggling creature.'[48] One witness called Ann Terry 'foolish,' while another described her as 'a very silly foolish girl, not capable of taking care of herself ... I believe sometimes she is not *compos mentis*.'[49] The juries in all of these cases rejected the claims of congenital infirmity and found the women guilty.

These convictions seem puzzling. Legal authorities often settled cases involving idiocy without a trial. Juries considered evidence of idiocy more credible than evidence of insanity because they believed they could verify the authenticity of idiocy more easily than they could establish that an offender was *non compos mentis*. These guilty verdicts suggest that jurors found the evidence presented unconvincing and that they doubted the longevity, severity, or sincerity of the women's conditions.

The second category of cases associated insanity with childbirth and the pain of labor. In 1723, Pleasant Bateman claimed that 'she was ill, and was in a fit when she was delivered, and had not her senses.'[50] Elizabeth Ambrook did not testify in her own defense, but at her trial in 1735 her sister-in-law told the court that when she asked Elizabeth why she threw her baby out the window, Elizabeth responded that 'she did not know what she did, for thro' the extremity of pain she thought the room was on fire when she threw it out.'[51] At her trial in 1769 Sarah Hunter said, 'I awaked in the morning and found there was a child: that frighted me very much. I was not sensible what I did. I can give no account how I did it.'[52] In 1771 Elizabeth Parkins told the court that she was 'taken very bad over night.' She explained in her defense: 'I went to cut the string [i.e. the umbilical cord] to ease myself: I was deprived of my senses, and do not remember any thing that I did.'[53]

In the descriptions of their psychological states during labor, many defendants commented on their level of responsibility for the crime. Some women denied having criminal intent. When a midwife examined Mary Shrewsbury in 1737, she asked 'how she could cut her child's throat so barbarously?' Shrewsbury insinuated that an external force had prompted her crime when she replied that 'the devil had given her strength, and not God.'[54] At her trial in 1755 Isabella Buckham said, 'I was not in my senses; I do not know what I said or did. Had I been in my senses I should have been very loth to have parted with it.'[55] In this unusual defense, Buckham admitted that she had killed her child, but she denied criminal intent.

Other women maintained the absence of criminal intention using the preparation defense. Pleasant Bateman said that 'she had made provisions for the child.' She called one of the witnesses for the prosecution who confirmed that she had made preparations five or six months before the birth and that 'she had several fits but a few days before, and she was not able to help herself in an hour's time after.'[56] Diana Parker made a similar claim in her trial in 1794. She told the court, 'I did not mean to make away with the child, I did not know what I was about. Here are some things that I made for the child; a shift, cap, etc.'[57]

In all of these cases the defendant made a narrow claim about the state of her mind during the crime itself. Each argued that the actual fact of childbirth produced a mental state during which she had no control over her behavior. The women's descriptions gave the impression that they did not remember this time and that they could take no responsibility for their actions. They did not deny that a murder took place, but they argued that their behavior was not criminal because they lacked malicious intent. They established the temporary nature of their insanity by introducing evidence about the preparations they had made for the birth of their child before the onset of labor.

As the century passed, the court showed increasing interest in the state of the defendant's mind at the time of the crime. Unlike other cases featuring the language of the mind, defense counsel, perhaps playing on the jury's sympathy for women accused of infanticide and the perceived link between insanity and childbearing, introduced evidence about psychological states, and judges and jurors responded to it with their own questions about the woman's mental capacity. In Hanna Perfect's trial in 1747 the court and the counsel for the defense questioned Mary Millet, a fellow servant, about the details of the crime. Counsel for the defense initiated a line of questioning about the state of the prisoner's senses, to which Millet responded, 'I believe she was stupefied.' At this point the judge intervened to ask, 'You believe she had not the government of her understanding?' Millet answered, 'No, I believe she had not.' Counsel for the defense followed this question with one about whether Perfect was 'a sensible woman at other times.' Millet responded that Perfect 'is a very sensible young woman' and that her general character was that of a 'very sober, honest girl.'[58]

At her trial in 1781, Elizabeth Harris said nothing in her own defense, but several witnesses responded to questions put to them by her counsel about her state of mind. Asked if the prisoner seemed 'much confused or afflicted,' the midwife, Sarah Tuffnel, replied that 'she seemed to give very odd answers at times, as if she was not quite right in her head.'[59] In the trial of Elizabeth Jarvis in 1800 the defense counsel asked Robert Whitfield, a surgeon who examined the child, whether 'a woman in strong labour is not always possessed of her faculties of reason?' Whitfield responded 'not always.'[60] In these examples the line of questioning attempted to tie the state of the woman's senses to her labor and drew a distinction between her character and mental capacity when she was in labor and when she was not. This line of questioning paralleled the distance put by the women accused of infanticide between their nurturing preparations for the birth and the disturbing effect of labor on their senses.

The court's interest in the defendant's state of mind mirrored William Hunter's psychological explanation for infanticide. Hunter explained that an illegitimate pregnancy affected a woman with 'an unconquerable sense of shame' who 'pants after the preservation of character' by causing her to feel 'overwhelmed with terror and despair.'[61] As a result of the emotional stress of concealing the pregnancy and trying to preserve their reputations, these women 'are overtaken sooner than they expected.' Hunter accounted for their behavior by pointing to 'their distress of body and mind [which] deprives them of all judgements and rational conduct; they are delivered by themselves ... in their fright and confusion ... insensible of what is passing.'[62] Hunter's assessment of the circumstances leading to the act of child murder legitimized the narratives that emerged in the trials by placing them in a medical context. It redefined infanticide as an involuntary result of the physical and emotional distress experienced by single women during pregnancy and childbirth.

Conclusion

This chapter has sought to deepen our understanding of the decline in convictions for infanticide in the eighteenth century. While scholars have pointed to the jury's sympathy with the single women accused of this crime, consideration of the culture of sensibility and its emphasis on experience and emotion explains the defenses made by some of those accused and suggests their reception by judges and juries. The development of excuses, spoken in the language of the mind, demonstrates the influence of sensibility on people of all social ranks of early modern English society and reveals a dynamic that existed between the single women accused of infanticide and those who heard their testimony.

The increased use of the pleas of mental excuse in infanticide cases from the 1730s and the 1740s and their acceptance by juries during the latter part of the century coincides with the emergence of the language and culture of sensibility discussed in chapter 3. The literature of sensibility modeled relations between classes in an attempt to teach Britain's emergent middle class how to respond to the most mundane of life's experiences as well as to its crises. An attempt to reconstruct the reception of the language of the mind in criminal court serves as a good way to suggest its implications well beyond literature.

The rise of sensibility had a distinct effect on what was said in court. Their use of the language of the mind may suggest that poor, ordinary single women were caught up in this new understanding of self and sensibility along with their masters and mistresses. When confronted with the crime of infanticide, they had to find a way to explain the accusations and their guilt to themselves and to their community. The stereotyped preparation defense did not serve this purpose. Instead, some women found alternate explanations that rested on the reconstruction and narration of experience and emotion. But the stakes for using the language of the mind to explain their crimes were high: the plea included an admission of guilt that could result in the defendant's conviction and execution.

Did defendants know that the culture of sensibility affected the reception of their pleas? The drop in convictions pre-dated the era of sensibility, but the acceptance of psychological pleas coincided with it. The cultural values of sensibility affected the justices of the peace who presided over the deposition process and the judges and jurors who listened to these pleas in court. The Old Bailey trials suggest that as the eighteenth century progressed, juries became more open to pleas of emotion in place of or along with the preparation defense. This increased association of infanticide, insanity, and single women in the second half of the eighteenth century set the stage for what Roger Smith describes as 'the legally exculpatory attitude towards [all] infanticidal women' in the nineteenth century.[63]

Jurors rejected the language of mental excuse in the earliest cases reviewed here, and one wonders why they did not embrace it immediately. One explanation certainly lies in the fact that the acceptance of an insanity plea for infanticide would have had a destabilizing effect on the law and would have necessitated the repeal of the statute of 1624. A different, extra-legal explanation might call on the history of sensibility. The translation of the crime of infanticide from a rational premeditated criminal act into the result of a mental illness coincided with the height of the circulation and consumption of fiction concerned with sensibility. The deployment of pleas of emotion reflects a cross-class concern with feeling, emotion, and the self.

The change in the reception of the pleas of the mind may bear relation to the changes in the didactic message conveyed by the cult of sensibility. Eighteenth-century writers of sensibility had inconsistent views of sensibility and class. While some saw sensibility as an equalizing characteristic shared across lines of class, for others 'it was the property more or less exclusively of the higher and more genteel orders.'[64] The latter conception of sensibility may account for the rejection of psychological and emotional excuses expressed in the pleas of poor single women accused of infanticide in the first half of the eighteenth century. As the century progressed, however, poor, single women increasingly appropriated the association of pregnancy, insanity, and infanticide while middling jurors began to accept the universality of a sensible self, vulnerable to displacement and shared by defendants and jurors alike. In the context of the culture of sensibility, the explanation for infanticide that pointed to a temporary 'phrenzy' brought on by a single woman's illegitimate pregnancy was received as sincere, inevitable, and exculpatory.

The individual self may not have been defined as part of the identities of the lower orders at the beginning of the century and may account for jury resistance to the narratives of emotion in the 1720s and 1730s. However, by the middle and late eighteenth century, middle-class sensibility necessitated a recognition of the subjectivity of the other. Rather than an act of generosity on the part of judges and jurors, this awareness of working-class pain and the acceptance of the subjectivity of the poor affirmed the middle-class viewers' notions of their superior sensibility and confirmed their belief that they could perform true compassion only though contact with suffering. Unlike an active premeditating murderess, a single woman, defined as the passive victim of male seduction and her own insanity, would elicit real compassion.[65]

The adjudication of infanticide made the eighteenth-century courtroom one site in the exchange of sensibility. Defendants performed their emotional repertoire acting out their roles as victims. By engaging with these sentimental narratives, judges and jurors affirmed their own superior sense of self and sensibility. The acceptance of the pleas of the mind from women accused of infanticide starting in the middle of the eighteenth century reflects a new language of emotion: it made explicit the sympathy that existed for women accused under the statute of 1624.

The single women who made a defense of temporary insanity at their trials for infanticide were aware of the association of all women's reproductive capacity with temporary insanity activated by pregnancy and child birth. Furthermore, they drew on middle-class notions of the impetuous nature of decision-making and behavior among the poor believed to be more pronounced among women and used to explain both the sexual act that produced the illegitimate pregnancy as well as the crime of infanticide. These female defendants constructed an explanation for their crimes that would have been believable to their listeners. However, female knowledge of the law and agency in the courtroom was undermined by the intervention of medical men who co-opted women's stories and interpreted them as predetermined, the effect of a displaced self.

The implications of the pleas of mental distress devastated the legal foundations of the 1624 statute and led to its eventual repeal in 1803.[66] This kind of testimony insisted on a shift in the legal mechanism with which the crime was ushered through the system: it traded on the insanity defense rather than the 'preparation defense.' This new understanding of the crime invalidated the assumptions of the statute of 1624 and presented a serious problem for the legal system by introducing an explanation for crime as an excuse for it. This problem was resolved with the statute's repeal in 1803, and the embrace of the narrative of temporary insanity for single women faced with a pregnancy outside of marriage. However, the language of emotion had much more destabilizing implications for the legal system in general. These new excuses threatened to redefine all crime as insanity by linking all behavior to psychological motives for which the defendant took (or could take) little or no responsibility. The potential repercussions of the language of emotion were not lost on legal authorities, who resisted four attempts to repeal the statute of 1624 between 1772 and 1776. These failed attempts were couched in the language of 'humanity and justice,' while the success of Lord Ellenborough in 1803 made an appeal for more certain punishment.[67]

The repeal of the statute of 1624 in 1803 resolved the problem posed by the language of mental states for cases of infanticide. It allowed the women accused of infanticide and their families as well as judges and jurors to embrace the narrative of temporary insanity for single women faced with a pregnancy outside of marriage. The nature of the excuse, its application to a relatively small group of defendants, and the implicit sympathy on which it depended allowed its acceptance in court. This case study reveals the importance of gender in the reception of all psychological pleas for all kinds of crimes and presages the creation of the always accountable subject by the end of the century. By admitting this excuse and defining its parameters as exceptional and applicable to recently delivered women because of the weakness of their female nature and its reproductive capacity, the legal system may have prevented the admission of other excuses that built upon the language of mental states. To assess the reception of the language of the mind in a broader range of cases we turn now to an examination of courtroom observers and their vigorous discussions of responsibility, emotion, and the self during the second half of the eighteenth century.

5

'An indulgence given to great crimes'? Sensibility, Compassion, and Law Reform

The previous three chapters have documented the salience of the language of mental states in the English courtroom in the eighteenth century. The vocabulary of psychological excuse reflected a wider discussion of the relationship between reason, emotion, and the self that permeated eighteenth-century culture. In the courtroom – with life, liberty, or property at stake – these ideas found their most intense use and provoked a debate about the limits of this language of excuse. The language of the mind destabilized the definition and determination of *mens rea*, criminal intent, the basis of all criminal law. Although legal codes and commentary had long recognized insanity as an excuse for crime, in the age of sensibility the language of mental excuse broadened this exculpatory category in unpredictable and uncontrollable ways. Eighteenth-century debates among legal reformers reveal a struggle to determine the limits of compassion, to identify legitimate exculpating states of mind, and to distinguish them from those considered within an individual's capacity for control and responsibility.

How did justices of the peace, jurors, and judges participate in the discourse of mental excuse? How did observers of England's courts, whose anxiety about the place of compassion in the courtroom we saw in chapter 2, respond to it? Trial accounts, judges' charges, pardon letters, and treatises on legal reform show that many in the courtroom spoke and understood the language of excuse. After a consideration of the use of this language by judicial authorities, we will turn our attention to observers of England's legal system and to those who sought to reform it. Their concerns about the language of mental excuse and its effects on the legal system led to proposals for reconciling compassion and justice and reintegrating the displaced self.

'Circumstances duly weighed': prosecutors, judges, jurors, and the vocabulary of excuse

The pressure on judges and juries to mitigate only increased in the eighteenth century. Faced with the harsh penalties outlined in England's 'bloody code' judges and jurors paid special attention to extenuating circumstances such as the defendant's gender, age, character, and reputation.[1] Judges and jurors may have welcomed the language of the mind with which defendants spoke of the stresses of daily life, drunkenness, financial hardship, and compulsion. Legal authorities may have even encouraged these excuses as a sorting mechanism of mitigation. This chapter shows how implicit cooperation between judges, jurors, defendants, and prosecutors served as an important conduit for the introduction of broader conceptions of mental distress into the legal discourse.

A rare piece of pre-trial evidence suggests the attention paid to the defendant's state of mind by justices of the peace who investigated crimes in the immediate aftermath of their discovery. When John Clarke examined William Ward on January 25, 1763, Clark noted that the suspect 'appeared to be in great confusion.' Clarke 'admonished him of the heinous nature' of his crime of arson and 'advised him to prepare for a further examination.' On January 26 Ward 'again answered little to the charge; and made a bad defense.' Clarke's elliptical notes suggest that on both days Ward made an incoherent defense. The phrase 'great confusion' summarized Clarke's opinion about Ward's state of mind rather than the facts of the case. Based on the evidence he collected and the 'fear of danger from this very man William Ward,' Clarke sent Ward to the county gaol. Clark probably had the Justices' Commitment Act (17 Geo. II, c. 5) in mind when he detained Ward; it empowered justices of the peace to apprehend offenders whom they considered dangerous. This case reveals the discretion that magistrates had in the pre-trial process. Clark seems to have taken action based on his observation of Ward's 'confusion' and potentially dangerous behavior rather than any clinical diagnosis.[2]

Judges and juries, victims and counsel for both the prosecution and the defense, participated in the development of a vocabulary of mental states, expanded its terminology, and struggled to set parameters for its use. The *Old Bailey Sessions Papers* reveal that rather than belonging exclusively to the accused, interest in states of mind articulated by the language of excuse circulated widely among all participants in the legal process.

The judge who presided at Samuel Prigg's trial for the murder of Thomas Girl in May 1746 charged the jury to find 'what condition of mind, or understanding the prisoner appeared to be [in] at the time this fact was done.' In a rare, though not unique, addendum to the trial transcript, the editors of the *OBSP* included lengthy 'hints of his lordship's charge to the jury, upon this melancholy case.'[3] These remarks reveal the kinds of arguments made in cases that disputed the prisoner's mental state and the judge's role in assessing their legal impact.

The trial began with a lengthy reconstruction of the events leading up to the crime. When asked to make his defense, the prisoner replied, 'I have nothing to say, I commit my cause to God.' Counsel questioned nine witnesses who appeared on his behalf who gave lengthy and detailed reports about the 'illness in his head.' They said he would 'sit and cry to himself,' 'talk'd very rambling,' 'seemed very melancholy,' and 'would talk of strange things, that we could not understand' including 'making away with himself.' Several witnesses told the court that he 'has not followed his business [as a pawnbroker and a plasterer] as he should have done this year or two' and that he would 'keep his bed for two or three days in a melancholy way.'[4]

The prisoner's attorney tried to convince the court that his client's illness had intensified in the six months prior to the crime and that Prigg was 'different to what he was formerly.' One witness said that the prisoner had come to her a month earlier 'exceedingly confused,' while another told the court that a week before the crime he had 'look'd very wild with his eyes.' Some of this testimony undermined the argument for uninterrupted insanity. Mary Fox claimed she had known the prisoner 'from a child.' She said that 'he has had his intervals at times; I have seen him very well at other times.' This contradictory testimony points to the problems with managing the language of excuse and may indicate why defense counsel would hesitate before introducing it. The prisoner's counsel urged the jury to believe that the crime had taken place during a period of lunacy, not during a lucid interval.[5]

The judge opened his charge by reminding the jurors that all the witnesses had agreed that Prigg's 'whole behavior was sensible in what he went to do' and that 'all his actions appeared to them as cool and as sensible.' The judge concluded that 'this is the evidence to maintain the indictment.' He recapitulated the defense 'made against it [i.e. the indictment],' describing the accused as 'a man that has lately lost his understanding, has been beside himself.' The judge continued, summarizing the legal commentary on the defense of insanity. 'I must tell you, that in point of law, a man void of all sense and understanding, so degraded to the condition of a brute, is no more answerable for such a fact, than the instrument by which he does it.' Was the judge simply continuing a judicial synopsis or hinting at his own opinion when he added, 'but then it must be one void of reason and understanding, and one known to be so'? In the next section of the charge, the judge described lunacy and reminded the jury of the offender's full culpability for crimes committed during a lucid interval. As if acknowledging that Prigg suffered from mental distress, the judge quoted some of the compelling testimony from the trial, giving it credence when he called it 'a candid and sure account.' On the other hand, the judge's use of the word melancholy to describe Prigg's condition could have served as yet another hint that he did not consider Prigg's mental state exculpatory.[6]

In the final section of his charge the judge examined the meaning of malice. He minced no words, telling the jury that 'in the present case, the manner of doing of it, if nothing more, implies malice.' So as to leave no doubts on this point, the judge continued: 'it was covered, and most effectually done ... in a manner, that no man could possibly make a defence against; that is all the evidence of the deepest malice.' This discussion directly followed the judge's use of the word melancholy, a mental state that Hale said caused 'excessive fears and griefs' but did not render its victims 'wholly destitute of the use of reason.' The mention of malice in such close proximity to melancholy again may have suggested the judge's bias to the jury. In what seems like an incongruous statement, he then tempered this implicit direction to convict with his concluding remarks. The judge advised the jury that

> if on the other hand, there is an evidence given to you, which induces you to think he was a man deprived of reason and understanding, that is an excuse allowed by the law; because unless a man has understanding, he cannot be guilty of any crime; for crimes are acts of the mind. A man deprived of his understanding, has no mind to govern him at all.[7]

Even this mitigating reminder set a strict standard for an insanity defense by demanding that jurors find the defendant 'deprived of reason and understanding' with 'no mind to govern him at all.' The jury found Samuel Prigg guilty and sentenced him to death.

How do we interpret this charge? The charge seems to oscillate between holding Prigg accountable for Girl's murder and excusing him as an 'irrational man.' The structure and content of the judge's words reveals his efforts to grapple with the language of excuse and the inconclusive evidence about states of mind presented at the trial. His charge illustrates how the psychological pleas articulated in court during the eighteenth century complicated the relationship between states of mind and legal responsibility.

The judge focused on the problem of partial insanity. His seeming indecision about how to weigh the testimony about mental distress reflects an attempt to apply Hale's guidelines. Hale advised judges that

> this partial insanity seems not to excuse them [offenders] in the committing of any offense for its matter capital; for doubtless most persons, that are felons of themselves, and others are under a degree of partial insanity, when they commit these offenses.

The judge responded in his charge to Hale's warning that 'it is very difficult to define the indivisible line that divides perfect and partial insanity but it must rest upon circumstances duly to be weighed and considered both by the judge and jury.'[8] The judge's charge closely followed Hale's admonition to strike a balance 'lest on the one side there be a kind of inhumanity toward the defects of human nature, or on the other side too great an indulgence given to great crimes.'[9] This charge reveals the judge's efforts to contain the language of excuse without denying the exculpatory nature of a legitimate plea of insanity.

The judge's equivocation reflected the dilemma faced by all judges and jurors ruling on cases involving excuses of partial lunacy. On the one hand, given the 'facts' surrounding the case they wished to hold the perpetrator responsible for the criminal act. On the other hand, they believed that someone considered *non compos mentis* lacked both the understanding and the intent that held a sane individual accountable for crime. Judges and jurors had to balance the exculpatory treatment that the law prescribed for offenders suffering from insanity with the concern that the mental conditions described by neighbors and relatives did not qualify as such. The precedent set by a lenient judge and jury could pose a threat of further violence to the community and undermine the rule of law.

In the second half of the eighteenth century the persistence and elaboration of the language of the mind reflects the fact that efforts to limit its use failed. Witnesses for the prosecution often broached the subject of the defendant's mental state before the accused presented his or her case. When they did so, the rising number of defense attorneys were quick to draw attention to this potentially exculpatory evidence, thereby amplifying the impact of the language of the mind.[10]

When he brought charges against Thomas Simkins for stealing a black gelding in 1751, the prosecutor, Anissiter Thomas, told the court that

Simkins said 'he never did such a thing before, and that he was out of his senses.' When asked by the prosecution's counsel 'is he out of his senses at times?' Thomas answered 'to me he appears as if he was.'[11] In the same session, Lucy Booth was tried for stealing over two pounds of brass from her employer, Richard Midwinter, a founder. Midwinter, the victim, told the court that when he confronted his servant, 'she said she was very sorry for it, and begged I'd forgive her, saying, she was sometimes out of her senses.' Another witness for the prosecution, George Garret, said that the accused 'owned she took it, and that she was out of her senses at the time.' The prosecuting attorney followed this comment by asking, 'did she seem to be out of her senses?' to which Garret responded, 'no, my lord, she did not.'[12] These examples demonstrate the presence of the language of mental incapacity and its many sources; compelled by its relevance, victims introduced it in court and obliged their lawyers to explain extenuating circumstances that could have weakened their case.

When witnesses for the prosecution introduced mental excuses in their testimony, they attracted the attention of the growing number of defense lawyers in the mid- and late eighteenth century. At Christopher Wade's 1755 trial for highway robbery, Francis Taylor, one of the prosecution's witnesses, said that the prisoner 'was not capable of giving any account of himself that night.' In his cross-examination, defense counsel returned to Taylor's comment, asking 'did you think he was in his senses?' Taylor responded, 'I can't really say; he spoke some things sensibly, but he was in a sad case.' In addition to 11 character witnesses, two women who saw the prisoner on the night in question bolstered the argument for Wade's mental distress when they said that the accused 'was not in his senses, and could not give reasonable answers.'[13] Especially when they did not initiate the use of this language, counsel for the defense pursued these references to states of mind in cross-examination and in their defense of the prisoner and translated them into the language of psychological excuse.

Sometimes defense attorneys planted their client's mental excuse early in the trial, thereby shaping subsequent lines of inquiry from both the defense and the prosecution. For example, at Daniel Dwite's 1756 trial for assault with the intent to steal, Dwite's lawyer cross-examined Thomas Kelley, the victim and the first witness to testify. He asked, 'was the prisoner in liquor?' to which Kelley responded 'I thought he look'd to be so when we took him up.'[14] The next witness, George Manner, a watchman, told the court spontaneously that when he apprehended Dwite, 'I took the prisoner up by the right arm, and said *hollo, what do you do here?* He seem'd to be a little in liquor.' This exchange forced the prosecutor's lawyer to ask John Folk, the third witness and also a watchman, 'was the prisoner fuddled?' Folk answered, 'he appear'd stupified; he could not tell where he was. I believe he was no ways in liquor, only frighted.'[15] Counsel for the defense shaped the courtroom dialogue by interjecting the issue of the prisoner's sobriety during the examination of the first witness. Each succeeding witness offered an opinion on the state of mind of the accused. By the time Dwite spoke, telling the court that he 'went to drinking with an acquaintance ... I remember I fell once ... but did not know where I was; and when I awaked in the roundhouse [prison cell] I could not tell where I was,' his plea could hardly have surprised those listening.[16] The prisoner did not say he was drunk, but the testimony of the prosecution's witnesses filled out the picture and put his words in the context of a drunkenness defense.

At Thomas Jacocks' murder trial in September 1766 a witness for the prosecution introduced evidence that led to a lengthy discussion of the prisoner's state of mind. Henry Gotobed, a witness for the prosecution, told the court that he responded to the victim's distress call at the Two Fighting Cocks on Finchley Common. According to Gotobed's testimony when he apprehended the prisoner, Jacocks 'was very much in liquor,' and 'had nothing to say, he was quite entirely in liquor.' On cross-examination, counsel for the defense asked, 'was the prisoner very much in liquor?' and Gotobed responded, 'he was quite stupid, I hardly think he knew what he did.' The next witness, John Caverly, said, 'the prisoner was very fuddled, he could hardly speak at all.' Again defense counsel pursued the issue by asking, 'was he very much in liquor?' to which Caverly replied, 'he was very much, he could hardly speak.'[17] Defense counsel so successfully raised the issue of drunkenness that by the time Jacocks told the court, 'I was fuddled, or I had never done such a thing,' the judge and the jury had ample preparation for his excuse and more than just the offender's word for his mental condition.[18]

Other cases suggest that victims, their witnesses, and their counsel believed that information about the offender's state of mind could have a mitigating effect on the jury's verdict. To prevent such an outcome prosecutors and their lawyers responded to such evidence to try to refute it. For example, when Samuel Toy stole several brass hinges and escutcheons from John Jenkins in 1756, he said in his defense, 'I know nothing concerning the affair. I was very much in liquor; and know no more that I took any thing away than he that is unborn.' The prosecuting attorney immediately turned to William Hopkins, one of his witnesses, and asked, 'was the prisoner in liquor?' to which Hopkins replied, 'he was a little in liquor, but not so much but he knew what he did.'[19] When James Aldridge, indicted for breaking and entering with intent to steal, told the court in 1765 that 'going along, I had got pretty much in liquor .... I do not know how I came by the lanthorn,' the *OBSP* reported cryptically that 'the prosecutor and watchmen were asked and they said he was quite sober.'[20]

In a similar though better documented interchange from 1766, the accused, Peter Deal, said in his defense, 'I got pretty much in liquor. I went upstairs, and took that handkerchief instead of my own.' Deal's lawyer seized on his client's potentially mitigating state of mind and turned immediately to the prosecutor, William Hibditch, to ask 'did the prisoner appear to be in liquor?' Hibditch replied, 'he did not appear to be at all in liquor.' The lawyer then turned to John Lee, another of the prosecution's witnesses, and asked, 'What do you say? Was he sober or not?' When John Lee answered that 'he did not appear to be in liquor,'[21] Deal's attorney shifted his line of questioning and asked whether perhaps the prisoner had brought his own 'bundle into the house' rather than taking the victim's. This new strategy succeeded no better than the first as each witness testified that he saw only one bundle of goods.

In the absence of defense counsel at William Smithson's Old Bailey trial for the theft of a trunk full of clothes in December 1778, mentioned in chapter 3, the presiding judge played an active role by querying the mental effects of a physical injury exacerbated by alcohol. William Barnet, one of the prosecution's witnesses, told the court that he 'found the prisoner in bed; he pretended to be asleep, or dead drunk, or something. I believe he was not drunk.'[22] When granted the opportunity to speak in his defense, Smithson said, 'I know nothing of the matter; I was very much in liquor; when I am in liquor I am out of my mind; I don't know what I say or do. I had a fracture in my head some years ago.'[23] After Smithson made his plea, the court asked one of the prosecutor's witnesses, Mathew Wilson, if 'he, [Smithson] when he fetched the trunk, appear[ed] to stagger, or seem unable to carry the trunk?' Wilson replied that 'he did not appear to me to be drunk; if he had been drunk he could not have carried it.' The victim then added, 'When we took him in bed, he appeared exceedingly stupid, whether it was real or affected, I cannot take upon me to say; he never stirred a limb, nor got out of bed till he was dragged out.'[24] This testimony showed the engagement of several witnesses and the presiding judge with the exact state of the offender's mind. Again, the prosecution's witness introduced the evidence about the offender's state of mind, and this information shaped the rest of the trial.

The question of the effect of alcohol on Smithson's mental capacity preoccupied all the witnesses who appeared on his behalf. Asked about a scar left by the prisoner's head fracture, Thomas Martin and Edward Pugh, both witnesses for the defense, replied that they had seen the scar on Smithson's head, but that they knew nothing about how he got it. Edward Robinson, who had known the prisoner for two years, said that he had heard about the scar. He went on to say that Smithson was 'afraid of getting too much in liquor; he is a remarkable sober man.' The judge pursued the subject asking, 'did you ever see him in liquor?' Robinson replied, I cannot say I have much.' The judge followed with another question, 'did you ever see him out of his mind?' to which Robinson also answered in the negative.[25]

Samuel Smith testified at length about the defendant's condition:

> I have known the prisoner between six and seven years; he always bore an excellent character. About three years ago I was informed he fell off the coach-box, and had his skull cracked. I have been in his company [and] when he is a little in liquor he is like a mad man.

The judge probed the issue: 'What do you mean by his being like a mad man when he is in liquor; do you mean that he is a violent outrageous man?' Smith replied, 'When he is in liquor he does not know what he says or does.' The court queried further, 'Do you think that he has that want of understanding, that he would drive his coach into the Thames?' Smith answered, 'I cannot say that. I know when he is in liquor he is quite out of his mind.'[26] Elizabeth Dennis said she had known Smithson for two and a half years and that 'he is a very honest man as far as I know; only when he is in liquor he is just as if he was out of his senses almost.' The court responded by asking, 'Do you think he is capable of knowing then what he does?' To this question Dennis replied, 'I don't think he is some times.'[27]

The unusual detail in this case illustrates a widespread familiarity and engagement with the language of excuse. Without the presence of a defense attorney, most of the trial revolved around the defendant's state of mind. The judge took the role of examiner and far from dismissing this evidence about Smithson's scar and the effects of liquor on his mind, his continued queries show a persistent effort to pin down the extent of the prisoner's accountability for his behavior. Like the charge in Prigg's case discussed earlier, this case reveals the judge's struggle to balance mental distress as a legitimate excuse with the need to assign responsibility. Pleas of mental distress expanded the jury's fact-finding role to include an assessment of the prisoner's state of mind and in the process increased the presence and the use of the vocabulary of excuse far beyond what the law allowed.

Further evidence that the language of mental states permeated all aspects of the trial comes from cases of manslaughter. In cases of manslaughter, 'the unlawful killing of another, without malice either express or implied,' defendants and their lawyers often cast the death as a result of a disagreement between friends or acquaintances.[28] Those convicted of this clergyable offense were usually branded in the hand and discharged. John Beattie has argued that by the second half of the eighteenth century a combination of fines and imprisonment replaced branding as judges and jurors felt the need to impose a more substantial punishment on those convicted of manslaughter.[29] Some evidence suggests that this trend to more severe punishment led to more explicit discussions of the character and personality of the accused and his or her susceptibility to provocation.[30]

Witnesses on behalf of James Mutter, accused of murder in 1751, described him as 'peaceable, sober, and discreet.' Alexander Coming said, 'I never heard him called a quarrelsome man. He always behaved himself quietly,' while James Reney said he was 'not a person of a rankorous disposition on any consideration.' A former landlady, Mrs. Cleland, said he 'always behaved quietly' and James Young described 'a sober young man, for I never saw him addicted to any passion whatsoever.' Margaret Green told the court, 'I never took him to be of a quarrelsome disposition, but of a mild good natured temper.'[31]

When Antonio de Silva killed Bartholomew Malahan in 1761 a similar discussion ensued. Asked about the prisoner's behavior, Francis Eagan said, 'He was always very peaceable. I saw him fight one night, and instead of stabbing the person, he gave me his knife.' Eagan explained that de Silva fought only because the two men 'had used him very ill.' Counsel for the defense then asked if de Silva 'used to quarrel and fight often' to which Eagan replied, 'I never saw him quarrel, but that one time.'[32] Four other witnesses appeared to corroborate Eagan's evidence. In answer to a question about whether de Silva was 'a quarrelsome man, or of a peaceable disposition?' John Randall described the accused 'as quiet a man as ever I saw: I saw him fight once, and before ever he begun, he said, I will not use my knife.' The next question queried the reason for the fight, to which Randall responded, 'Smith challenged him [de Silva].' Counsel pursued the subject asking, 'Is the prisoner addicted to passion, or not?' to which Randall replied 'he is not, he will sooner take two affronts, than give one.' Ann Kennedy rounded out this picture of a peaceful and quiet man testifying that 'I have often seen him strive to make peace, but never saw him quarrel; I have seen him take many affronts, but never saw him give any,' while Daniel Venbury described 'a harmless, civil man' who responded to his provocation peacefully.[33] Evidence of the accused as 'harmless,' 'quiet,' 'peaceable,' and by no means 'addicted to passion,' implicated the deceased as the source of a tremendous and unreasonable provocation to which the prisoner had no recourse but violence. The defense attorneys configured their questions to elicit these assertions about the capacity of both the defendant and the deceased to control their emotions and to deflect the issue of malicious intent from the offender to the victim.

In some manslaughter cases the courtroom discussion scrutinized the victim's temper and disposition so much that the deceased seemed the object of prosecution. At his Old Bailey trial for the murder of Richard Jasper in June 1761, Joseph Brice told the judge:

> I am extremely sorry that I am obliged to appear before your lordship in this court, for a crime of this nature. The evidence is such, that I hope will convince the whole world that I could not avoid coming to the extremity that I did, which was owing to the violence of the deceased.[34]

Several witnesses testified that with his dying words, 'I was the aggressor,' Jasper exonerated Brice of all wrongdoing.[35] John Medley, the keeper of the coffeehouse where the two men met, testified that he overheard Jasper, the deceased, provoke Brice, the accused. Defense counsel inquired about the victim, 'what sort of a man was he [Jasper] for temper?' Medley answered that 'when he had been drinking, he was a very quarrelsome, proud, haughty man, as ever I saw in my life.' Defense counsel continued, 'Was he so when he had been drinking only?' Medley replied: 'I have seen him quarrel at other times, when he has been sober, but he was not so bad as when in liquor; he was a very proud man.' Defense counsel pursued the issue further asking, 'was he a passionate man in general?' to which Medley responded, 'yes, a little hasty and passionate, what we call a hot man.'[36] This line of questioning reveals a striking concern with the victim's emotional temperament and its effect on his behavior.

Brice's lawyer continued to probe these issues by asking Medley, 'is Mr. Brice of that disposition?' to which Medley replied 'I never knew Mr. Brice offend any body in my life; he is a very quiet man as can be.' Medley continued, 'I never heard Mr. Brice have any words with any body; he was very quiet and peaceable as any man I ever knew in my life.' Later in the trial counsel for the prosecution asked James Ford, a friend of the Brice family, about the prisoner's 'character as to humanity.' Ford answered, 'I never in my life heard any thing of his being liable to quarrel or being of a hot disposition.'[37] The jury's conviction of Brice for manslaughter attested to a consensus that emerged during the trial that the responsibility for the death of Richard Jasper rested with Richard Jasper, specifically his 'hot,' 'hasty,' and 'passionate' temperament.

As Chief Justice of the King's Bench, Sir Dudley Ryder (1691–1756), presided at the Old Bailey criminal trials from 1754 until the year of his death. His synopses of cases from four sessions of the court survive.[38] They provide a unique perspective on the language of excuse and allow us to draw some conclusions about the effect of this language in specific cases. Like other judges, Ryder kept notes to help him remember particular details for summation, jury instruction, and post-verdict proceedings. In his notebook Ryder underlined evidence he found especially relevant or compelling. Although Ryder did not comment explicitly about the language of excuse or its prevalence, of the 50 cases, 12 mention state of mind.

At Alexander Barrow's October 1754 trial for stealing a silver-handled sword, witnesses for the prosecution and the defense mentioned the prisoner's 'madness.' Ryder paid special attention when James Barlow told the court that 'before he [the prisoner] came to the justice he pulled down all the wainscot and tore off his shirt like a madman.'[39] Ryder again underlined the testimony of Alexander Leigerwood, a constable on duty the night of the crime, who said he had known the prisoner for 'some time before.' Leigerwood said of Barrow: 'He behaved like a [crazy] at the roadhouse and broke up the wainscot. I don't think he was not solid in his sense. I never knew of his being out of his senses till this night.' Barrow denied any knowledge of the crime. In his defense he called a witness who had known him for eight years. The witness testified to the prisoner's honesty, but he added that 'indeed of late he has *behaved in a very* odd manner both before and since this. He had a very good character. He lived with [Paterson] bookseller. Since he left him I have taken him to be a madman.'[40] The notes on this case ended with a verdict of not guilty.[41] Ryder's emphases suggest that he found the evidence about Barrow's state of mind both relevant and convincing.

In April 1756 Robert Ogle's case first came to trial, as discussed in chapter 2. Ryder's baffling notes leave us absolutely no clue about how he felt about the defendant, the case, or the issue of insanity. The prisoner's counsel, Mr. Lucas 'moved to put off the trial on affidavit of the prisoner's insanity.' Ryder responded to this request by asking the prisoner 'whether he gave instruction to his counsel to move this?' Ogle replied that 'he was not ready to produce his witnesses, and had been under a course of physic, but had given no other reasons.' We know that Ryder postponed the trial until the next session, but what motivated his decision – Ogle's response, his general appearance, or his lawyer's motion – remains hidden.[42]

The question of insanity resurfaced in the same session when Robert Waites, indicted for stealing money, stood mute when asked 'whether he had any questions to ask.' Ryder noted that he '*only stared and would not speak, as if mad.*' Ryder's notes continued,

> the witness says that when he was with them the prisoner was in his sense; but when he was brought before the justice he appeared to be very much terrified and seemed out of his mind, and [the witness] said that last week he saw him [the accused] and appeared very well.[43]

The emphases, combined with Ryder's description of the defendant 'as if mad,' suggests his interest in the offender's state of mind: did he suffer from partial insanity, a phase of lunacy or was this a case of counterfeit?

Ryder's notebooks also include a diary in which he recorded his experiences as an assize judge on the Home Circuit during the summers of 1754 and 1755. On Friday August 9, 1754 at Chelmsford in Essex Ryder heard the case of Frances Cheek, accused of murdering her six-month-old child. In the lengthiest and most detailed account of his reasoning in a case involving possible insanity, Ryder's notes reflect the judicial anxiety that surrounded pleas of mental illness. A neighbor found Cheek 'kneeling over the body of [her] child, cut plainly with a chicken hook lying by bloody.' When asked why she did it, Cheek 'said nothing but that she should be hanged and knew nothing of the matter.' A clergyman who saw her after the crime testified that 'she was then distracted.' Unlike his case notebooks, in which Ryder recorded Old Bailey trials almost verbatim, the diary summarized evidence without attributing it to specific witnesses or recording their words. In the Cheek case Ryder concluded that 'she was two days after clearly not out of her senses, nor now at her trial nor during the intermediate time, nor any evidence given of her having been disordered before, but one witness said she was a hasty passionate woman.'[44] When he charged the jury, Ryder told them 'they must consider whether she did the fact, and if so whether she was out of her senses when she did the fact, immaterial whether she was so afterwards when she reflected what she had done.'[45]

In his concern to corroborate Cheek's insanity defense, Ryder looked to a history of mental distress or an episode of lunacy before the crime.

A telling disagreement between the judge and the jury ensued. The jury 'first said they were satisfied she killed the child but doubted her sanity.' Despite his own admission that Cheek 'looked wild and disturbed' at her trial, Ryder 'explained again to them the nature of the case rather against the prisoner' and sent them back to deliberate further. An hour and a half later, the jury brought in a conviction. Ryder noted that he 'told them I was very well satisfied' and pronounced a death sentence to be followed by dissection – the ultimate punishment.[46] As discussed in chapter 4, the conviction rate for infanticide had dropped by the second decade of the eighteenth century, so this 1754 conviction stands out as unusual. Ryder did not mention Cheek's marital status, but the absence of a husband at the trial and the failure of the insanity defense, suggests she may have been a single woman. Her case documents the shifting cultural understanding of the discourse about insanity in infanticide trials. While pleas of mental distress by single women at the Old Bailey were more successful by the 1740s and the language of excuse convinced Cheek's jury that she suffered from mental distress when she killed her child, Dudley Ryder did not yet accept the act of infanticide itself as proof of insanity.

The contrast between Cheek's case and a case of 'total insanity' tried on August 14, 1755 is quite striking. The trial of *R* v. *Sullivan* generated none of the anxiety or tension apparent in the Cheek case. Ryder empanelled a jury to 'enquire' whether the defendant, 'indicted for felony, and appearing now as last assizes a lunatic,' 'stood mute willfully or by visitation of God.' The jury found that it was 'by visitation of God.' Ryder agreed that Sullivan appeared 'in court very mad' and dispatched the case quickly by ordering the defendant's confinement.[47]

On the issue of drunkenness Ryder's notes leave some intriguing silences. When Peter Duinby stood accused of stealing salmon from Joseph Russel in April 1755, Ryder seems to have discounted the defendant's intoxication. The prosecution's witness, Benjamin Tompson, gave extensive testimony about the prisoner's state of insobriety, and the *OBSP* records a lengthy interrogation of the mental state implied by the word 'fuddled.'[48] Ryder did not include any of the nuances of this discussion of drunkenness in his notes, nor did he underline Tompson's conclusion, 'I now believe he was fuddled at that time.' Instead Ryder summarized Duinby's statement that 'he knew nothing of the matter, he was so fuddled.'[49] Ryder's emphasis on the first half of the sentence, and his failure to note the verdict or his opinion about it suggests the obviousness of a guilty verdict and the dismissal of this prisoner's drunkenness as a legitimate extenuating circumstance.[50]

Dudley Ryder's notebook and diary raise as many questions as they answer. The notes corroborate my findings from the *OBSP* and from the Northern Circuit depositions that even when it elicited no explicit comment in the court record, or when it was not supposed to be relevant at all, evidence about the mind and mental distress drew the attention of the court. However, Ryder did not underline all the testimony that referred to mental distress, and in cases where he did so, he underlined other unrelated details. None of his notes comments specifically about the insanity defense or the language of excuse. On the other hand, his underlining betrays an interest in the defendants' psychological states and suggests their relevance to him. It is impossible, however, to draw a conclusion about how he weighed this evidence and what other factors (the defendant's looks or gestures, the witnesses for the prosecution and the defense, the prosecutor's credibility, to name just a few) contributed to his opinions in these cases.

To examine further the significance of the language of the mind in the second half of the eighteenth century we must move to sources that document the legal process after conviction. In their petitions for pardon, addressed to the Home Office, convicted felons, their relatives, and supporters appealed for mitigation.[51] The secretary of the Home Office, established in 1782, sent these appeals to the judge who presided at the trial for his opinion on the case, and in response the judge attached a letter in which he supported or opposed the request. If he endorsed the prisoner's petition, the judge could recommend the commutation of sentence, a conditional pardon, or a free pardon.[52]

These sources reveal the importance and weight ascribed to the offender's state of mind both by prisoners and their families and by judges who considered mental distress a legitimate extenuating circumstance, regardless of whether they granted the pardon. The cases sampled here testify to the richness of the language of the mind as well as its subtlety and nuance. In crafting these petitions, their writers argued for the authenticity of an offender's distressed psychological state and appealed to the emotions and sensibility of the legal officials who considered the applications. The petitions illustrate the intersection of the language of the mind with the language of sensibility because the same document drew on both to make a case for pardon.

When they raised the issue of mental distress, the petitions often alluded to the defendant's history of insanity and impaired ability to distinguish right from wrong. The petition for James Husband, convicted of theft from a shop in 1784, described an offender who 'now is and during his whole life time has been insane ... incapable of knowing the nature of the offence for which he now stands convicted.'[53] Dated April 13, 1786, the petition on behalf of Decima Chapple, accused of receiving stolen goods, asserted that Chapple did what 'she was not conscious to be a crime, providence not having blessed her with an understanding capable of clearly distinguishing right from wrong.'[54] The petition explained that Decima had lived a life 'uniformly honest, simple, and inoffensive' and attributed her crime to her limited understanding, 'that slender capacity now most probably impaired by the natural infirmities of age.'[55] The next year Amelia Gill tried to procure a pardon for stealing cloth by describing herself as 'sometimes a little flighty from a decline of life.'[56] While these petitioners made a claim for the prisoner's idiocy, history of mental distress, and old age, others argued for temporary or partial insanity.

James Hyde, who petitioned for his wife Eleanor in 1784, described his 'very distracted situation on account of his wife, for whom he entertains a great affection.' In addition to his avowal that Eleanor had no previous criminal history, he pledged for her 'sincere repentance,' 'sorrow and contrition.' Hyde further suggested that 'the pungent distress of mind which she [Eleanor] has suffered, from the dreadful situation to which she has reduced her parents husband and friends' – presumably as a result of her crime – caused his wife to miscarry.[57] When James Askoe petitioned for pardon in February 1787, he explained that 'unhappy imbecility of mind occasioned by a violent fever'[58] caused him to steal a horse. Samuel Aderton said he stole a horse in 1788 in 'a momentary frenzy occasioned by the dissolute behavior of his wife, which he had discovered just before the commission of the felonious act.'[59] These petitioners referred to a wide range of mental states they attributed to the very real effect of daily stress on their psychological states, their physical health, and their behavior.

Evidence that judges took seriously these claims of mental distress comes even from letters arguing against a pardon. After Susanne Winton's conviction for theft and arson in 1786, the chaplain of the gaol, a Mr. Underwood, told the judge that 'the prisoner had not so good an understanding as most girls her own age.' In his letter the judge summarized his previous investigation of this issue. He asked 'if he [Underwood] thought she had not a capacity to distinguish good and evil, or that she did not know the iniquity of the offences for which she was convicted?' Based on Underwood's response that 'he could not say he thought that,' the judge opposed any pardon and 'thought her a proper object for punishment.' The judge's letter cited 'the evidence against her [which] moved her to be of a competent understanding' and the premeditated nature of the crime 'as it appeared that she had set fire to the barn in consequence of a previous deliberate plan and for the purpose of robbing the house, which she afterwards affected.'[60]

In his rejection of the petition, the judge cited the case made at Winton's trial by her defense counsel. 'For tho' counsel were employed for her, they never ventured to put a question to any of the witnesses called on her behalf respecting her intellect.'[61] The attorney's omission of this evidence supports my assertion that, in general, defense counsel hesitated to introduce evidence about mental states that was not patently obvious in the demeanor of the accused. The judge's response, however, indicates that he expected that any questions of mental incapacity, in this case Underwood's letter insinuating idiocy or retardation, would be raised at trial and suggests that one's case for a pardon would be weakened if they were not. The judge disputed the sincerity and truthfulness of Winton's mental incompetence rather than the exculpatory nature of such a defense. This correspondence demonstrates his effort to apply a standard for the excuse of mental impairment; Winton fell short. The prisoner's intent, 'a previous deliberate plan,' executed 'for the purpose of robbing the house,' proved her culpability for the crime.

When two merchants from Bristol petitioned on behalf of Thomas Davis in 1787, they too described the prisoner's 'weakness of understanding.' They claimed that Davis' 'stupidity and ignorance' made his crime of forgery ineffective and that he 'was incapable of injuring society by any attempts of this nature.' The judge agreed that

> the prisoner did appear to me to be as asserted in the petition, grossly ignorant and stupid, but not to such a degree of incapacity, as would amount to a legal defence or as would at all have justified an acquittal, or the supposition of insanity.[62]

The judge who presided at Joseph King's trial in 1788 applied a similar rationale when he concluded that 'the defense set up was insanity, some insane or strange acts were given in evidence on his trial, but none to show want of understanding in the commission of the imputed felony.'[63] Like the judge in Winton's case, these judges compared the prisoner's state of mind with an exculpatory state of insanity and found the offenders did not meet the criteria.

Mental excuses such as drunkenness and compulsion also appeared in the judges' correspondence. John Wood explained that he 'was unfortunately and without any previous intention induced' to commit highway robbery. In his petition from 1783 Wood explained that his crime resulted 'through the wicked machinations and devices of a notorious rogue whom he accidentally met with at a public house and who by his art and ingenuity induced him to drink so liberally as to throw him into a state of total intoxication.'[64] Similarly, Thomas Truss alleged in 1784 that 'he was in liquor' when he stole poultry and that he 'was drawn into the snare of evil designed persons not thinking the crime to be of so great magnitude.'[65] Petitioners for Joseph Nicholas Smith in 1788 alleged that 'had he not been intoxicated and overinfluenced ... he would not have committed' highway robbery.[66] These petitioners argued that their drunkenness made them vulnerable to temptation and the compulsion of company. In the same year, William Baker's petitioners, who included the sheriff and the grand jurors from the Warwick assizes, declared that 'the unhappy convict ... was in a state of intoxication at the time of the offence.' They explained that they did not offer this explanation 'as apologizing for the crime imputed to him but in hopes that the effect of liquor and not the malevolence of his mind induced him to a commission of the crime.'[67] The middling sort who petitioned on Baker's behalf articulated an understanding of responsibility that separated drunkenness and evil intent. Some judges agreed.

When Robert Williams stole a horse in 1785, he pleaded 'drunkenness in his excuse.' The judge recommended a free pardon because 'in fact he was in liquor in the evening of the 5 April' and that 'in his conduct the next day there was the folly and extravagance of drunken men.'[68] In the same year James Oakes appeared on a list of prisoners considered for a pardon. The presiding judge summarized the crime and recommended a free pardon because 'he was extremely in liquor at the time and upon the whole there appears to me some doubt as to the felonious intention.'[69] The judge assessing William Smith's case in 1786 expressed far more suspicion of Smith's 'supposition that his crime was the effect of intoxication.' Citing the 'pains taken to conceal his theft, by wrapping the sheet round his waist' the judge concluded that the evidence 'argues too much deliberation to admit of any excuse from drunkenness.'[70] These cases demonstrate the assumptions that offenders, petitioners on their behalf, and legal authorities shared about drunkenness and its results: a loss of physical control and diminished legal accountability. The assessment of responsibility in these cases rested on the question of intent. Just as petitioners tried to link the offender's state of mind to a lack of criminal intent, so judges applied a similar formula for pardon.

In their post-trial efforts to secure a pardon some prisoners associated their mental distress with poverty. In his petition for pardon dated March 23, 1784, John Carney blamed 'distressed circumstances at the time of committing this crime' for the robbery of $10\frac{1}{2}$d. The prisoner explained that a war wound left him prone to periodic mental impairment. 'Your petitioner, in consequence of such fracture in his skull, is at intervals not perfectly in his senses as was the case when he committed this crime.' He attributed his crime to 'the pressure of poverty working on a delirious brain [which] produced this fatal crime.'[71] According to Carney, the anxiety and stress of poverty aggravated his physical injury and led to insanity and crime.

Although other petitioners did not make an explicit connection between insanity and poverty, they suggested that mental distress caused by their impoverishment compelled the crime. John Hewitt explained in 1784 that he had a wife and two children 'totally destitute at that inclement season of the common necessaries of life.' After the rejection of his appeal for poor relief from parish officials, 'a fit of despair' produced 'the rashness to violate the laws of his country.'[72] The same year a letter in favor of John Lenney noted that the offender's unemployment before the crime left him 'for four days in want of the common necessaries of life, and that one of the articles stolen was a loaf of bread, which he with great eagerness devoured.'[73] Two letters written by the Duke of Richmond on behalf of Francis Danger in 1786 declared that the offender 'was drove to it [highway robbery] by distress' and that he 'was induced to commit this rash action from a temporary distress, but without the least degree of violence or premeditation.'[74] In April of the same year a letter supporting Francis Coath explained that the prisoner's physical disability and large family made him 'incapable of procuring a sufficient quantity of food to enable them to exist on.' Consequently, his 'family have been frequently driven to the greatest distress and misery and have been impelled by extreme hunger to have recourse to several thefts.'[75] The language of excuse in the pardon petitions makes a more explicit case for poverty-induced mental distress than depositions or trial transcripts. In a last effort to save their lives, petitioners reinterpreted the issue of criminal intent by linking desperation, mental distress, and crime to depict overwhelming, unrestrained compulsion. The legitimacy of these psychological pleas, brought by men in an overwhelming majority of cases, drew on traditional understandings of the male responsibility to provide for their family. Like the cases of infanticide that assumed a dormant feminine potential for insanity that could be activated by pregnancy and childbirth, these cases argued for an insanity innate to men and activated by the failure to fulfill their roles as providers.

How did judges respond to these excuses? The evidence points to a limited acceptance. When he reviewed Joseph Partridge's case in 1786, the judge summarized the events that led to the sentence of transportation for seven years. The letter then listed several extenuating circumstances, including the judge's impression that Partridge 'appears ... to have been impelled to the commission of this crime by distress,' and recommended him for a pardon.[76] In the same year, William Adair concluded that Peter Ogier's theft of household furniture 'appeared to have been done from the pressure of great distress.'[77] A letter from 1787 on behalf of John Smith, written to the judge by a magistrate, asserted that 'it was his first offence and committed through distress.'[78] When the judge in Luke Hoyle's case from 1786 rejected the prisoner's petition, he explained that 'the prisoner had money in his pocket at the time,' so 'it was clear that he was not impelled to the commission of the crime by the pressure of immediate want.'[79] Just as in the case of William Smith, who did not seem intoxicated enough, this judge doubted Hoyle's truthfulness about his poverty rather than rejecting the idea that poverty did create 'pressure' that compelled crime.

While these judges recognized the link between mental distress and crime, other letters reveal certain reservations about the validity of these excuses in criminal law. In the case of John Smith, convicted of street robbery in 1784, the judge recommended against a pardon saying that

> there is no reason to apprehend that his circumstances, if he should now be pardoned would be less distressed, than he alleges they were, or that he would have more virtue to resist the temptation arising from that distress.'[80]

This judge believed that 'temptation' arose from distress, but he did not think that the explanation justified a pardon. Similar ambivalence about responsibility and states of mind emerged in the sources relating to Thomas Bax. When George Morgan died a few days after a fight with Bax in 1786, the judge advised a verdict of manslaughter because 'the law in that case made such an allowance for the frailty of human passions, as to extenuate the crime.' In response to the prisoner's petition for a pardon, however, the judge recommended 'severe punishment,' in this case a year's imprisonment, because 'it appeared to me that the prisoner had given a very intemperate scope to his passion and such as merited a severe punishment.'[81] This case provides a good example of the co-operation between legal authorities and defendants who used the language of the mind and delineated its limits. In the same letter the judge allowed an extenuating psychological explanation for crime to reduce the severity of punishment while simultaneously containing its exculpatory scope to exclude it as an outright excuse.[82]

When he wrote a letter urging the pardon of William Rose in 1784, Edward Venables Vernon (1757–1847) demonstrated the prevalence of the language of excuse and the acceptance of the idea that psychological and social forces could temporarily cloud an offender's moral judgment and impair one's capacity for self-restraint. A curate in Sudbury, later named Archbishop of York, Vernon explained that Rose stole 'through unavoidable misfortunes' that 'reduced [him] to the greatest distress. And I am told, that himself, his wife and five small children were almost starving when he committed the crime.' Vernon concluded his letter by declaring that several members of the grand jury and 'many other most respectable characters would most heartily join' him to support the petition for a man 'esteemed by them rather unfortunate than culpable.'[83] Vernon's words summarized the cultural understanding of moral responsibility as a shifting and changing entity in which the offender's mental state had a direct bearing on criminal intent, culpability, and accountability. When any participant introduced arguments based on this conception of responsibility into the criminal process, everyone who participated in the legal system was forced to confront the disjuncture between theoretical standards for exculpatory states of mind and those created by lived experience and eighteenth-century conceptions of the self. The pardon petitions document the struggle of judicial authorities to define legitimate, exculpatory states of mind, to contain the inevitable expansion of the language of mental distress, and to regulate its application during the trial and after conviction.

'A case of great compassion': sensibility at trial

As discussed in chapter 2, legal authorities were deeply concerned about the shifting definition of criminal responsibility and discussed at length the appropriate proximity of sensibility and justice. The relationship between sensibility and justice disturbed members of the legal establishment and observers of England's courts alike. Some warned of the destabilizing influence that pleas of diminished responsibility had on sensible, compassionate jurors. Other reformers urged jurors to sympathize or be 'compassionate' with criminals who argued that they did not have full control of their behavior or full accountability for their actions.

Dudley Ryder's notes betray a similar anxiety about the role of emotion in the jury's deliberation and by extension in his own assessment of responsibility. Regarding a trial of October 23, 1754, he wrote, 'I spoke to the jury on the head of compassion exercised in this particular case of pickpocket.' Ryder seemed satisfied with the result of his charge 'And the jury found him <u>guilty of the indictment generally</u>.' He noted that 'the aldermen Bethel and Alsop both said they were much pleased with what I said to the jury.'[84] In the case of Thomas Rolf, indicted for highway robbery, repeated mention of the prisoner's distress shaped the trial that took place before Ryder on October 25, 1754. Four of the prosecution's five witnesses testified about the prisoner's unemployment, his pregnant wife, his regret, and his report that he 'did it for want.' Ryder underlined all these details as well as the testimony from witnesses on Rolf's behalf who mentioned his 'excellent character,' his 'necessity,' and his 'wife and two small children.'[85]

In his charge to the jury Ryder spoke to the issue of compassion. 'I summed up exactly and told the jury the prisoner had the best of characters and that evidence might outweigh doubtful evidence, but compassion could not justify finding contrary to truth.' After the jury convicted Rolf, he wrote, '<u>I told the jury they did right, but it was a case of great compassion</u>.'[86] When the jury 'desired I would intercede for him,' presumably referring to a pardon, Ryder reminded them that the Recorder of London 'would have an opportunity of representing it fully to His Majesty.' Ryder's final comment on the case reveals the effect of such testimony on him. Ryder admitted that 'indeed I never in all my life met with a robbery on the highway so clearly proved to be the effect of mere necessity and committed for want of necessaries to maintain himself, wife big with child, and two infants,' but he did not indicate that he would take an active role in appealing for the prisoner.[87] Ryder's notes and emphases suggest that he believed that any consideration of Wolf's circumstances must be reserved until after trial and that the jury's verdict should reflect the 'facts of the case' alone. Ryder also revealed his personal struggle to distance his identity as a man of feeling and sensibility from his persona as a judge charged with guiding the assessment of legal responsibility.

The separation of justice and sensibility did not, however, lead Ryder to repress his sensibility completely or to portray himself as an unfeeling man, insensitive to the emotional testimony he heard. A suggestive incident from his diary exposes the intersection of mental excuse, legal judgment, and emotion. When he handed down the death sentence of Frances Cheek, convicted of the murder of her six-month-old infant in

August 1754 (discussed above), Ryder reported that 'I made a very proper speech extempoare [*sic*] and pronounced it with dignity.' In his notebook, Ryder described his feelings as he pronounced the death sentence on Frances Cheek: 'I was so affected that the tears were gushing out several times against my will.'[88] Self-conscious about the public nature of his emotional response, Ryder noted that 'it was discerned by all the company – which was large – and a lady gave me her handkerchief dipped in lavender water to help me.'[89]

Was Ryder oblivious to the irony of his claim to have cried against his will while sentencing to death a woman who some believed acted against her will? His use of the phrase 'against my will' implied his failure to distance sensibility from the legal setting. Yet his feelings did not prevent him from securing Cheek's conviction. By leaving his show of emotion until the pronouncement of the death sentence, Ryder achieved what he deemed an appropriate balance of emotion and justice. He enforced justice by insisting on a conviction and displayed sensibility when reading the death sentence. In his performance Ryder attempted to reclaim his authority as a judge and the authority of middle-class masculinity in the face of the threats of defendant initiative and the emphasis on feminine emotions in the culture of sensibility. When he directed the jury to convict Frances Cheek, he asserted his judge's authority over the trial, restricted the ethos of sensibility to middling jurors and judges, and reconstituted the trial as the setting for the traditional masculine values of reason, indifference, and stoicism. Ryder's tears at the sentencing may have signaled some limited consideration of compassion as appropriate only at the post-trial phase of the criminal legal process.

Some evidence from the correspondence with the Home Office suggests that petitioners deliberately appealed to sensibility to try to procure the judge's sympathy for their cause in an effort to reduce the severity of a non-capital sentence or to escape execution. In 1787 John Smith apologized for the lengthy epistle he wrote to Lord Sydney (1733–1800) who served as Home Office secretary from 1783 until 1789. Smith said he hoped that 'my many misfortunes distress and miserable situation plead my excuse, and hope that you will not be deaf to the tender feelings of compassion.' Smith appealed to Sidney's sensibility by raising the issue of mental distress when he wrote '[I] hope that urgent necessity, and an uneasy state of mind which is only bounded by despair, will plead in your lordship's breast and be a powerful advocate in my favor.'[90] James Askoe's petition dexterously combined mental excuse and sensibility in 1787. He thanked the judge for granting him a reprieve based on 'compassion to your petitioner's unhappy imbecility of mind occasioned by a violent fever' and requested a full pardon.[91] The correspondence with the Home Office mixed psychological explanations for crime with the language of emotion and sensibility to argue for mitigation. The evidence suggests that these petition writers implicitly appealed to the sensible reader, one who, moved by the pain of others, responded to passion with compassion.

Some pardon letters written on behalf of convicted felons by 'respectable' 'men of character' reveal the appeal of social equals to each other's sensibility and compassion. In 1785 a letter on behalf of John Jacob declared: 'we firmly believe he [Jacob] will never be guilty of any thing hereafter unworthy of your grace's unbounded goodness and humanity should you think him worthy of your grace's compassion.' In case this entreaty did not convince the judge who read it to grant the pardon, the petitioners assured him that they knew about his 'humanity and benevolence to the unfortunate and distressed.'[92] A letter for George Owen from 1785 conveyed the expectation that its reader would respond positively because the extenuating circumstances cited by the author 'may have some influence with a person of your feeling and good nature.'[93] Implying that their feelings motivated their own behavior these petitioners urged an assessment of legal responsibility that relied on a combination of justice, emotion, and sensibility.

The middling men who supported Matthew Barker's petition for pardon in 1784 referred directly to the effects of feelings on their behavior. They explained that 'a more lamentable case upon the whole has been seldom seen, [and] a more general and anxious compassion was we believe never excited in all ranks of men.'[94] They alleged that 'impelled by his pity for the very extraordinary case of the prisoner ... Mr. Blake was therefore deterred by his humanity from executing the prisoner.' A note, perhaps from the judge who presided at Barker's trial, read: 'my feelings have induced me to concur in a petition to your lordship.' Another writer, 'actuated ... by the purest motives of compassion within my own breast and appealing as I do to your lordship's great humanity,' claimed that he took the liberty to make the appeal 'impelled' by 'every dear dictate of my reason and every better sensibility of my heart.'[95] Although these emotional appeals seem formulaic, their readers could not have easily dismissed them without risking their reputations for compassion and sensibility.

Some letters anticipated the discomfort aroused by introducing sensibility into a discussion of legal responsibility. Thomas Beever concluded his letter for Matthew Barker in 1784 with an explicit disclaimer about sensibility:

> As the gratification alone of your tenderness and humanity on this occasion will I conceive be too indulgent to your feelings to leave it necessary for me to offer arguments to stimulate you to compliance with my request, I will not affront you with the use of any.[96]

Beever promised not to transgress by making an argument for sensibility in a legal context and not to pressure the judge by implying that he would lack humanity and feeling if he did not comply with the request. Beever's pledge not to resort to the language of sensibility speaks to the potency of such an argument. By denying his appeal to emotion, his reference to the subject may have actually strengthened his appeal to sensibility. In another example from 1787 when Richard Burke wrote on behalf of Thomas Davis, Burke enhanced the credibility of those who signed Davis' petition, 'merchants of eminence in business, fortune, and character,' by stating that

> none of these with whom I am personally acquainted and I am so acquainted with most of them, are likely to be swayed to this application, by mere favor to a prisoner or general tenderness, and that in this case they cannot be influenced by particular tenderness to Davis, as he is an utter stranger in Bristol.[97]

This evidence points quite strikingly at the discomfort aroused by the introduction of the language of sensibility into a legal context and echoes Fielding's warning about the 'tender-hearted and compassionate.'[98] Courtroom observers and legal reformers warned that the proximity of sensibility and justice would have lasting and profound effects not only on individual cases but on the legal system at large. The vocabulary of the mind and the compassion it elicited in jurors occluded the definition of criminal intent and undermined the process of assigning responsibility for crime.

Solitary confinement

Thus far this chapter has sought to examine judicial reactions to the language of the mind in pre-trial depositions, trial transcripts, and petitions for pardon. Another response to the language of the mind was the creation and designation of new forms of punishment.

While some reformers advocated the union of sensibility and justice, they did not recommend a higher acquittal rate, and I do not wish to argue that judges and jurors who sought to apply the ethos of sensibility to their juridical duties did so by acquitting or pardoning prisoners more often. The discussion of sensibility and justice did, however, lead to an examination of the causes of crime. Some of the explanations for crime that emerged in the late eighteenth century pointed to the offender's displaced self and inadequate sensibility, both viewed as threats to law and order; in the work of some commentators, solitary confinement emerged as the corrective for both. Although not all who engaged in the debates about penal reform endorsed solitary confinement and some expressed skepticism about this form of punishment, the advocates of solitary confinement incorporated language of the mind similar to that used by participants in the courtroom.[99]

In his *Rambler* essay from November 1750, Johnson discussed the unrealistic 'expectation of uniformity of character' in the face of 'the power of desire, the cogency of distress, the complications of affairs or the force of partial influence.'[100] Almost as if he were speaking to a jury assessing the merits of a defendant's case, Johnson advised that 'such is the state of all mortal virtue, that it is always uncertain and variable.' While he did not condone moral lapses, Johnson urged his readers to weigh the good and the bad that coexist in an offender carefully. 'Let none too hastily conclude that all goodness is lost, though it may for a time be clouded and overwhelmed; for most minds are the slaves of external circumstances.'[101] For Johnson the displaced self concealed a good and virtuous one; even in 'the loose, and thoughtless and dissipated, there is a secret radical worth, which may shoot out by proper cultivation.' With 'the breath of counsel and exhortation' this 'spark of heaven, though dimmed and obstructed, is yet not extinguished ... but may be kindled into flame.'[102] Johnson's essay urged rehabilitation.

In another essay Johnson advised that 'retirement from the cares and pleasures of the world has been often recommended as useful to repentance' because 'sorrow and terror must naturally precede reformation.' In solitude 'austerities and mortifications are means by which the mind is invigorated and roused, by which the attractions of pleasure are interrupted, and the chains of sensuality are broken.' Johnson referred here to the contrition made necessary by ordinary human fallibility rather than crime, but legal reformers seeking alternatives to the death penalty echoed the call for seclusion with the hope for 'a change of life.'[103]

In the late eighteenth century English legal reformers set out to create Johnson's 'breath of counsel' in order to redirect or reintegrate criminal selves.[104] John Howard (1729–1790) led the program of penal reform in the 1770s. Howard's belief in the power of incarceration as an instrument of moral reform emphasized the discipline of the prisoner's body, but more importantly, the rehabilitation of his or her conscience. Howard's *State of the Prisons in England and Wales* published in 1777 inspired members of parliament endeavoring to design an alternative to transportation which had been interrupted by the American War of Independence. William Eden and William Blackstone authored the Penitentiary Act (19 Geo. III, c. 74) which passed in 1779. The act prescribed hard labor, religious instruction, and solitary confinement as the means to rehabilitation.[105]

For Manasseh Dawes, the offender's sensibility comprised the object of punishment. He suggested that 'to restrain moral actions which prove absolutely adverse to men's happiness, application should be made to their minds.'[106] Dawes believed that punishments such as slavery or transportation would correct the psychological deficiency that caused crime by making 'men sensible of their crimes.'[107] In 1785 William Paley surmised that 'of the reforming punishments which have not yet been tried, none promises so much success as that of solitary imprisonment.' The project, 'to raise up in him reflections on the folly of his choice, and to dispose his mind to such bitter and continued penitence, as may produce a lasting alteration in the principles of his conduct,' set out to reform the offender's thoughts.[108] For both Dawes and Paley, rehabilitation was a question of sensibility and psychology.

In his discussion, Paley alluded to a treatise by Jonas Hanway (1712–1786) on *Solitude in Imprisonment* (1776).[109] Hanway proclaimed solitary confinement 'the most humane and effectual means of bringing malefactors ... to a right sense of their condition.'[110] He complained about criminals who lacked 'a due sense of the offences they have been guilty of' and severe laws that allowed 'numbers [to] escape condemnation' through 'tenderness of evidence – the quirks of the law – the mercy of judges – the humanity of juries – and the clemency of the most benignant of sovereigns.'[111] Instead, Hanway urged the 'wonderful effects of a judicious severity, blended with such mercy and compassion as will operate on the native ingenuousness of the mind.'[112] Solitary confinement promised punishment and reformation; it satisfied reformers who wished to introduce sensibility into the legal setting without compromising the rule of law.

For Hanway, as for all who recommended a mix of sensibility and justice, 'if we do not maturely consider the cause of an offence, as well as the offence itself, our sentences will always be defective.'[113] Hanway identified the problems facing England as the results of trade and prosperity:

> In a trading nation, citizens will sometimes leave their families in distress; many persons become insane at this period of time ... we live in the same climate, in the same plenty, and are addicted to the same violence of temper; and the more vicious we are rendered by the force of affluence, the more insanity and sickness there will be.[114]

For some, prosperity and affluence overwhelmed and over-stimulated the emotions, producing too much sensibility and eroding one's self-control. The psychological toll of prosperity displaced the true self.

Hanway, like Johnson, attributed crime to a self displaced by 'warmth of temper, ignorance, *drunkenness*, or being exposed to the *arts of seduction*.' But he insisted that they 'are not therefore *irreclaimable*.'[115] Hanway based his proposal on the assertion that 'man is a reasoning, as well as a passionate creature.'[116] The 'same foul streams' bring 'the love of pleasure, in preference to the love of God, till our passions and appetites are inflamed.'[117] These unrestrained passions cause 'infernal ambition,' 'restless vanity,' and 'robbery and murder,'[118] but the inculcation of Christian values would 'restore the prisoner to the world and social life in the most *advantageous* manner.'[119] In order to effect a permanent reformation and to 'reduce those to a sense of reason and religion,' Hanway proposed '*solitude*, cutting the prisoner off from all means of evil.'[120]

Echoing Johnson, Hanway wrote that the solitary prison cell would 'awaken the hearts and understandings' and 'restore [prisoners] to the world, upright and honest' through the 'tears of repentance.'[121] Solitary confinement would change a prisoner through '*affliction* ... the truest friend to *repentance*: solitude will create affliction, such as arises from a *consciousness of guilt*.'[122] Consciousness of guilt relied on a coherent self. The advocates of solitary confinement hoped that the imposition of pain would redirect the prisoner's sensibility and awaken the sense of responsibility.

Hanway referred to the 'flutter of mind' caused by poverty and vice.[123] In response to these irrational impulses that displaced the self, he recommended solitary confinement to give the prisoner 'time to consider' and an opportunity for him to contemplate 'his *immortal* part' and to '*open his mind*.'[124] Hanway and other proponents of solitary confinement believed that given the time to reflect, the offender would reform. They characterized this scheme as a 'gentle treatment' and promised that it would 'bring them [prisoners] to their right mind.'[125] Although

Hanway carefully distinguished the sort of mental distress that caused crime from insanity, he believed that offenders suffering a displaced self needed 'time and solitude' to 'restore them to themselves.'[126]

In 1792 John Brewster (1753–1842) published a pamphlet *On the Prevention of Crimes, and on the Advantages of Solitary Imprisonment* in which he reiterated many of the points made by Hanway. Brewster stated quite emphatically in his introduction that

> it is a matter of the greatest moment to society to give a right direction to the mind of man and to endeavor to improve those dispositions which might otherwise become the sources of misery and misfortune.[127]

Citing the failure of 'punishments, which however heavily they fettered the body, never reached the mind,' Brewster praised solitary confinement for its endeavor to find 'that spark of honest ambition, which, however latent, is yet to be found in most minds.'[128] Like Johnson before him, Brewster affirmed the existence of a universal, true, good self, however obscured or concealed.

This new form of punishment would make 'the perpetrator himself ... sensible of his fault.'[129] For prosecutors, this new punishment would circumvent the 'compassion for the sufferer' that Paley and Fielding warned would result from 'excessive correction.'[130] The isolation of solitary confinement promised to achieve these goals because it would 'correct the understanding' and 'convince the judgment' of a criminal, but it did not compromise severity.[131] 'Buried in a solitude where he has no companion but reflection, no counsellor but thought [he] ... will find ... the severest punishment he can receive.'[132] Solitude would 'inspire [the offender] with a degree of horror, which he never felt before. This impression is greatly heightened by his being *obliged to think.*'[133] Brewster believed that by suffering pain, the prisoner, 'left alone, and feelingly alive to all the stings of remorse' would experience a complete reformation.[134]

Some social critics like William Godwin (1756–1836) denounced solitary confinement as 'uncommonly tyrannical and severe' and doubted that it could serve as an 'article of reformation.'[135] Josiah Dornford (1764–1797) refuted the charge that 'some men are not to be managed' when he asserted that 'bold, daring, impudent offenders [should] be shut up by themselves to reflect for a few days in a dark room, and they will soon be of a better mind.'[136] Although the prescriptive literature cited here and the actual practice of solitary confinement always diverged and the enthusiasm for this new form of punishment faded soon after its implementation, the earliest advocates of solitary confinement believed that it offered the best chance for the criminal's rehabilitation based on experience with the displaced self and the theory of sensibility as played out in the criminal trial.[137]

Hanway and other proponents of solitary confinement relied on the existence of what Johnson called 'secret radical worth' and 'a spark of heaven.' They believed that most criminals suffered from a good self displaced by drunkenness, distress, or temptation, the result of uncontained and misdirected sensibility. Although they did not believe that such an offender suffered from insanity, they did suggest that mental distress 'dissipates his mind' and 'benumbs his senses.'[138] They believed that the pain of solitude would restore the offender's sensibility, its moral perception and acuteness of feeling, and reintegrate the displaced self. Solitary confinement provided its advocates a means to negotiate sensibility and justice: it recognized the prisoner's culpability and allowed for his/her conviction while accommodating compassion and the culture of sensibility through the circumvention of capital punishment.

Conclusions

At every stage of the legal process participants in England's legal system employed the vocabulary of mental distress when they tried to explain or excuse crime. Rich and nuanced descriptions of mental states appealed to the eighteenth-century sensibilities of defendants and prosecutors, judges and jurors by negotiating the line between responsibility for crime and new understandings of sensibility and the self. Some feared that these mental excuses destabilized the signification and determination of *mens rea*, criminal intent.

The language of diminished responsibility did not go unnoticed by observers of England's judicial system. Some legal commentators sought to prevent further crime by enforcing the harsh penalties of the 'bloody code.' They recommended the separation of justice and sensibility and the containment of compassion. Other legal reformers believed that 'to prevent crimes, is to have the nature of them well understood.'[139] They endorsed the convergence of sensibility, compassion, and justice and acknowledged the displacement of the self.

Although solitary confinement appealed to reformers of all stripes with its promise to combine severity and compassion, it did not shore up the definition of *mens rea*. Even those who accepted insanity as a legitimate excuse for crime wished to circumscribe the language that could be used to describe mental states. Although willing to accept the language of excuse as a reason for mitigation, they did not necessarily wish to define psychological distress as exculpatory in the fullest sense of the word. The trial of James Hadfield would bring these issues into sharp focus in May 1800.

6

The End of Excuse?
James Hadfield and the
Insanity Plea

War, inflation, national debt, high prices, food shortages, fear, suspicion, and crisis marked Great Britain on the eve of the new century. Both Whigs and Tories felt the tension, anxiety, and sense of impending social, political, and economic crisis in 1790s. While the Tories decried the French Revolution as a threat to tradition, monarchy, and social order, the Whigs and Jacobin radicals mourned the repression of 'English liberty,' and their own apparent failure to bring the values of the French Revolution to Britain.[1] When James Hadfield (1771–1841) fired at George III on May 15, 1800 as the king entered the royal box in Drury Lane Theatre, the panic aroused by the would-be regicide reverberated within a culture preoccupied with issues of rebellion, loyalty, monarchy, and millenarianism.[2]

Hadfield's treason trial took less than six hours and ended with a verdict of 'not guilty, he being under the influence of insanity at the time the act was committed.' The acquittal led Parliament into an emergency session where the House of Commons passed the 'Act for regulating Trials for High Treason and Misprision of High Treason,' known as the Treason Bill of 1800 (39&40 Geo. III, c. 93) and the 'Act for the Safe Custody of Insane Persons Charged with Offenses' (39&40 Geo. III, c. 94). The Treason Bill reduced the murder or attempted murder of the king to an ordinary felony, thereby denying those accused of these crimes the special rights granted to defendants in political trials. The 'Act for the Safe Custody of Insane Persons Charged with Offenses,' known as the Criminal Lunatics Act, legislated the automatic, indefinite incarceration of anyone acquitted by reason of insanity for treason, murder, or any other felony. The act limited bail for persons indicted for criminal offenses who claimed mental impairment and allowed the indefinite incarceration of suspects who seemed to suffer from mental illness.

Scholarship on the Hadfield case offers two interpretations of the role of the case in the history of the insanity defense. Nigel Walker and Joel Eigen minimized its place in the history of insanity pleas, arguing that Hadfield's case had relatively little impact on the number of insanity defenses submitted in the nineteenth century.[3] Others, most prominently Richard Moran, assigned the case a special importance based on the passage of the Criminal Lunatics Act and the legislated incarceration of offenders acquitted on the basis of insanity.[4]

In the context of this book, however, a different perspective on Hadfield emerges. Moran suggested this interpretation in the conclusion to his article about the case:

> It might be said that the trial of James Hadfield marked the abolition of the insanity defense, not its origin, since in most jurisdictions a successful defense of insanity now leads to automatic confinement for an indefinite period of time.[5]

Rather than decriminalizing behavior or creating an easy way for defendants to avoid criminal prosecution, the Hadfield decision and the passage of the Criminal Lunatics Act (which eventually led to the promulgation of the M'Naughten Rules in 1843) reduced the number of pleas that defendants could introduce in court, circumscribed the language that could be used to describe mental states, and dictated harsher punishments for those *acquitted* as insane.[6] These decisions heralded new, medicalized and criminalized descriptions of defendants as pathological and replaced the supple language of excuse that had seen such elaboration in the eighteenth century. The new medical language within the 'lawyerized' trial replaced the phenomenon illustrated in this study that allowed defendants and others who spoke on their behalf to broaden the category of exculpatory mental states and define these states as temporary and unrelated to the defendant's true self.

The crime

James Hadfield 'sat in the second row from the orchestra, but toward the middle of the pit' on the evening of Thursday, May 15, 1800. 'Just as his majesty entered his box, and was bowing to the audience with his usual condescension,' Hadfield rose from his seat and 'levelling a horse pistol toward the king's box, fired it.'[7] According to the newspaper accounts no one saw the perpetrator in time to prevent the shot, but 'providentially a gentleman who sat next him, Mr. Holyroyd, of

Scotland Yard had the good fortune to raise the arm of the assassin, so as to direct the contents of the pistol toward the roof of the box.' The audience shouted 'seize the villain – shut all the doors!' but the king remained calm, and looked down at his would-be assassin with 'the most perfect composure' while the queen displayed 'the most dignified courage.' The theatergoers standing nearby and some of the musicians from the orchestra quickly seized Hadfield and rushed him into the musicians' room. The crowd shouted 'shew the villain!' and the orchestra played 'God save the king.'[8]

While the audience joined in anthem, the king's would-be assailant underwent an examination by several men who noticed that he wore an officer's waistcoat. The man declared that 'he had no objection to tell who he was. It was not over yet – there was a great deal more and worse to be done. His name was James Hadfield.' Despite his attempted regicide, Hadfield told his inquisitors that he had served in the Fifteenth Light Dragoons and that he 'had fought for his king and country.'

When the Prince of Wales, (the future George IV (r. 1820–1830)) and the Duke of York, Frederick of Hanover (1763–1827), entered the room, Hadfield looked at the latter and declared 'I know your royal highness – God bless you. You are a good fellow. I have served with your highness.' He pointed to his face and said,

> I got these, and more than these in fighting by your side. At Lincelles I was left three hours among the dead in a ditch, and was taken prisoner by the French. I had my arm broke by a shot, and eight sabre wounds in my head; but I recovered, and here I am.[9]

Hadfield's disfiguring scars covered his face and head. A deep cut over his eye, a long scar on his cheek, and one on his temple left physical reminders of the psychological and physical trauma he had suffered during his service in the army.

Hadfield told his examiners that following his discharge from the army, he had returned to London and made a good living as a silversmith. He explained that 'being weary of life,' he bought a pair of pistols from Mr. Wakelin, a hairdresser and broker. On the morning of the assassination attempt, he borrowed a crown from his master, Solomon Hougham, bought some powder, and went to the house of Mrs. Mason in Red Lion Street where he drank a beer. Afterwards, he tested the pistols in the yard behind the pub, and finding one 'good for nothing' he discarded it. Then he used lead to cast himself two slugs, loaded his pistol, and left for the theater.

At this point in the interrogation, the magistrate, Sir W. Addington, arrived. He noted pragmatically that the position of Hadfield's pistol when he shot at the king would determine the criminal charge. Addington asked Hadfield 'what had induced him to attempt the life of the best of sovereigns?' to which Hadfield replied that he

> had not attempted to kill the king. He had fired his pistol over the royal box. He was as good a shot as any in England; but he was himself weary of life – he wished for death, but not to die by his own hands. He was desirous to raise an alarm; and wished that the spectators might fall upon him. He hoped that his life was forfeited.[10]

Looking for motive, Addington asked Hadfield if he belonged to the London Corresponding Society. Hadfield replied in the negative, but he did say that he belonged to the Odd Fellows Club and a Benefit Society. When asked if he had any accomplices, Hadfield put his hand on his heart and denied it.[11]

The Times described Hadfield as 'extremely collected' throughout his examination, but *Bell's Weekly Messenger* reported that at this point in the interrogation he began 'to shew manifest signs of mental derangement.' He spoke

> in a mysterious way of dreams and of a great commission he had received in his sleep: that he knew he was to be a martyr, and was to be persecuted like his great master, Jesus Christ. He had been persecuted in France; but he had not yet been sufficiently tested. He knew what he was to endure, but he begged Sir W. Addington to remember that Jesus Christ had his trial before he was crucified. He said many other incoherent things in the same style.[12]

Following this outburst, several witnesses were brought in to provide further information about the accused. William Wakelin, from whom Hadfield bought his pistols, corroborated the assailant's story. Wakelin told the investigators that 'he knew very little of Hadfield, but knew where he worked and had heard a good character of him, but that the least drink affected his head.' Several other witnesses who knew Hadfield from Mrs. Mason's rooming house where he lived with his family, confirmed this fact and 'said they ascribed this to the very severe wounds he had received in the head. The least drink quite deranged him.'[13]

Hadfield's examination ended with this evidence. When the performance finished and the theater emptied, the investigators found the slugs in the orchestra below the royal box.[14] Hadfield was committed to Cold Bath Fields, but at midnight the Privy Council, fearful of a larger unchecked conspiracy, called him and the important witnesses to the office of the Home Secretary, the Duke of Portland, for another examination to find out if there were any accomplices.[15] Finally, they charged Hadfield with high treason, committed him for trial, and sent him to Newgate Gaol by hackney coach.

The next morning the Privy Council met again to review the evidence against Hadfield. His co-workers testified that Hadfield had met a man who assured him that 'he had had Jesus Christ in keeping five years in Mount Sion, and that he was soon to visit this world.'[16] The man, a cobbler by the name of Bannister Truelocke (1750–1830), was immediately apprehended in Islington. Truelocke was described as 'much possessed with an opinion of the speedy return of our Saviour' and apparently 'he had possessed the prisoner also' with his millenarian beliefs as 'they both seem to be religiously mad.' Truelocke 'talked very rationally on any other subject but religion.' He called himself 'the true descendant of God!' and declared his resolution to 'destroy the world in the course of three days.'[17] A clerk reported that he had heard Truelocke tell Hadfield 'it was a shame there should be any soldiers; that Jesus Christ was coming; and [that] we should have neither king nor soldiers.'[18] Truelocke's testimony ended with his incarceration in the house of correction at Cold Bath Fields.

Press accounts reported that James Hadfield was born in London, the son of a coachman. He made a living as a silversmith and, according to the papers, 'he was not in distress.' He said he had had two wives 'one the best woman in the world, the other a very bad woman, but of her he was the most fond.' The newspapers reported that 'he is much scarred' and several witnesses described 'severe wounds' on his head.[19] At his arraignment at the Court of King's Bench on June 18, 1800 Hadfield 'appeared very composed and conducted himself with decency and propriety.' He pleaded not guilty, and in a written petition that contradicted his earlier assertion that 'he wished for death,' he expressed a desire for a defense but declared his inability to 'procure proper legal assistance' 'by reason of his poverty.' In his petition he asked for Thomas Erskine and Serjeant Best as his defense team with Charles Humphries as his solicitor. The men, who had no prior knowledge of Hadfield's request, accepted.[20]

Reading the Hadfield trial

On June 26, 1800 James Hadfield stood trial for high treason: 'compassing and imagining the death of the king.' In his opening remarks, the attorney general, John Mitford (1748–1830),[21] told the jury to 'discharge from your minds every thing which you have heard upon the subject, *to attend solely to the evidence which will now be given to you.*'[22] Throughout his speech, Mitford anticipated the insanity defense, noting that given the number of witnesses to the crime and the other physical evidence 'there can be no doubt of his guilt, if some excuse cannot be offered.'[23] He did not argue against insanity as a valid excuse for crime, but he refuted the legitimacy of an insanity defense for Hadfield, arguing that his was *'a deliberate act'* and promising to show that 'before the act, at the time of the act, and after the act, he had that degree of understanding which enabled him to form a judgment of that which he proposed to do, of that which he did, and of that which he had designed.'[24] Mitford concluded that 'when a man has that degree of understanding, however deranged his state of mind may have been at other times, the law says, and the safety of the world requires, that he should be responsible to justice for the act which he has so done.'[25]

To refute the legitimacy of Hadfield's legal insanity, Mitford cited Coke and Hale. He referred to the cases of Edward Arnold who tried to kill Lord Onslow in 1723 and Lawrence Shirley, Lord Ferrers who killed his steward in 1760. Both of these trials had revolved around the insanity defense and discussions of its rightful application and each case reestablished the standard of proof that hinged on whether the offender had 'that competent degree of reason which enabled the person accused to judge whether he was doing right or wrong.'[26] Mitford reiterated that

> if a man is completely deranged, so that he knows not what he does, if a man is so lost to all sense, in consequence of the infirmity of disease, that he is incapable of distinguishing between good and evil – that he is incapable of forming a judgement upon the consequences of the act which he is about to do, that then the mercy of our law says, he cannot be guilty of a crime.[27]

Mitford summarized his position affirming *mens rea* by saying that 'the will, to a certain degree, is the essence of the crime.'

Mitford agreed that idiots, children, madmen, and lunatics could not be held responsible for a crime of which they were 'perfectly unconscious.' Nonetheless, he warned jurors that 'we must be very cautious; – it is not every frantic and idle humour of a man that will exempt him from justice, and the punishment of the law.'[28] Mitford restated the 'wild beast test' explaining that exculpatory insanity left a man 'totally deprived of his understanding and memory,' unable to know 'what he is doing any more than an infant, than a brute, or a wild beast.'[29] Acknowledging a range of mental states, Mitford urged jurors to 'weigh *the degree of discretion* which the person accused possessed' according to their behavior 'in the ordinary intercourse of life.'[30] He instructed the jury to hold defendants responsible for their crimes if they 'possessed that competent understanding which enabled them to discern good from evil.'[31]

John Mitford's opening remarks set out the dilemma faced by the English legal system in the eighteenth century. Mitford wished to frame the insanity defense as an all-or-nothing proposition. Quoting Coke and Hale and referring to the state trials of Edward Arnold and Lord Ferrers, Mitford wished to limit the qualifications for exculpation to 'absolute madness' and 'a total deprivation of memory.'[32] At the same time Mitford admitted that despite the guilty verdicts, both of the earlier cases involved some kind of insanity.[33] Judge and jury concurred 'that Arnold's mind was deranged' and 'that it was deranged even with respect to my Lord Onslow himself.' In that case, the fact that 'he had a steady and resolute design and used all proper means to effect it' became the basis of a guilty verdict. In the Ferrers case many witnesses agreed that Ferrers 'occasionally laboured under the misfortune of insanity.'[34] Mitford explained the guilty verdict reached by the House of Lords in 1760:

> that it was not necessary that a person [who] committed a crime should have the full and complete use of his reason, but as my Lord Hale emphatically expresses himself, a competent use of it; whether he had that use of it which was sufficient to have restrained those passions which produced the crime; and that if there be thought design, and faculty to distinguish the nature of actions, to discover the difference between moral good and evil.[35]

Mitford used the Ferrers case to induce the jury to consider the lucid intervals between bouts of occasional insanity. He charged the jury to decide whether Hadfield experienced a lucid interval when he tried to kill the king, and whether he 'had that capacity of mind which was capable of forming intention, whether he weighed the motives, proceeded deliberately, and knew the consequences of what he did.'[36]

Mitford and the countless judges and jurors who listened to the language of mental excuse in depositions and trials throughout the eighteenth century, faced a serious problem: how to assess the apparently legitimate states of insanity with which Hadfield was known to have suffered prior to his crime. Mitford could not ignore Hadfield's disfiguring physical and mental injuries and his discharge from the army, 'partly on account of the state of his mind.'[37] Looking at Hadfield's scarred face, it was easy to imagine the mental wounds he carried with him. But Mitford concluded that Hadfield had acted 'as other men would do upon similar occasions' and that 'he was capable, therefore, of assigning a reason for the act which he was then doing,' that 'he had a competent degree of reason to distinguish upon all these particulars, and he did distinguish.'[38] Although Mitford acknowledged that after the crime Hadfield 'was then in a kind of heat and agitation,' he maintained that Hadfield's interrogators testified 'how far he appeared to them to be in the possession of his understanding, and conscious of the act that he had done, and of the consequence of that act – that he knew that, by the law, his life was forfeited.'[39]

Mitford ended his opening remarks by admitting 'that a man ... perhaps may be at some times deranged, and ... never perhaps perfectly recover the sanity of his mind,' but he asserted that such a person 'may yet be guilty of crimes, and may be punished for those crimes.'[40] This statement rested on a comment regarding the self particularly relevant to this study:

> there is a natural impression upon the mind of man, of the distinction between good and evil, which never entirely loses hold of the mind whilst the mind has any capacity whatever to exert itself – nothing but total and absolute debility deprives the mind of any man of that.[41]

Mitford's reference to 'a natural impression upon the mind of man' echoed the Cambridge Platonist writers who posited the existence of an innate ability to distinguish between good and evil. While Mitford's comment assumed the universality of such an ability, he asserted that most criminals broke the law in full knowledge of the wrongful nature of their behavior. His remark paralleled those made by defendants and other witnesses both in pre-trial depositions and in trial transcripts; but defendants claimed that circumstance displaced a good self, while Mitford contested exactly this point and rejected the assumption that a mind that could distinguish good from evil would necessarily choose the righteous path.

Given the ample evidence proving that Hadfield had committed the crime, the crown's prosecution revolved around establishing Hadfield's deliberate criminal intent. Asked repeatedly if 'his countenance exhibited any marks of agitation at the time his majesty entered, immediately prior to the discharge of his pistol,' and if they observed 'any thing particular in his conduct or behavior,'[42] witnesses answered that they noticed nothing out of the ordinary. One man who sat next to Hadfield at the Drury Lane Theatre said that he regarded the accused as 'a pitiable object, from the severe wound he had upon his cheek, and the appearance of a ball extracted from his temple.'[43] Another, who sat behind Hadfield in the theater, reported that after he shot at the king, Hadfield stood on the bench 'seemingly very much agitated and confused.'[44]

The Duke of York testified that Hadfield had served as one of his orderlies. He described Hadfield's disposition during the interrogation as 'perfectly collected' and said that he spoke 'as connectedly as could possibly be.' Joseph Richardson, one of the men present at Hadfield's interrogation in the music room of the theater, told the court that the accused 'constantly denied that he had any intention to take away the king's life.' Asked whether he made the denial 'under the impression of lunacy, or of a collected man knowing what he was speaking of,' Richardson replied that he 'saw no one indication of lunacy about him whatever.' He said that Hadfield had told his examiners:

> gentlemen, do not give yourselves all this trouble; use me well, and I will tell you the whole truth. I am a man tired of life; my plan is not to take away my own life, I sought therefore to get rid of it by other means; I did not mean to take away the life of the king but I thought this attempt would answer my purpose well.[45]

Hadfield's co-workers, William Harman and Thomas Dicks, reported on Hadfield's demeanor before the crime. Dicks described Hadfield as 'more soldier than ever' on the day of the shooting, but he said that 'he seemed duller, not so cheerful in sprits.' Although 'he seemed lower in sprits,' Dicks denied that 'there was any thing the matter with his head' or that there had been anything 'disjointed in his conversation.'[46] Shortly after Dicks spoke, the prosecution completed its presentation of the evidence, and the defense counsel rose to speak.

Thomas Erskine began his opening remarks by extolling the virtues of King George III and the English legal system. He commended the sovereign's 'calm and forbearance.' He praised the rationality and restraint of a criminal process that 'covered [the offender] all over with the armour of the law' providing him a copy of the indictment, legal counsel, and the right to challenge jurors as well as a mandated 15-day 'quarantine' between the arraignment and trial 'lest the mind should be subject to the contagion of partial affections.'[47] Erskine turned immediately to the critical issues of the case. He qualified his general agreement with the attorney general by summarizing the problem in cases of mental excuse:

> the law, as it regards this most unfortunate infirmity of the human mind ... aims at the utmost degree of precision; but there are some subjects ... upon which it is extremely difficult to be precise. The general principle is clear, but the application is most difficult.[48]

Erskine maintained the rule of *mens rea* arguing that accountability rests on the 'reason of man,' and that 'the deprivation of reason acquits him of crime.' He pointed out that 'so fearfully and wonderfully are we made, so infinitely subtle is the spiritual part of our being, so difficult is it to trace with accuracy the effect of diseased intellect upon human action' that questions about the line that separated peculiarity from insanity, and accountability from exculpation, confounded even the best judges.[49]

Erskine then continued with a discussion of insanity and the civil law. He pointed out that because of the 'extreme difficulty of tracing with precision the secret motions of a mind deprived by disease of its soundness and strength' contracts are voided with anyone considered *non compos mentis*, no matter what the cause. In criminal cases, on the other hand, 'there must be a TOTAL *deprivation of memory and understanding.*' Erskine lingered over the interpretation of this phrase and concluded that 'no such madness ever existed in the world.'[50] He asserted that only idiocy rendered a person in 'a state of prostrated intellect, as not to know his name, nor his condition, nor his relation toward others,' while the majority of those who suffer from insanity

> not only had memory, in my sense of the expression – they have not only had the most perfect knowledge and recollection of all the relations they stood in toward others, and of the acts and circumstances of their lives, but have, in general, been remarkable for subtlety and acuteness.[51]

This description of insanity matches the nuanced narratives of mental excuse brought to court by defendants and witnesses throughout the eighteenth century.

Erskine argued that only a minority of insanity defenses featured a defendant whose 'mind is stormed in its citadel, and laid prostrate under the stroke of frenzy.' In these people 'all the ideas are overwhelmed – for reason is not merely disturbed, but *driven wholly from her seat.*' According to Erskine, '*such persons alone (except idiots) are wholly deprived of their UNDERSTANDINGS.*' In other cases of insanity 'reason is not driven from her seat, but distraction sits down upon it along with her, holds her, trembling, upon it, and frightens her from her propriety.'[52] This manifestation of mental disease featured delusions 'which so overpower the faculties, and usurp so firmly the place of realities, as not to be dislodged and shaken by the organs of perception and sense.' But Erskine maintained that both of these categories of mental excuse 'are not only extremely rare, but never can become the subjects of judicial difficulty. There can be but one judgment concerning them.'[53] These were the clear-cut cases in which the accused obviously suffered from mental illness during a crime for which he or she could not be held responsible. Erskine's characterization of these cases reveals his familiarity with English courts, the excuses made by defendants, and the decisions that jurors faced.

As easy as the first two categories might seem, cases in the third category 'frequently mock the wisdom of the wisest in judicial trials.' In these cases 'the delusions are not of that frightful character, but infinitely various, and often extremely circumscribed.' But as Erskine pointed out, 'imagination (within the bounds of the malady) still holds the most uncontrollable dominion over reality and fact.' Exhibiting at once a subtle understanding of mental states and a knowledge of the language of excuse that echoed in the eighteenth-century courtroom, Erskine continued:

> Such persons often reason with a subtlety which puts in the shade the ordinary conceptions of mankind: their conclusions are just, and frequently profound; but the premises from which they reason, when within the range of the malady, are uniformly false; – not false from any defect of knowledge or judgment; but, because a delusive image, the inseparable companion of real insanity, is thrust upon the subjugated understanding, incapable of resistance, because unconscious of attack.

Erskine's schema defined 'the true character of insanity' as 'delusion ... where there is no frenzy or raving madness.'[54]

Erskine's defense stood on his contention that Hadfield's crime 'was the immediate, unqualified offspring of the disease.' He argued that 'the relation between the disease and the act should be apparent' and that in order to qualify as legitimate, the delusion in question must 'proceed upon something which has no foundation or existence.'[55] He urged the jury to evaluate the evidence presented by the prosecution in light of his caveat that 'insane persons frequently appear in the utmost state of ability and composure, even in the highest paroxysms of insanity, except when frenzy is the characteristic of the disease.'[56]

The final portion of Erskine's opening statement confronted the relationship between responsibility and the ability to distinguish good from evil. He dismissed this guideline as 'too general in this mode of considering the subject.' Erskine reiterated the doctrine of *mens rea* and maintained that a conviction should follow 'if malicious mischief, and not insanity, had impelled him [Hadfield] to the act' while a finding that 'he came to the theatre ... under the dominion of the most melancholy insanity that ever degraded and overpowered the faculties of man' should precede an acquittal. Erskine restated his charge to the jury to decide

> whether the prisoner, when he did the act, was under the uncontrollable dominion of insanity, and was impelled to it by a morbid delusion; or whether it was the act of a man who, though occasionally mad, or even at the time not perfectly collected, was yet not actuated by the disease, but by the suggestion of a wicked and malignant disposition.[57]

Careful to distance himself from those cases discussed in the previous chapters of this study in which a range of emotional states were deployed in court to justify or excuse a variety of crimes, Erskine exclaimed the need for strict legal criteria for mental disease lest 'every departure from sober, rational conduct, would be an emancipation from criminal justice.'[58] He denied making 'any appeal addressed only to [the jury's] compassion,' and urged the jurors not 'to give the rein to compassionate fancy.'[59]

After this lengthy discussion of delusion, insanity, and legal responsibility, Erskine introduced his client as a 'gallant, loyal' soldier who suffered disfiguring wounds to the head in service to the king. These scars, according to Erskine, distinguished Hadfield's condition from 'insanity arising from the spiritual part of man as it may be affected by hereditary taint – by intemperance, or by violent passions.' Instead, this case resembled idiocy in its permanent effect. Hadfield's 'species of madness' manifested itself as 'violent agitation [that] fills the mind with the most inconceivable imaginations, wholly unfitting it for all dealing with human affairs according to the sober estimate and standard of reason.'[60] Erskine explained that Hadfield's illness caused him to believe he had 'constant intercourse with the Almighty Author of all things.' Hadfield believed that the world was coming to an end and that 'he was to sacrifice himself for its salvation.' Not wishing to commit the crime of suicide, he went to the theater and shot at the king hoping that 'by the appearance of crime his life might be taken away from him by others.'[61]

Erskine declared that 'this bewildered, extravagant species of madness' took hold of Hadfield immediately after he received his wounds and persisted through his discharge, to the fateful day that he shot at the king, and to the present. To prove the immovability of the illness, Erskine described Hadfield's attempt to kill his infant son on Tuesday, May 13, two days before he shot at the king. Believing that he acted 'in obedience to the superior commands of heaven,' Hadfield 'came to the bed of the mother, who had this infant in her arms, and endeavoured to dash out its brains against the wall.' Erskine argued that had he succeeded in killing his son, Hadfield certainly would have been found not guilty of murder. This supposition of Erskine's resonates exactly with the findings discussed in chapter 4 that showed the consistent acquittal of married parents who committed infanticide. Erskine used this incident to illustrate his point that the deprivation of memory was a fiction maintaining that 'the prisoner knew perfectly that he was the husband of the woman, and the father of the child; – the tears of affection ran down his face at the very moment that he was about to accomplish its destruction.' Erskine explained that at the moment he tried to kill his son Hadfield could have had a rational conversation about 'every circumstance of his past life and every thing connected with his present condition, *except only the quality of the act he was meditating.*' Erskine attributed Hadfield's assault on his son to 'the over-ruling dominion of a morbid imagination.' After this lengthy account, Erskine asked the jurors to consider the shooting of the king as analogous to an incident of infanticide committed by a married father.[62]

Erskine brought his lengthy opening remarks to a close by maintaining his total support of English law and the existing guidelines for an insanity defense. He upheld the convictions of Arnold and Ferrers: while he acknowledged that they had 'violent passions' and 'wild and turbulent manners,' he contended that no 'morbid delusion overshadowed [their] understanding.'[63] For Erskine, a legitimate insanity defense rested on the existence of delusions that had no basis in 'actual circumstances and real facts.' He urged the jurors to evaluate the case based on this definition and expressed confidence that 'your sound understandings will easily enable you to distinguish *infirmities* which are *misfortunes* from *motives* which are *crimes.*'[64] At the same time he called on them to judge Hadfield 'rigidly by the evidence and the law.' Claiming that he 'made no appeal to your passions – you have no right to exercise them.'

he advised jurors to put compassion and feeling aside while they decided the case.[65]

His opening remarks complete, Erskine and his co-counsel, Serjeant Best, began a presentation of the evidence: witnesses who described Hadfield's conscientious service as a soldier, his loyalty to the crown, his injuries, and his subsequent mental condition. Those who served with him told the court that during the hospital stay when he was recovering from the wounds he suffered in the Battle of Lincelles, Hadfield acted like 'a person insane,' that he was 'quite deranged,' and that he looked 'like a man that was out of his mind.'[66] A physician, Dr. Alexander Creighton (1763–1856), attributed Hadfield's condition to 'injuries done to the brain' and corroborated the contention that although the illness began when Hadfield was wounded in 1793, it did not manifest itself constantly, that 'when any question concerning a common matter is made to him, he answers very correctly; but when any question is put to him which relates to the subject of his lunacy, he answers irrationally.' Creighton explained that 'it requires that the thoughts which have relation to his madness should be awakened in his mind, in order to make him act unreasonably.'[67] Members of Hadfield's family poignantly described their constant struggle to care for him as he descended into madness each spring and summer since his discharge from the army and his return home in 1796. Members of the household told the court about their attempts to contain Hadfield's millenarian prophesies, blasphemous talk, threats of violence, frenzied fits, and his assault on his son a few days before the attempt on the king's life. The family members reported that Hadfield had apparently visited with one Bannister Truelock in his agitated state.

After 12 witnesses had testified, Lord Kenyon (1732–1802), Chief Justice of the King's Bench, broke in to ask if Erskine had almost completed presenting his evidence. When Erskine responded that he had 20 more witnesses to examine, Kenyon asked Mitford and the prosecuting team if they could call any witnesses to contradict the evidence offered by the defense. Kenyon observed that Erskine's witnesses 'bring home conviction to one's mind, that at the time he committed this offence, and a most horrid one it is, he was in a very deranged state.' Kenyon implied that an acquittal was likely when he said, 'I do not know that one can run the case very nicely; if you do run it very nicely, to be sure it is an acquittal.'[68] Kenyon's comments, and his choice of the word *nicely*, suggest that he saw acquittal as the appropriate resolution of the case despite the fact that Hadfield's condition did not match the legal definition for exculpatory insanity. Kenyon described Hadfield as 'a most dangerous member of society,' and he acknowledged to the attorney general that 'it is impossible that this man with safety to society can be suffered, supposing his misfortune is such, to be let loose upon the public.' Mitford said only that he had no knowledge of Hadfield's illness since his discharge from the army.

Kenyon ended the trial by proposing that 'the prisoner, for his own sake, and for the sake of society at large, must not be discharged.' In order to preserve the 'safety of society,' Kenyon suggested that Hadfield 'should be properly disposed of, all mercy and humanity being shown to this most unfortunate creature.' Kenyon then asked the jury whether Hadfield 'was not so under the guidance of reason, as to be answerable for this act.' Erskine registered his agreement that 'the safety of the community requires that this unfortunate man should be taken care of.' William Garrow (1760–1840) then suggested that in order to provide some resolution to the case, the jury ought to render a verdict, 'that they acquit the prisoner of this charge, he appearing to them to have been under the influence of insanity at the time the act was committed.'[69] The jury obliged immediately. Without leaving the room or conferring for long, they found Hadfield 'not guilty; he being under the influence of insanity at the time the act was committed.'[70] With this verdict the four-hour trial came to a close.

Four days later, on June 20, 1800, John Mitford introduced a bill in the House of Commons to address the concerns raised by Hadfield's acquittal. At the second reading of the bill on July 1, it was separated into two bills that both passed on July 28, 1800. The first, an 'Act for regulating Trials for High Treason and Misprision of High Treason' (39&40 Geo. 3, c. 93), made those accused of treason subject to the same treatment as defendants charged with any ordinary felony. This meant that these cases were no longer tried at King's Bench and that the accused no longer had the right to defense counsel. The second bill passed that day, the 'Act for the Safe Custody of Insane Persons Charged with Offences' (39&40 Geo. 3, c. 94), mandated the incarceration of all defendants found not guilty by reason of insanity. As discussed in chapter 2, some offenders found insane and acquitted had been incarcerated in the past, but the new statute mandated and regularized the practice and prohibited remanding criminal lunatics to the custody of their families. The new law also allowed for the preventive detention of suspected offenders who suffered from mental illness.

The Criminal Lunatics Act had four sections. The first created the special verdict, not guilty but insane, and applied it *ex post facto* to James Hadfield. The second section called for the detention without bail of persons indicted for criminal offenses who were found to be insane at their arraignment. This section also mandated the detention of suspects who appeared insane when they were 'brought before any court to be discharged for want of prosecution,' and the third section made it difficult to bail these suspects. The fourth section empowered members of the Privy Council to apprehend anyone who seemed mentally ill who tried to enter one of the king's palaces or places of residence.[71]

The attorney general explained the need for the Criminal Lunatics Act

> because it has been found that persons who have done the most shocking acts, and who have been acquitted on the ground of being deranged in their intellects, having been allowed to go at large, have afterwards committed similar acts again.[72]

Mitford's opposition to Catholic Emancipation, the repeal of the Test and Corporation Acts, and the Slave Trade Abolition bill allows us to put his sponsorship of the Criminal Lunatics Act in a different context. This legislation was not just the response of an attorney general who had lost a case. Instead it was a rejoinder to Erskine and his successful argument in favor of Hadfield's acquittal. This legislation reads like a rebuttal to the *Man of Feeling*, and fits into a political agenda that attacked the expansion of the rights of the disenfranchised seeking to circumscribe the rights of non-elites, be they Irish, dissenters, slaves, or lunatics.

In support of the bill, William Windham (1750–1810), the secretary of war, contended that 'madmen ... were influenced by the fear of punishment more than by any other consideration, and to a degree much beyond the impression it made on other men.'[73] This statement clearly contradicted all English legal precedent and practice. John Nicholls (1745–1826) protested that 'never did the law of England sanction the punishing [of] a madman' because 'the will was necessary to constitute a crime.' Nicholls explained his objection to the bill on the grounds that 'the punishment of a madman could not operate as a prevention.'[74] The solicitor general, Sir William Grant (1752–1832), had the final word. He 'questioned whether the plea of madness, with regard to any crime, could be admitted' and added that 'it was doubtful whether there were many persons so mad as not to be capable of being influenced by such a fear.'[75] The debate ended on this note, and both bills passed.

Hadfield remained in custody at Newgate Gaol until October 10, 1800 when he was transferred to Bethlem Hospital. He escaped in 1804 but was captured shortly afterward and was returned to Newgate. He remained there a further 12 years until, in 1816, Bethlem opened a new wing for criminal lunatics. Hadfield lived the rest of his life there until his death from tuberculosis in 1841.[76]

Other contemporary insanity trials

Scholars have credited Thomas Erskine's oratory genius with Hadfield's acquittal. Certainly his opening remarks and his redefinition of delusion made brilliant use of subtle legal reasoning to nuance the category of exculpatory insanity. Erskine's defense, however, reflected the cultural tensions that riddled eighteenth-century criminal legal practice. The inspiration for his logic came, by his own admission, from 'all the cases which have filled Westminster Hall with the most complicated considerations.'[77] As evidenced above, Erskine was familiar with the language of mental excuse and its persistent use by defendants and other participants in the legal process.

Erskine went on to explain that those

> lunatics and other insane persons who have been the subjects of [those cases], have not only had memory, *in my sense of the expression* – they have not only had the most perfect knowledge and recollection of all the relations that stood in toward others, and of the acts and circumstances of their lives, but have, in general, been remarkable for subtlety and acuteness.[78]

Erskine referred to the cases of explicit insanity that came before the courts as well as those that echoed with the language of mental excuse. The issue was unresolved because

> defects in their reasonings have seldom been traceable – the disease consisting in the delusive sources of thought. All their deductions within the scope of the malady, being founded upon the *immoveable* assumption of matters as *realities*, either without any foundation whatsoever, or so distorted and disfigured by fancy, as to be almost nearly the same thing as their creation.[79]

Erskine's claim that the total deprivation of memory and understanding was a legal fiction resonated with Lord Kenyon and the other lawyers who participated in Hadfield's prosecution or his defense. Many of these same lawyers, most prominently William Garrow, had participated in the same debate, with the same parameters, employing the same vocabulary at other trials that featured an insanity defense.

The Hadfield case parallels findings among the cases of insanity that came before the Old Bailey between 1780 and 1800. Questions about the prisoner's state of mind, the manifestations of his/her insanity, the exact timing of these incidents, and their authenticity shaped these cases. Judges repeatedly directed jurors 'to judge whether at the moment of committing that fact he was not a moral agent, capable of discerning between good and evil, and of knowing the consequences of what he did.'[80] Despite the predictability of many of the arguments made in these cases, the outcomes of these trials were far from consistent, and it is almost impossible to discern why some offenders were convicted while others were acquitted.

The discussion of the ability to distinguish good from evil raised another theme that the Hadfield case shared with more typical Old Bailey trials that featured an insanity defense: the question of the self, specifically the good self. In his prosecution of Hadfield, John Mitford asserted that 'there is a natural impression upon the mind of man, of the distinction between good and evil.' Mitford claimed that this inherent impression 'never entirely loses hold of the mind whilst the mind has any capacity whatever to exert itself – nothing but total and absolute debility deprives the mind of any man of that.'[81] Mitford's guidelines suggested that any emotional distress or mental agitation, confusion, derangement, or turmoil short of 'total and absolute debility' left intact the ability to tell good from evil and proved the offender's evil intent.

But what about cases of temporary insanity, or what the judge in John Simpson's case from April 1786 called 'an insanity, temporary in its nature, which arose in consequence of a particular circumstance taking effect only during a particular period'?[82] In the Old Bailey cases, lawyers and judges often interrogated the character of the accused to discern whether a good self existed 'independent of madness.'[83] The witness who described Richard Crutcher in September 1797 as 'deranged in his mind' also told the court that he was 'perfectly honest and of perfect integrity.'[84] In April 1800 Bryan Broughton described Henry Piers as 'a very eccentric and inconsistent character, a man that seemed to be at war with his own interest in general,' but Boughton continued that 'when in possession of a sound mind, [Piers was] incapable of doing an action morally wrong.'[85]

How did the court interpret this evidence? In Francis Parr's January 1787 trial witnesses described the accused as 'a very honest upright man,' 'a very just and very worthy man,' and 'disordered in his mind.' In his closing remarks the judge who presided summarized the evidence against Parr, and he instructed the jurors that while 'it has been established by a number of very respectable witnesses, that this unfortunate man has been a man of excellent character,' they should disregard this evidence 'if the facts [of the crime] are clear.' On the other hand, the judge told the jury that if they doubted the credibility of the evidence against Parr, 'the prisoner certainly ought to have the benefit of that character in a strong degree.'[86] With his somewhat confusing directions the judge tried to separate this evidence about character from the facts of the case.

The judge then launched into a lengthy speech about the insanity defense in which he attempted to disassociate mental state from the evidence about character. He proposed that 'circumstances are easily produced by perturbation of guilt, more especially in people who have led good lives, and who cannot deviate far without great perturbation of mind.'[87] The judge implied that a person of good character was more susceptible to the insanity caused by guilt. His instructions support the findings in chapters 3, 4, and 5 in which poor men and most women were assumed to have less control of their feelings and emotions and more susceptibility to crime. He dissuaded jurors from trying to explain a crime committed by a generally righteous person with insanity and urged them instead to disconnect character and reputation from state of mind. This judge's attempt to achieve such a separation contradicted the instincts of most judges and jurors in the eighteenth century charged with the task of assessing a defendant's *mens rea*. The persistent questions about character in discussions of an offender's mental state suggest that most judges and juries took seriously the task of finding the true self. They sought to resolve cases that mentioned insanity by determining the orientation of the suspect's moral compass.

Conclusion

Is it surprising that Erskine secured an acquittal even though Hadfield's delusion did not reveal itself in the wild, raving behavior typically associated with defendants who submitted an insanity defense? As I have shown, throughout the eighteenth century defendants and witnesses on their behalf had often described mental incapacity that did not manifest itself as total depravity of memory or understanding as though it should be exculpatory. Of course, the Old Bailey trials were not state trials and the political context of Hadfield's act made his trial much more serious. Nevertheless, even the threat of regicide in the midst of Britain's war with France did not convince the jury to convict James Hadfield. Why?

Certainly Erskine's skill deserved part of the credit for the success of his argument, as did Hadfield's head wounds, dramatic, physical markers of his mental condition. But the case and the legislation that followed are significant because together they represent an attempt by England's legal and legislative bodies to resolve issues that had been debated, discussed, and settled inconsistently throughout the eighteenth century.[88] Thomas Erskine did not present his defense of James Hadfield as a radical change in the definition of criminal responsibility, but this was in fact his argument. Erskine successfully redefined the issue of criminal responsibility and delusion by sidestepping the right–wrong test as the measure of 'perfect' or 'total' insanity. This new standard of proof played on the unresolved problem of mental states that plagued the English legal system in the century prior to Hadfield's trial.[89]

The psychological pleas articulated in court during the eighteenth century complicated the relationship between states of mind and legal responsibility. Hale foreshadowed this problem when he warned judges and juries of the complexities of pleas that drew on insanity. The challenge was to strike a balance 'lest on the one side there be a kind of inhumanity toward the defects of human nature, or on the other side too great an indulgence given to great crimes.'[90] Judges at insanity trials held at the Old Bailey echoed Hale's warning in their charges to juries 'for it would be highly dangerous to the public, if every suspicion of a disordered mind; if every circumstance that shewed not a regular, an orderly conduct, should be admitted in extenuation of such crimes.'[91] Furthermore, 'the bare enormity of the offence' could not serve as 'a foundation to excuse the man who could be wicked enough to commit it' lest the legal system dismiss every violent or inexplicable crime as the effects of a 'defect of will' for which the offender bore no responsibility.[92]

Achieving the balance between humanity and accountability challenged the legal system to draw a line invisible to the mortal eye. In order to preserve the 'safety of society' Kenyon suggested that Hadfield 'should be properly disposed of, all mercy and humanity being shown to this most unfortunate creature.'[93]

Erskine's brilliance lay in his ability to show that the completely displaced self, totally deprived of memory and understanding as proposed by the prosecution, was as much of a fiction as the permanently coherent self demanded by the legal system. The trial established a consensus among legal authorities that neither existed and this concurrence led to the Criminal Lunatics Act. The verdict in Hadfield's trial and the legislation that followed his acquittal created a new legal and cultural category of person. The new category assumed a separation between the true self and the displaced self and reflected a legal acknowledgement of the split. While the good self earned an acquittal, the displaced self deserved punishment.

At a cultural level, this new consensus signaled the replacement of what Karen Halttunen has called the 'depravity narrative' with the 'disease narrative.'[94] Eighteenth-century moral philosophers challenged earlier conceptions of the sinful self and the constant struggle against universal human depravity by proposing alternative ways of thinking about the acquisition of morality. Whether one agreed with Locke about the *tabula rasa* or sided with Shaftesbury's innate moral sense, the Enlightenment emphasized the human potential for goodness. The explanation for crime that pointed to a diseased self was much more compelling than a depravity model because it presented crime as deviance from an assumed, good norm rather than a corroboration of an inherent, essential evil. With Hadfield's acquittal and confinement, the state achieved two seemingly contradictory outcomes: the jury's acquittal on the basis of insanity acknowledged the displaced self while Hadfield's incarceration consolidated the legal subject whose punishment was assured regardless of the defendant's mental state.

Why end a study of short trials with a lengthy one? Why conclude a book about unknown defendants with a famous one? The Hadfield case is qualitatively different from the other cases that have been the focus of this discussion, yet the arguments articulated in it rehearsed the same questions that surrounded every case that mobilized the language of excuse throughout the eighteenth century. The fact that Hadfield had tried to kill George III catapulted his act and the debate surrounding the insanity defense into the headlines and into statutory law.

What were the consequences of Hadfield's trial? Some scholars have argued that they were few: Hadfield's acquittal did not change the rules for insanity defenses; judges, jurors, and lawyers did not adopt Erskine's theory about delusions as the test for excusable insanity; and the number of acquittals for insanity neither rose nor fell as a result. Other historians argue that Hadfield's acquittal and subsequent incarceration had profound effects on the English legal system and English politics because the Criminal Lunatics Act enabled the state to confine those it considered politically threatening without a hearing or a trial.[95]

Neither of these interpretations of Hadfield fully discloses the importance of the trial as a cultural event. The trial itself staged eighteenth-century anxieties and preoccupations with sensibility, reason, and emotion and struggled to resolve legal inconsistencies. Following Hadfield's acquittal, the stakes for talking about insanity rose, especially for suspects who faced possible incarceration without trial based on the suspicion of mental instability. The new categories that emerged from Hadfield's case reflected the instability of the doctrine of *mens rea* at the end of the eighteenth century. Hadfield's case represented a response to this instability: the creation of the subject constituted by legal, medical, and scientific institutions that essentialized the self and limited its freedom.

7

From Self to Subject

To explore crime, responsibility, and the self in the eighteenth century, this study has drawn upon the methods and concerns of legal, cultural, and social history. These three approaches can, I argue, complement one another to provide a broader and more nuanced view of legal responsibility and individual and national identity. Using the courtroom to study the history of the self and subject has enabled me to reconstruct common individual's unique perceptions of themselves – perceptions often absent from histories of the self that portray it only in elite or middling terms. An engagement with the culture of sensibility reveals the forces that shaped the language of mental excuse and its reception by legal authorities. The insights about self and subjectivity generated by this study contribute to our understanding of the relationship between the individual and the state and look toward the impact of these developments on the formation of Britain as a nation.

Joining legal, cultural, and social history opens a different perspective on crime and the law in eighteenth-century England. A thorough understanding of legal process is essential to a study of crime and deviance. Only by studying crime within its immediate legal context can one fully appreciate the stakes of the arguments made in court and the basis for the evidence left to us. But rather than treating the law as a closed system outside of society or culture, I place the excuses made by participants in the legal process in the context of the culture that produced them and the relations of power that constrained them. By combining these approaches rather than blending them, one can preserve the integrity of each methodology even while transgressing its boundaries.

In the eighteenth century the English criminal trial developed from the 'accused speaks' trial to the 'lawyerized,' adversarial trial that emerged by the nineteenth century. As Langbein has shown, the structure and practice of the earlier trial compelled the accused to 'serve as an informational resource' about the crime and the circumstances surrounding it.[1] Given the prominent place reserved for the voice of the accused, it should not surprise us that when forced to speak, defendants took the initiative to tell their story of their crime, developing their own vocabulary with which to describe their responsibility in relation to their state of mind.

In their attempts to envision this process, historians of crime sometimes portray the intimidating and unfamiliar courtroom setting as overwhelming and frightening to the common people processed by the legal system.[2] I would urge us to think about the 'accused speaks' trial as a *potentially* empowering experience, an opportunity for creativity and agency. Like gallows speeches, the accused could use his or her knowledge of the law to 'spin' the events and evoke as much sympathy as possible.[3] The sophistication of the excuses described in this study, as well as their uncontainable, unpredictable effects on the legal process and on the definitions of crime and culpability, may have contributed to the decisions of judges to hand over the management of the trial to lawyers and in so doing to silence the accused.

The language of mental excuse was a consistent part of the criminal trial in the eighteenth century. Its amplification within the context of discussions of the self and of sensibility caused great anxiety to those who participated in the legal process and those who observed them. The state trials of Edward Arnold in 1724, James Bradshaw in 1746, Lawrence Shirley, Lord Ferrers in 1760, and James Hadfield in 1800, brought recurring attention to these issues at intervals throughout the eighteenth century. These trials received much attention in the press and raised difficult questions about the relationship between crime, responsibility, mental states, and accountability, transmitting the discomforts of their unresolved nature to the legal world and the public at large.

Beyond the exceptional instances of 'obvious' insanity pleas, the language of mental excuse that permeated English courtrooms in the eighteenth century created a rich, complex, nuanced discourse about responsibility. My study of this discourse has revealed contemporary preoccupations with definitions of masculinity, femininity, and status that had profound implications for the emerging categories of class, criminal, and citizen. Within the context of Enlightenment discussions of the self and the era of sensibility, these psychological pleas, couched in a vocabulary of mental states, won a limited acceptance from judges and jurors who recognized that one's mental state might prompt unintended crime.

In eighteenth-century England some defendants and other witnesses used the language of mental states to excuse their behavior, but their vocabulary and its implications destabilized the criminal process. The willingness of judges and jurors to agree that 'crimes are acts of the mind' and to accept that these mental excuses threatened the definition of *mens rea*, the very foundation of legal process.[4] Participants in England's legal system equated the self with morality and moral understanding. As Charles Taylor noted in the introduction to his study of the history of the western self: 'selfhood and the good, or in another way selfhood and morality, turn out to be inextricably intertwined themes.'[5] Their testimony inverted the identification of the self with moral understanding: for these defendants the very fact that they had done something immoral proved that they were not themselves. The legal system could not, however, recognize this inversion without jeopardizing its integrity because the vocabulary of the mind and the displaced self could make holding anyone responsible for crime almost impossible. *Tout comprendre, c'est tout pardonner.*

While eighteenth-century concerns with emotion and sensibility ushered in the eventual acceptance of the defense of insanity, the Hadfield decision in 1800 and the M'Naughten Rules that followed in 1843 circumscribed the language that could be used to describe mental states and mandated incarceration for those found not guilty by reason of insanity. In the nineteenth century medicalized and criminalized descriptions of patients replaced the permeable language of the eighteenth century that had allowed defendants and others who spoke on their behalf to broaden the category of exculpatory mental states and define them as temporary and unrelated to the defendant's true self and sensibility. While mental excuses continued to function in the legal discourse of the nineteenth century, the circle of persons empowered to deploy them in court was restricted. Defendants and their witnesses were barred from introducing these terms, defining them, or arguing for them. In the nineteenth century the arbitration of the language of excuse and its promotion to diagnosis or special verdict became the purview of physicians and lawyers alone.[6]

It has been argued that by the mid-nineteenth century medical and scientific discourses and institutions essentialized the self by defining insanity, homosexuality, and criminality as pathologies that encompassed one's entire identity.[7] How did this happen and why? This study suggests that the origins of the process were well underway by the middle of the eighteenth century. Throughout this book the term self has referred to one's sense of a cohesive, continuing, singular identity. Far from a unified, immutable essence, the eighteenth-century self, as described by defendants in court, was contingent, highly unstable, and often displaced by a wide range of psychological states. Although this self was socially and culturally constructed and reconstructed by experience and circumstance, it was that construction that became a means of agency as participants in the trial presented themselves in ways they believed might win the jury's sympathy and result in an acquittal or at least a mitigated sentence.

The passage of the Criminal Lunatics Act in 1800 attempted to contain the self as a legal category by allowing the consideration of mental states in an assessment of guilt and circumscribing their exculpatory effect by mandating incarceration for those found not guilty by reason of insanity. This development signaled the constitution of the legal subject with limited agency. I do not wish to argue that the subject irrevocably replaced the self by the end of the eighteenth century or that the transition from self to legal subject was an irreversible step toward the consolidation of the power of the state or its legal institutions. By gesturing toward the outlines of a legal subject, the legal institutions involved wished to strengthen their hold on a permeable self too susceptible to changing passions and emotions. Although the courts would continue to trade in stories about the self, the self was increasingly subordinated to the subject. While the history of the insanity plea in the nineteenth century shows that Hadfield's case by no means resolved the relationship between mental states and criminal responsibility, it did signal a permanent change in the way that the language of mental excuse could be presented in legal proceedings.[8]

The resolution reached in Hadfield's trial acknowledged the displaced self and attempted to create a legal subject who could be confined regardless of the state of his or her self at the time of the crime. Questions of character, social background, and state of mind continued to assert their influence on assessments of responsibility and accountability in the nineteenth century as they still do today.[9] Nevertheless, the growth of wide-scale incarceration in the late eighteenth and nineteenth centuries meant that most convicted felons faced confinement and were subject to attempts to rehabilitate the self. The creation of the subject allowed for consideration of the emotional and psychological constraints on the offender's capacity to control his or her behavior without negating legal assumptions about free will and the demands for accountability. In other words, James Hadfield was found not guilty, but he spent the last 41 years of his life confined by the state.

What effect did these legal developments have on culture and politics outside the courtroom? The new economy of sensibility and responsibility helped to forge an alliance between middle-class juries and well-born judges that would shape British politics in the modern age. The agreement between judges and jurors to admit mental states as part of the assessment of guilt and accountability contained implicit assumptions about the inability of certain defendants, specifically poor working men, vagrants, and women, to manage their life experiences, to contain their emotions, and to control their behavior. The implications of this assumption about the susceptibility of these groups to a more volatile and uncontrolled psychology helped to solidify a consensus shared by middling men and aristocrats that limited the agency of women and poor men as criminals actors and as citizens.

With the passage of the Criminal Lunatics Act, the explanation of mental displacement no longer worked to excuse criminal behavior. Instead it necessitated preventive detention. Although they might avoid the death penalty, convicted felons who claimed to have committed a crime because of a displaced self, suspects who seemed to suffer from mental illness, and even those tried and acquitted on the grounds of insanity were to face confinement in order to rehabilitate them, protect the rest of society from future danger, and defend the legal system from charges of impotence. Those convicted of lesser crimes who did not qualify for transportation would face incarceration and the discipline of the prison, including solitary confinement, in hopes that punishment and religious instruction would bring these 'malefactors ... to a right sense of their condition' and inculcate 'a due sense of the offences they have been guilty of.'[10] The combination of an insanity plea and enforced incarceration allayed long-held fears about the dangerousness associated with lunacy and the apprehensions about counterfeit while accommodating new ideas about the susceptibility of working men and women to the destabilized self.

The assumption that poor men and women were more prone to mental instability and less able to control themselves reduced their agency as criminals and had profound implications in the political realm. The political crises of the long eighteenth century – from the Glorious Revolution, continuing through the debate set off by John Wilkes and the war in the North American colonies, to the French Revolution – began the process of re-imagining the state and its subjects. This process consolidated the British state in the nineteenth century and lasted through the Fourth Reform Bill of 1885 and the creation of the welfare state after the Second World War. Equality before the law was an integral part of the widespread discussions of Britishness and representation in the eighteenth century that defined the qualifications of active citizenship. Central to this discussion was a definition of responsibility that actively excluded women and poor men. The property qualification that always accompanied the franchise was often justified as a badge of the respectable nature of its owner and that owner's stake in his society. Given the widespread preoccupation with emotions and mental states, respectability and property became evidence of an emotional and psychological control and controlled sensibility that qualified one as responsible. The alliance between middling jurors and aristocratic and middling judges effectively circumscribed criminal and political working class and female agency by solidifying the link between citizenship, responsibility, and emotional control. This definition of citizenship had profound implications for the British Empire and its colonial subjects as well.[11]

Class and gender emerge as the hinges of these legal, political, and cultural developments. The British defined their mission to civilize around their cultural superiority, priding themselves on a social order that made a sharp distinction between masculinity and femininity. The threat posed to middle-class masculinity by the culture of sensibility and its encouragement of men to import what were represented as 'female' qualities into formerly masculine realms caused a backlash. This reaction against the cult of feeling attempted to reinscribe middle-class British masculinity with traditional male traits and to distance it from emotion, spontaneity, empathy, and compassion so integral to the eighteenth-century 'man of feeling.'

Like the groundbreaking work published 30 years ago in *Albion's Fatal Tree*, this study demonstrates the centrality of the criminal law to the political narrative. The alliance between the middle class and the aristocracy in Britain is usually depicted emerging in 1832 with the Great Reform Bill. Although that fact is certainly true, one history of that alliance goes back to the dynamic between judges, jurors, and defendants in the eighteenth-century criminal courtroom. The affinity that middle-class jurors found with aristocratic judges defined them as allies who heard the pleas of poor working men and women with a combination of sympathy and distance. An analysis of legal history within the context of social and cultural history can reveal the subtle relationships among emotion, responsibility, gender, class, and citizenship in the eighteenth century.

Notes

1 Crime, Culture, and the Self

1. *Post and Gazetteer*, May 16, 1800, p. 2.
2. The Treason Act of 1696 (7–8 Will. III c. 3) provided counsel to those accused of treason.
3. T.B. Howell, ed., *A Complete Collection of State Trials and Proceedings for High Treason and Other Crimes and Misdemeanors*, 34 vols. (London, 1820), 27: 1356.
4. Nigel Walker, *Crime and Insanity in England*, 2 vols. Vol. 1: *The Historical Perspective* (Edinburgh, 1967), pp. 68–72.
5. My definition of language is influenced by J.G.A. Pocock's definition and interpretation set out in the Introduction to *Virtue, Commerce, and History: Essays on Political Thought and History, Chiefly in the Eighteenth Century* (Cambridge, 1985), especially pp. 1–28.
6. Pocock, *Virtue, Commerce, and History*, p. 7.
7. Miranda Chaytor, 'Husband(ry): Narratives of Rape in the Seventeenth Century,' *Gender and History* 7 (1995): 378–9. Chaytor's article provides a thorough analysis of the structure of depositions and their interpretation.
8. J.H. Baker, 'Criminal Courts and Procedure at Common Law, 1550–1800,' in *Crime in England, 1550–1800*, ed. J.S. Cockburn (Princeton, 1977), pp. 15–48; J.S. Cockburn, *A History of English Assizes from 1558 to 1714* (Cambridge, 1972); idem, 'Early Modern Assize Records as Historical Evidence,' *The Journal of the Society of Archivists* 5 (1975): 215–31.
9. The scholarship on representation is quite extensive. For discussions of early modern England, see Frances Dolan, *Dangerous Familiars: Representations of Crime in England, 1500–1700* (Ithaca, 1994); Marion Gibson, *Reading Witchcraft: Stories of Early English Witches* (New York, 1999); Malcolm Gaskill, *Crime and Mentalities in Early Modern England* (Cambridge, 2000); and Joy Wiltenburg, *Disorderly Women and Female Power in the Street Literature of Early Modern England and Germany* (Charlottesville, VA, 1992). For a more general discussion, see Catherine Gallagher and Thomas Laqueur, eds., *The Making of the Modern Body: Sexuality and Society in the Nineteenth Century* (Berkeley, CA, 1987); Ludmilla Jordanova, *Sexual Visions: Images of Gender in Science and Medicine between the Eighteenth and the Twentieth Centuries* (Madison, WI, 1989); and Sara Maza, 'Stories in History: Cultural Narratives in Recent Works in European History,' *American Historical Review* 101 (1996): 1493–1515.
10. The work on sensibility is tremendously rich and provocative. Some of the most helpful insights for this study emerged from Nancy Armstrong, *Desire and Domestic Fiction: A Political History of the Novel* (Oxford, 1987); G.J. Barker-Benfield, *The Culture of Sensibility: Sex and Society in Eighteenth-Century Britain* (Chicago, 1992); Barbara Benedict, *Framing Feeling: Sentiment and Style in English Prose Fiction, 1745–1800* (New York, 1994); R.F. Brissenden, *Virtue in Distress: Studies in the Novel of Sentiment from Richardson to Sade* (New York, 1974); Alan T. McKenzie, *Certain, Lively Episodes: The Articulation of Passion in*

Eighteenth-Century Prose (Athens, GA, 1990); John Mullan, *Sentiment and Sociability: The Language of Feeling in the Eighteenth Century* (Oxford, 1988); Adela Pinch, *Strange Fits of Passion: Epistemologies of Emotion, Hume to Austen* (Palo Alto, CA, 1996); Janet Todd, *Sensibility: An Introduction* (London, 1986); Ann Jessie Van Sant, *Eighteenth-Century Sensibility and the Novel: the Senses in Social Context* (Cambridge, 1993); Anne C. Vila, *Enlightenment and Pathology: Sensibility in the Literature and Medicine of Eighteenth-Century France* (Baltimore, 1998).

11. According to Charles Taylor 'selfhood and the good, or in another way selfhood and morality, turn out to be inextricably intertwined themes.' *Sources of the Self: The Making of the Modern Identity* (Cambridge, MA, 1989), p. 3. Taylor traces the association of responsibility and the self in western culture to Plato. Studies of the early modern self since Taylor include Leo Damrosch, *Sorrows of the Quaker Jesus: James Naylor and the Puritan Crackdown on the Free Spirit* (Cambridge, MA, 1996); Roy Porter, ed., *Rewriting the Self: Histories from the Renaissance to the Present* (London, 1997); and Dror Wahrman, 'The English Problem with Identity in the American Revolution,' *American Historical Review* 106 (2001): 1236–62; idem, 'On Queen Bees and Being Queens: A Late-Eighteenth-Century "Cultural Revolution"?' in *The Age of Cultural Revolutions: Britain and France, 1750–1820* (Berkeley, 2002), pp. 251–80; and idem, *The Invention of the Modern Self* (New Haven, 2004).

12. Michael MacDonald, *Mystical Bedlam: Madness, Anxiety, and Healing in Seventeenth-Century England* (Cambridge, 1981), chapter 4. Carol Neely, 'Recent Work in Renaissance Studies: Did Madness Have a Renaissance?' *Renaissance Quarterly* 44 (1991): 776–91.

13. Martin Weiner's study of the nineteenth century, *Reconstructing the Criminal: Culture, Law, and Policy in England, 1830–1914* (Cambridge, 1990), examines the Victorian preoccupation with the relationship between criminality and self-regulation or mastery of the self.

14. Michael Grossberg, *A Judgment for Solomon: The d'Hauteville Case and Legal Experience in Antebellum America* (Cambridge, 1996), p. xii.

15. The dichotomy between popular and elite culture is most starkly portrayed in surveys of the period, for example in Douglas Hay and Nicholas Rogers, *Eighteenth-Century English Society: Shuttles and Swords* (Oxford, 1997); Roy Porter, *English Society in the Eighteenth Century* (London, 1982); Lawrence Stone, 'Social Mobility in England, 1500–1700,' *Past and Present* 33 (1966): 16–55; E.P. Thompson, 'Patrician Society, Plebian Culture,' *Journal of Social History* 7 (1974): 382–405; idem, 'Eighteenth-Century English Society: Class Struggle Without Class,' *Social History* 10 (1978): 133–65; Keith Wrightson, *English Society, 1580–1680* (New Brunswick, 1982), chapter 1; idem, 'The Social Order of Early Modern England: Three Approaches,' in *The World We Have Gained: Histories of Population and Social Structure* ed. Lloyd Bonfield, Richard Smith, and Keith Wrightson (New York, 1986), pp. 177–202. In histories of crime, a similar breach informs John Brewer and John Styles, eds., *An Ungovernable People? The English and their Law in the Seventeenth and Eighteenth Centuries* (London, 1980); 'Introduction,' Anthony Fletcher and John Stevenson, eds., *Order and Disorder in Early Modern England* (Cambridge, 1985), pp. 1–40; V.A.C. Gatrell, *The Hanging Tree: Execution and the English People, 1770–1868* (Oxford, 1994); Douglas Hay, Peter Linebaugh, John G. Rule,

E.P. Thompson, and Cal Winslow, eds., *Albion's Fatal Tree: Crime and Society in Eighteenth-Century England* (New York, 1975); Peter Linebaugh, *The London Hanged: Crime and Civil Society in the Eighteenth Century* (Cambridge, 1992); and E.P. Thompson's *Whigs and Hunters: The Origins of the Black Act* (New York, 1975).

16. Richard Wightman Fox, 'Intimacy on Trial, Cultural Meanings of the Beecher-Tilton Affair,' in *The Power of Culture, Critical Essays in American History*, ed. Richard Wightman Fox and T.J. Jackson Lears, (Chicago, 1993), p. 131.

17. Along with all the depositions from the Northern Circuit from 1660 to 1800, I read all the cases from the *OBSP* from 1680 to 1714 and sampled 13 years between 1715 and 1800. For more on the depositions, see J.S. Cockburn, 'The Northern Assize Circuit,' *Northern History* 3 (1968): 118–30; idem, *Calendar of Assize Records, Home Circuit Indictments, Elizabeth I and James I*. Vol. I: *Introduction* (London, 1985). John Langbein has written extensively about the *OBSP* as an historical source. See 'The Criminal Trial before the Lawyers,' *The University of Chicago Law Review* 45 (1978): 263–316; and idem, 'Shaping the Eighteenth-Century Criminal Trial: A View from the Ryder Sources,' *The University of Chicago Law Review* 50 (1983): 1–136. The publication of the *OBSP* is described by Michael Harris in 'Trials and Criminal Biographies: A Case Study in Distribution,' in *Sale and Distribution of Books from 1700*, ed. Robin Myers and Michael Harris (Oxford, 1982), pp. 1–36. Simon Devereaux explores the relationship between the accuracy of the *OBSP* and ideas about 'public justice' in the late eighteenth century in 'The City and the Sessions Paper: "Public Justice" in London, 1770–1800,' *Journal of British Studies* 35 (1996): 466–503.

18. My analysis is influenced by scholarship on law, narrative, and culture, including Peter Brooks and Paul Gewirtz, eds., *Law's Stories: Narrative and Rhetoric in the Law* (New Haven, 1996); Patricia Ewick and Susan Silbey, eds., *The Common Place of Law: Stories from Everyday Life* (Chicago, 1998); Daniel Farber and Suzanna Sherry, 'Telling Stories out of School: An Essay on Legal Narratives,' *Stanford Law Review* 65 (1993): 807–57; Robert Hariman, ed., *Popular Trials: Rhetoric, Mass Media, and the Law* (Tuscaloosa, 1990); 'Legal Storytelling,' special issue, *Michigan Law Review* 87 (1989); Martha Merrill Umphrey, 'The Dialogics of Legal Meaning: Spectacular Trials, the Unwritten Law, and Narratives of Criminal Responsibility,' *Law and Society Review* 33 (1999): 393–423; and J.B. White, *Heracles' Bow: Essays on the Rhetoric and Poetics of the Law* (Madison, WI, 1985). Literature and law is a growing field that has influenced my interpretation of legal sources. See Jonathan Grossman, *The Art of Alibi: English Law Courts and the Novel* (Baltimore, 2002); Hal Gladfelder, *Criminality and Narrative in Eighteenth-Century England: Beyond the Law* (Baltimore, 2001); Laura Hanft Korobkin, *Criminal Conversations: Sentimentality and Nineteenth-Century Legal Stories of Adultery* (New York, 1998); Alexander Welsh, *Strong Representations: Narrative and Circumstantial Evidence in England* (Baltimore, 1992).

19. For an overview of criminal process, see Baker, 'Criminal Courts and Procedure at Common Law,' in *Crime in England*, pp. 15–48. For more on justices of the peace, see Lionel Glassey, *Politics and the Appointment of Justices of the Peace, 1675–1720* (Oxford, 1979); and Norma Landau, *The Justices of the Peace, 1679–1760* (Berkeley, 1984). For more on reading depositions, see Gaskill, *Crime and Mentalities*; idem, 'Reporting Murder: Fiction in the

Archives in Early Modern England,' *Social History* 23 (1998): 1–30; and Gibson, *Reading Witchcraft*.

20. New work on popular literature has overturned earlier ideas about the readership of crime pamphlets. New studies show that crime literature appealed to a fairly wide audience of 'readers' and 'hearers' that included the wealthy and educated as well as artisans and laborers. On literacy and reading in early modern England, see Jonathan Barry, 'Literacy and Literature in Popular Culture: Reading and Writing in Historical Perspective,' in *Popular Culture in England, c. 1500–1850* (New York, 1995), pp. 69–94; John Brewer, *The Pleasures of the Imagination: English Culture in the Eighteenth Century* (New York, 1997); David Cressy, *Literacy and the Social Order: Reading and Writing in Tudor and Stuart England* (Cambridge, 1980); idem, 'Literacy in Context: Meaning and Measurement in Early Modern England,' in *Consumption and the World of Goods*, ed. John Brewer and Roy Porter (London 1993), pp. 305–19; R.A. Houston, *Literacy in Early Modern Europe: Culture and Education, 1500–1800* (London, 1988); James Raven, Helen Small, and Naomi Tadmor, eds. *The Practice and Representation of Reading in England* (Cambridge, 1996); and Tessa Watt, *Cheap Print and Popular Piety, 1550–1640* (Cambridge, 1991). For more on popular literature in early modern England, see Bernard Capp, *Astrology and the Popular Press: English Almanacs, 1500–1800* (London, 1979); idem, 'Popular Literature,' in *Popular Culture in Seventeenth-Century England*, ed. Barry Reay (London, 1985), pp. 198–243; Robert Collinson, *The Story of Street Literature: Forerunner of the Popular Press* (London, 1973); Gatrell, *Hanging Tree*; Andrea McKenzie, 'Making Crime Pay: Motives, Marketing Strategies, and the Printed Literature of Crime in England, 1670–1770,' in *Criminal Justice in the Old World and the New: Essays in Honour of J.M. Beattie*, ed. Greg T. Smith, Allyson N. May, and Simon Devereaux (Toronto, 1998); Isabel Rivers, ed., *Books and their Readers in Eighteenth-Century England* (Leicester, 1982); Leslie Shepard, *The History of Street Literature* (Newton Abbot, 1973); idem, *The Broadside Ballad* (London, 1962); Margaret Spufford, *Small Books and Pleasant Histories: Popular Fiction and Its Readership in Seventeenth-Century England* (Cambridge, 1981).

21. Cockburn, *Introduction*.

22. The form and function of crime literature is the subject of a wide range of scholarship. Ian Bell, *Literature and Crime in Augustan England* (London, 1991); Lincoln B. Faller, *Turned to Account: The Forms and Functions of Criminal Biography in Late Seventeenth- and Early Eighteenth-Century England* (Cambridge, 1987); idem, *Crime and Defoe: A New Kind of Writing* (Cambridge, 1993); Andrea McKenzie, 'Lives of the Most Notorious Criminals: Popular Literature of Crime in England, 1675–1775' (PhD diss., University of Toronto, 1999); idem, 'Martyrs in Low Life? Dying "Game" in Augustan England,' *Journal of British Studies* 42 (2003): 167–205; Michael McKeon, *The Origins of the English Novel, 1600–1740* (Baltimore, 1987); Linebaugh, *London Hanged*; John Richetti, *Popular Fiction before Richardson: Narrative Patterns, 1700–1739* (Oxford, 1969); J.A. Sharpe, ' "Last Dying Speeches": Religion, Ideology and Public Execution in Seventeenth-Century England,' *Past and Present* 107 (1985): 144–67; Robert R. Singleton, 'English Criminal Biography, 1651–1722,' *Harvard Library Bulletin* 18 (1970), 63–83; Ian Watt, *The Rise of the Novel: Studies in Defoe, Richardson and Fielding* (London, 1963).

23. Cynthia Herrup, *A House in Gross Disorder: Sex, Law, and the 2nd Earl of Castlehaven* (Oxford, 1999), p. 6.
24. *Ibid.*
25. Natalie Davis, *Fiction in the Archives: Pardon Tales and Their Tellers in Sixteenth-Century France* (Palo Alto, 1987), p. 112.
26. *Ibid.*, p. 4.
27. *Ibid.*, p. 112.
28. Hay, 'Property, Authority, and the Criminal Law,' in *Albion's Fatal Tree*. The issues explored in *Albion's Fatal Tree* are developed by Thompson in *Whigs and Hunters*, especially pp. 258–69.
29. For more on the issues of criminal process and mitigation, see J.M. Beattie, *Crime and the Courts in England, 1660–1800* (Princeton, 1986); Cockburn, *Crime in England*; J.S. Cockburn and Thomas A. Green eds., *Twelve Good Men and True: The Criminal Trial Jury in England, 1200–1800* (Princeton, 1988); Gatrell, *Hanging Tree*; Thomas A. Green, *Verdict According to Conscience: Perspectives on the English Criminal Trial Jury, 1200–1800* (Chicago, 1985); Cynthia Herrup, *The Common Peace: Participation and the Criminal Law in Seventeenth-Century England* (Cambridge, 1987); idem, 'Law and Morality in Seventeenth-Century England,' *Past and Present* 106 (1985): 102–3; Peter King, 'Decision-Makers and Decision-Making in English Criminal Law, 1750–1800,' *The Historical Journal* 27 (1984): 26–49; idem, *Crime, Justice, and Discretion in England, 1740–1820* (Oxford, 2000); John Langbein, 'Albion's Fatal Flaws,' *Past and Present* 98 (1983): 96–120; Linebaugh, *The London Hanged*; and J.A. Sharpe, *Crime in Seventeenth-Century England: A County Study* (Cambridge, 1983).
30. Tim Hitchcock, Peter King, and Pamela Sharpe, *Chronicling Poverty: The Voices and Strategies of the English Poor, 1640–1840* (London, 1997), p. 2.
31. Taylor, *Sources of the Self*.
32. Expressions of this mentality are found in Paul Seaver, *Wallington's World: A Puritan Artisan in Seventeenth-Century London* (Palo Alto, 1986) and in contemporary diaries and pamphlets. For an analysis of identity in this period, see Michael Mascuch *Origins of the Individualist Self: Autobiography and Self-Identity in England, 1591–1791* (Palo Alto, 1996). For more on religious belief in the seventeenth century, see Patrick Collinson, *The Religion of the Puritans* (Oxford, 1982); William Hunt, *The Puritan Moment: The Coming of Revolution in an English County* (Cambridge, MA, 1983); and Alexandra Walsham, *Providence in Early Modern England* (Oxford, 1999).
33. Karen Halttunen, *Murder Most Foul: the Killer and the American Gothic Imagination* (Cambridge, MA, 1998); Michel Foucault, *Discipline and Punish: The Birth of the Prison*, translated by Alan Sheridan (New York, 1977); and Wiener, *Reconstructing the Criminal*.
34. Foucault, *Discipline and Punish*, p. 194.
35. Raymond Martin and John Barresi, *The Naturalization of the Soul: Self and Personal Identity in the Eighteenth Century* (New York, 2000), p. 2.
36. By popular I mean definitions that differed from and expanded on the strict medical or legal definitions of mental distress. These definitions and understandings of insanity certainly were not restricted to the lower orders although they circulated there as well as among other social groups. For more on popular conceptions of insanity, see Joel Eigen, *Witnessing Insanity: Madness and Mad-Doctors in the English Court* (New Haven, CT, 1995); R.A. Houston, *Madness and Society in Eighteenth-Century Scotland* (Oxford,

2000); Michael MacDonald, *Mystical Bedlam*; Michael MacDonald, 'Popular beliefs about mental disorder in early modern England,' in *Heilberufe und Kranke im 17. und 18. Jahrhundert die Quellen und Forschungssituation*, ed. W. Eckart and J. Geyer-Kordesch (Munster, 1982), pp. 148–73; Roy Porter, *Mind-Forg'd Manacles: A History of Madness in England from the Restoration to the Regency* (London, 1987); Peter Rushton, 'Lunatics and Idiots: Mental Disability, the Community, and the Poor Law in North-East England, 1600–1800,' *Medical History* 32 (1988): 34–50; Walker *Crime and Insanity*.

37. Walker, *Crime and Insanity*, vol. 1, pp. 68–72.
38. Richard Moran, 'The Origin of Insanity as a Special Verdict: The Trial for Treason of James Hadfield (1800),' *Law and Society Review* 19 (1985): 488.
39. Walker, *Crime and Insanity*, vol. 1, p. 70.
40. This argument was made starkly in Andrew T. Scull's *Museums of Madness: The Social Organization of Insanity in Nineteenth-Century England* (London, 1979) and in a more nuanced and qualified way in *The Most Solitary of Afflictions: Madness and Society in Britain, 1700–1900* (New Haven, CT, 1993).
41. Eigen, *Witnessing Insanity* and Porter, *Mind-Forg'd Manacles*.
42. My cultural analysis of legal sources owes much to the scholars who have come before me. Laura Gowing, *Domestic Dangers: Women, Words, and Sex in Early Modern London* (Oxford, 1996); Herrup, *A House in Gross Disorder*; Chaytor, 'Husbandry: Narratives of Rape in the Seventeenth Century;' and Garthine Walker, *Crime, Gender, and Social Order in Early Modern England* (Cambridge, 2003).
43. Karen Halttunen, 'Humanitarianism and the Pornography of Pain in Anglo-American Culture,' *American Historical Review* 100 (1995): 304–5; Todd, *Sensibility*, chapter 1; Mullan, *Sentiment and Sociability*.
44. Howell, ed., *State Trials*, vol. 27, 1356.
45. Nigel Walker characterized the outcome of Hadfield's trial as:

> an acquittal in name only, for it tacitly admitted that the doctrine of *mens rea* could not safely be applied to the insane. A criminal lunatic might be as morally innocent as a man who had done harm by accident or in self-defense, but the danger of treating him as innocent was too great. The solution was to pay lip-service to his innocence but use the law to make sure he remained in custody.

Walker, *Crime and Insanity*, vol. 1, p. 81.

46. On providence, see Barbara Donagan, 'Providence, Chance, and Explanation: Some Paradoxical Aspects of Puritan Views of Causation,' *Journal of Religious History* 11 (1981): 385–403, idem, 'Godly Choice: Puritan Decision Making in Seventeenth-Century England,' *Harvard Theological Review* 76 (1983): 307–34; idem, 'Understanding Providence: The Difficulties of Sir William and Lady Waller,' *Journal of Ecclesiastical History* 39 (1988): 433–44; Hunt *The Puritan Moment*; Keith Thomas, *Religion and the Decline of Magic* (New York, 1971), pp. 78–112; Walsham, *Providence*; and Blair Worden, 'Providence and Politics in Cromwellian England,' *Past and Present* 109 (1985): 55–99. Walsham makes a strong case for providentialism's wide appeal beyond the ranks of puritans who counted themselves among the elect. Of course regulation of crime never relied exclusively on providence. Regulatory mechanisms expanded at every level during the sixteenth and seventeenth centuries. Steve Hindle, *The State and Social Change in Early Modern England, c. 1550–1640* (London, 2000).

47. In other contexts authorities articulated social and economic explanations for crime, pointing to poverty, enclosure, urbanization, illness, and disability among other factors. For examples, see Paul Slack, *Poverty and Policy in Tudor and Stuart England* (London, 1988); and idem, *The Impact of Plague in Tudor and Stuart England* (London, 1985).

48. John Taylor, *The Unnatural Father or, A Cruell Murther committed by one John Rowse of the Town of Ewell, ten miles from London in the County of Surry Upon two of his owne Children* (London, 1621), p. 18.

49. Peter Lake, 'Deeds against Nature: Cheap Print, Protestantism and Murder in Early Seventeenth-Century England,' in *Culture and Politics in Early Stuart England*, ed. Kevin Sharpe and Peter Lake (Palo Alto, CA, 1993), pp. 257–83.

50. *The Bloudie Booke, or, The tragical and desperate end of Sir John Fites (alias) Fitz* (London, 1605), pp. 3, 20.

51. *Ibid.*, p. 11.

52. *Ibid.*, p. 12.

53. *Ibid.*

54. *Ibid.*, pp. 12–13.

55. Taylor, *Unnatural Father*, p. 1.

56. *Ibid.*, p. 3.

57. *Ibid.*, p. 11.

58. *Ibid.*, p. 12.

59. *Heavens Cry Against Murder, or, A true Relation of the Bloudy and unparallel'd Murder of John Knight* ... (London, 1657), pp. 2, 3.

60. *Ibid.*, pp. 3, 4.

61. *Ibid.*, p. 4.

62. Lake, 'Deeds against Nature,' in *Culture and Politics*, pp. 257–83. Early modern conceptions of the social order are set out by Wrightson in 'The Social Order in Early Modern England: Three Approaches,' in *The World we have Gained*, and by Fletcher and Stevenson, 'Introduction' in *Order and Disorder*.

63. Lake, 'Deeds Against Nature,' in *Culture and Politics*, p. 274.

64. Taylor, *Unnatural Father*, p. 14.

65. *Ibid.*, p. 6.

66. *Ibid.*, p. 7.

67. *Bloudie Booke*, p. 20.

68. *Ibid.*, pp. 24–5.

69. 'Heavens Cry', p. 7.

70. Walsham, *Providence*, especially chapter 2; Peter Lake, 'Protestantism, Arminianism and a Shropshire Axe-Murder,' *Midland History* 15 (1990): 37–64; and idem, 'Deeds against Nature,' in *Culture and Politics*.

71. For more on these providential narratives, see Peter Lake, 'Popular Form, Puritan Content? Two Puritan Appropriations of the Murder Pamphlet from mid-Seventeenth-Century London,' in *Religion, Culture and Society in Early Modern Britain*, ed. Anthony Fletcher and Peter Roberts (Cambridge, 1994), pp. 313–34; and idem, 'Deeds against Nature,' in *Culture and Politics*.

72. Walsham, *Providence*, chapter 1; and John Stachniewski, *The Persecutory Imagination: English Puritanism and the Literature of Religious Despair* (Oxford, 1991).

73. Seaver, *Wallington's World*, p. 120.
74. Alan Macfarlane, ed., *The Diary of Ralph Josselin, 1616–1683* (London, 1976), December 11, 1669, p. 550.
75. Ibid., December 12–16, 1669, p. 551. See also the entry on March 13, p. 552.
76. Seaver, *Wallington's World*, p. 87.
77. *Ibid.*
78. Macfarlane, *The Diary of Ralph Josselin*, June 4, 1650, p. 205.
79. For more on the *Athenian Mercury*, see George Starr, *Defoe and Casuistry* (Princeton, 1971), chapter 1. On spiritual autobiography, see Starr, *Defoe and Spiritual Autobiography* (Princeton, 1965).
80. Keith Thomas, *Man and the Natural World: A History of the Modern Sensibility* (New York, 1983). For more on the relationship between science and religion in the seventeenth century, see Michael Hunter, *Science and Society in Restoration England* (Cambridge, 1981); John Redwood, *Reason, Ridicule and Religion: The Age of Enlightenment in England, 1660–1750* (Cambridge, MA, 1976); Richard S. Westfall, *Science and Religion in Seventeenth-Century England* (Ann Arbor, 1958).
81. On the retreat of providence from mainstream thinking, see Steven Shapin, *A Social History of Truth: Civility and Science in Seventeenth-Century England* (Chicago, 1994); Barbara Shapiro, *Probability and Certainty in Seventeenth-Century England: A Study of the Relationships between Natural Science, Religion, History, Law, and Literature* (Princeton, 1983); idem, *A Culture of Fact: England 1550–1750* (Ithaca, 2000); and Walsham, *Providence*, conclusion. Regarding providence and crime, see Gaskill, *Crime and Mentalities*; idem, 'The Displacement of Providence'; and Halttunen, *Murder Most Foul*, especially chapter 7.
82. James Guthrie, *The Ordinary of Newgate, his account of the behaviour, confession, and dying words of the malefactors who were executed at Tyburn on ... 24 December 1744 ...* (London, 1744–5), p. 47.
83. James Guthrie, *The Ordinary of Newgate, his account of the behaviour, confession, and dying words of the malefactors who were executed at Tyburn on ... 17th of February 1743 ...* (London, 1744), p. 81.
84. James Guthrie, *The Ordinary of Newgate, his account of the behaviour, confession, and dying words of the malefactors who were executed at Tyburn on ... 13th February 1739 ...* (London, 1739–40), p. 7.
85. Raymond Williams, *The Long Revolution* (London, 1961), p. 46.
86. Herrup, 'Law and Morality,' pp. 110–11; idem, *The Common Peace*. For the Anglo-American context, see Halttunen, *Murder Most Foul*, chapter 1.

2 'Of the Persons Capable of Committing Crimes': Pleas of Mental Distress in the Courtroom

1. T.B. Howell, ed., *A Complete Collection of State Trials and Proceedings for High Treason and Other Crimes and Misdemeanors*, 34 vols. (London, 1820), 19: 921–2.
2. *Ibid.*, 945.

3. W.S. Lewis, ed., *The Yale Edition of Horace Walpole's Correspondence*, 48 vols. (New Haven, 1960), 21: 403, 410–11. By a unanimous vote, Ferrers was found guilty and sentenced to death by hanging followed by dissection and anatomization. He was hanged on May 5, 1760. The details of the scandalous case and its relationship to more ordinary trials in the eighteenth century are the subject of my forthcoming article, 'Madness on Trial: Lord Ferrers and the Insanity Defense.'

4. John Brewer and John Styles, eds., *An Ungovernable People? The English and their Law in the Seventeenth and Eighteenth Centuries* (London, 1980), p. 14.

5. Cynthia Herrup, *The Common Peace: Participation and the Criminal Law in Seventeenth-Century England* (Cambridge, 1987); Peter King, *Crime, Justice, and Discretion in England, 1740–1820* (Oxford, 2000); idem, 'Decision-Makers and Decision-Making in English Criminal Law, 1750–1800' *The Historical Journal* 27 (1984): 51–8; J.A. Sharpe 'Enforcing the Law in the Seventeenth-Century English Village,' in *Crime and the Law: The Social History of Crime in Western Europe since 1500*, ed. V.A.C. Gatrell, Bruce Lenman, and Geoffrey Parker (London, 1980), pp. 97–119; and Keith Wrightson, 'Two Concepts of Order: Justices, Constables and Jurymen in Seventeenth-Century England,' in *An Ungovernable People*, pp. 21–46.

6. King, 'Decision-Makers and Decision-Making;' Thomas W. Laqueur, 'Crowds, Carnival and the State in English Executions 1604–1868,' in *The First Modern Society: Essays in English History in Honour of Lawrence Stone*, ed. A. L. Beier, David Cannadine, and James Rosenheim (Cambridge, 1989), pp. 305–56.

7. See the case studies in Brewer and Styles, *An Ungovernable People* and E.P. Thompson, *Whigs and Hunters: The Origins of the Black Act* (New York, 1975). Garthine Walker has a nuanced response to these earlier works in her discussion of conceptions of authority and agency in *Crime, Gender, and Order in Early Modern England* (Cambridge, 2003), chapter 6, especially pp. 210–27.

8. Nigel Walker pioneered the scholarship on the history of criminal insanity in *Crime and Insanity in England*, 2 vols. Vol. 1: *The Historical Perspective* (Edinburgh, 1967). See also Joel Eigen, *Witnessing Insanity: Madness and Mad-Doctors in the English Court* (New Haven, CT, 1995); idem, ' "I Answer as a Physician": The Assertion of Opinion over Fact in pre-McNaughten Insanity Trials,' in *Legal Medicine in History*, ed. Catherine Crawford and Michael Clark (Cambridge, 1994), pp. 167–99; idem, 'Delusion in the Courtroom: The Role of Partial Insanity in Early Forensic Testimony,' *Medical History* 35 (1991): 25–49; idem, 'Intentionality and Insanity: What the Eighteenth-Century Juror Heard,' in *The Anatomy of Madness: Essays in the History of Psychiatry*, 3 vols. Vol. 2: *Institutions and Society*, ed. William Bynum, Roy Porter, and Michael Shepherd (London, 1985), pp. 34–51. For the nineteenth century, see Roger Smith, *Trial by Medicine: Insanity and Responsibility in Victorian Trials* (Edinburgh, 1981). For attitudes to insanity in the early modern world, see A. Fessler, 'The Management of Lunacy in Seventeenth-century England: an Investigation of Quarter-sessions Records,' *Proceedings of the Royal Society of Medicine*, 49 (1956): 901–7; R.A. Houston, *Madness and Society in Eighteenth-Century Scotland* (Oxford, 2000); Michael MacDonald, *Mystical Bedlam: Madness, Anxiety, and Healing in Seventeenth-Century England* (Cambridge, 1981); idem, 'Popular Beliefs about Mental Disorder in Early Modern England,' *in Heilberufe und Kranke im 17. und 18. Jahrhundert die Quellen und*

Forschungssituation, ed. W. Eckart and J. Geyer-Kordesch (Munster, 1982), pp. 148–73; Roy Porter, *Mind-Forg'd Manacles: A History of Madness in England from the Restoration to the Regency* (London, 1987); Peter Rushton, 'Lunatics and Idiots: Mental Disability, the Community, and the Poor Law in North-East England, 1600–1800,' *Medical History* 32 (1988): 34–50; Akihito Suzuki, 'Lunacy in Seventeenth- and Eighteenth-Century England: Analysis of Quarter Sessions Records,' Part 1, *History of Psychiatry* 2 (1991): 437–56; idem, 'Lunacy in Seventeenth- and Eighteenth-Century England: Analysis of Quarter Sessions Records,' Part 2, *History of Psychiatry* 3 (1992): 29–44.

9. Nigel Walker, 'The Insanity Defense before 1800,' *The Annals of the American Academy of Political and Social Science* 477 (1985): 25–30. For more on the origins of the pardon, see Naomi Hurnard, *The King's Pardon for Homicide before A.D. 1307* (Oxford, 1969) and Stanley Grupp, 'Some Historical Aspects of the Pardon in England,' *American Journal of Legal History* 7 (1963): 51–62.

10. Henry de Bracton, *On the Laws and Customs of England*, 4 vols., ed. and trans. Samuel Thorne (Cambridge, MA, 1968), 2: 384. Although attributed to Bracton, the authorship of *On the Laws and Customs of England* is disputed.

11. Matthew Hale, *The History of the Pleas of the Crown*, 2 vols. (London, 1736), 1: 31–2.

12. William Blackstone, *Commentaries on the Laws of England*, 4 vols. Vol. 4: *Of Public Wrongs* (1769), Introduction by Thomas A. Green (Chicago, 1979), p. 20.

13. MacDonald, *Mystical Bedlam*, pp. 123–6; Walker, *Crime and Insanity*, vol. 1, pp. 42–4. For more on medieval pardons of insane offenders, see Hurnard, *The King's Pardon*, chapter 7; Thomas A. Green, *Verdict According to Conscience: Perspectives on the English Criminal Trial Jury, 1200–1800* (Chicago, 1985), pp. 24, 30; and Walker, 'Insanity before 1800,' p. 27.

14. Douglas Hay set out the place of the 'bloody code' in his groundbreaking essay, 'Property, Authority, and the Criminal Law,' in *Albion's Fatal Tree: Crime and Society in Eighteenth-Century England*, ed. Douglas Hay, Peter Linebaugh, John G. Rule, E.P. Thompson, and Cal Winslow (New York, 1975), pp. 17–63. My qualified view of his interpretation owes much to Joanna Innes and John Styles, 'The Crime Wave: Recent Writing on Crime and Criminal Justice in Eighteenth-Century England,' *Journal of British Studies* 25 (1986): 380–435, especially, pp. 420–30, John Langbein, 'Albion's Fatal Flaws,' *Past and Present* 98 (1983): 96–120; and Randall McGowen, ' "He Beareth not the Sword in Vain": Religion and the Criminal Law in Eighteenth-Century England,' *Eighteenth Century Studies* 21 (1988): 192–211.

15. King, 'Decision-Makers and Decision-Making'; and idem, *Crime, Justice, and Discretion in England, 1740–1820*.

16. Thompson, *Whigs and Hunters*, pp. 258–69.

17. The relationship between popular and elite culture in the early modern period has received considerable attention. For more, see Brewer and Styles, *An Ungovernable People?*; Anthony Fletcher and John Stevenson, eds., *Order and Disorder in Early Modern England* (Cambridge, 1985), especially the introduction; Douglas Hay and Nicholas Rogers, *Eighteenth-Century English Society: Shuttles and Swords* (Oxford, 1997); Peter King, 'Edward Thompson's Contribution to Eighteenth-Century Studies: The Patrician–Plebeian Model

Re-examined,' *Social History* 21 (1996): 215–28; Robert Malcolmson, *Popular Recreations in English Society, 1700–1850* (Cambridge, 1973); E.P. Thompson, *Customs in Common: Studies in Traditional Popular Culture* (New York, 1993); idem, 'Eighteenth Century English Society: Class Struggle Without Class,' *Social History* 3 (1978): 133–65; idem, 'Patrician Society, Plebeian Culture,' *Journal of Social History* 7 (1974): 382–405.

18. J.M. Beattie, *Crime and the Courts in England, 1660–1800* (Princeton, 1986), chapter 2 and King, *Crime, Justice, and Discretion*, chapters 2–4.

19. Beattie, *Crime and the Courts*, pp. 268–9. For more on informal means of prosecution, see Martin Ingram, 'Communities and Courts: Law and Disorder in Early-Seventeenth-Century Wiltshire,' in *Crime in England, 1550–1800*, ed. J.S. Cockburn (Princeton, NJ, 1977), pp. 110–34 and Robert Shoemaker, *Prosecution and Punishment: Petty Crime and the Law in London and Rural Middlesex 1660–1725* (Cambridge, 1991).

20. For more on the pre-trial process, see King, *Crime, Justice, and Discretion*, chapters 2, 3, and 4.

21. 2&3 Philip and Mary c. 10 (1555), *Statutes of the Realm*, 9 vols (London, 1810) 4: 286.

22. *Ibid.*

23. *Ibid.*

24. J.H. Baker, 'Criminal Courts and Procedure at Common Law, 1550–1800,' in *Crime in England*, p. 33. The office of the clerk of assize and his responsibilities are described in The *Office of the Clerk of Assize Containing the Form and Method of the Proceedings at the Assizes, and General Gaol-Delivery, as also on the Crown and Nisi Prius Side* (London, 1682). For more on these officers of the court, see J.S. Cockburn, 'Seventeenth-Century Clerks of Assize – Some Anonymous Members of the Legal Profession,' *American Journal of Legal History* 13 (1969): 315–32; idem, *History of Assizes* (Cambridge, 1974), chapter 5; and idem, *Calendar of Assize Records, Home Circuit Indictments, Elizabeth I and James I*. Vol. 1: *Introduction* (London, 1985).

25. Beattie, *Crime and the Courts*, p. 271.

26. *Ibid.*, pp. 273–6.

27. *Ibid.*, pp. 277–80.

28. These assumptions about the special case of murder have been questioned by Malcolm Gaskill, 'The Displacement of Providence: Policing and Prosecution in Seventeenth- and Eighteenth-century England,' *Continuity and Change* 11 (1996): 341–74; and idem, *Crime and Mentalities in Early Modern England* (Cambridge, 2000), chapter 7.

29. Maria White, 'Westminster Inquests' (MA thesis, Yale University, 1980), pp. 1–9. For more on coroner's bills as historical sources, see R.F. Hunnisett, 'The Importance of Eighteenth-century Coroners' Bills,' in *Law, Litigants and the Legal Profession*, ed. E.W. Ives and A.H. Manchester (London, 1983), pp. 126–39.

30. Based on my estimates, the Northern Circuit assizes probably tried between 20 and 30 prisoners a day. For more on the assize, see Cockburn, *History of Assizes*, pp. 110–24; Beattie, *Crime and the Courts*, chapters 6, 7, and 8; Green, *Verdict According to Conscience*, chapter 7; King, *Crime, Justice, and Discretion*, chapters 7–8. The choice of an assize town depended on the size of its population and its relative importance in the circuit. For more on the Northern

Circuit, see J.S. Cockburn, 'The Northern Assize Circuit,' *Northern History* 3 (1968): 118–30.

31. For those practices that distinguished London's Old Bailey from the assize circuit, see Allyson May, *The Bar and the Old Bailey, 1750–1850* (Chapel Hill, 2003), pp. 14–23. For more on conditions in jails during the seventeenth and eighteenth centuries, see John Langbein, 'The Criminal Trial before the Lawyers,' *The University of Chicago Law Review* 45 (1978): 263–316; idem, 'Shaping the Eighteenth-Century Criminal Trial: A View from the Ryder Sources,' *The University of Chicago Law Review* 50 (1983): 1–136; Beattie, *Crime and the Courts*, pp. 288–309; and Peter Linebaugh, 'The Ordinary of Newgate and His Account,' in *Crime in England*, pp. 246–68.

32. Until 1732 indictments were written in Latin. Depositions were always taken in English.

33. Based on his research in Surrey, John Beattie found that 87 percent of those accused of property offenses were indicted in peacetime while 82 percent of bills were found 'true' during wars. Bills found ignoramus were generally destroyed. Beattie, *Crime and the Courts*, p. 405. The grand jury reached its decision by a majority vote. Baker, 'Criminal Courts and Procedure,' in *Crime in England*, p. 19. For more on the grand jury, see Zachary Babington, *Advice to Grand Jurors in Cases of Blood: A Social and Administrative Study* (London, 1677); and John Morrill, *The Cheshire Grand Jury, 1625–1659* (Leicester, 1976).

34. In order to prevent them from finding an error 'on the face of the record' which would provide grounds for the reversal of the judgment against them, the accused were not allowed to see their indictments. Baker, 'Criminal Courts and Procedure,' in *Crime in England*, pp. 34, 45–6. For more on guilty pleas and plea bargaining, see A.W. Alschuler, 'Plea Bargaining and its History,' *Columbia Law Review* 79 (1979): 1–43; Cockburn, *Introduction*, pp. 65–70, 131–3; and John Langbein, 'Understanding the Short History of Plea Bargaining,' *Law and Society Review* 13 (1979): 261–72. Langbein discusses the discouragement of guilty pleas in 'Criminal Trail before the Lawyers,' pp. 277–9. In cases of treason and misdemeanor, refusal to plead was considered a confession of guilt while in cases of felony those who remained mute were subjected to the *peine forte et dure*, the pressing to death of a prisoner. Cockburn, *History of Assizes*, p. 117. By 12 Geo III, c. 20, passed in 1772, standing mute was considered a guilty plea and the *peine fort et dure* was abolished. Beattie, *Crime and the Courts*, pp. 337–8.

35. Baker, 'Criminal Courts and Procedure,' in *Crime in England*, p. 34.

36. Once the jury trials began, the grand jury continued its work ruling on indictments which were then turned over to the court. Baker, 'Criminal Courts and Procedure,' in *Crime in England*, p. 33.

37. For more on the trial during the sixteenth and seventeenth centuries, see Green, Verdict *According to Conscience*, chapters 4–6; J.S. Cockburn, 'Twelve Silly Men? The Trial Jury at Assizes, 1560–1670,' in *Twelve Good Men and True: The Criminal Trial Jury in England, 1200–1800*, ed. J.S. Cockburn and Thomas A. Green (Princeton, NJ, 1988), pp. 158–81; and in the same volume, Green, 'Retrospective,' pp. 358–99.

38. Thomas Smith, *De Republica Anglorum* (1583), ed. Mary Dewar (Cambridge, 1982), p. 113.

39. *Ibid.*

40. Cockburn, *Introduction*, p. 109; idem, 'Trial by the Book? Fact and Theory in the Criminal Process, 1558–1625,' in *Legal Records and the Historian*, ed. J.H. Baker (London, 1978), pp. 69–71; Beattie, *Crime and the Courts*, p. 342; John Langbein, *The Origins of Adversary Criminal Trial* (Oxford, 2003), p. 15. Langbein speculates that the justice of the peace could send his clerk to testify in his place. 'Criminal Trial before the Lawyers,' p. 281. Norma Landau has written extensively about the justices of the peace in the seventeenth and eighteenth centuries in *The Justices of the Peace, 1679–1760* (Berkeley, 1984). Landau calls the justices of eighteenth-century metropolitan London 'a byword for corruption' in 'The Trading Justice's Trade,' in *Law, Crime, and English Society, 1660–1830*, ed. Norma Landau (Cambridge, 2002), p. 46. For more on justices of the peace in the eighteenth century, see King, *Crime, Justice, and Discretion*, pp. 110–25.

41. Smith, *De Republica*, pp. 113–14.

42. *Clerk of the Assize*, p. 48.

43. Defendants were not sworn until 1898. *Langbein, Origins*, pp. 52–3.

44. James Fitzjames Stephen explained that defense counsel was unnecessary because 'in order to convict a prisoner the proof must be so plain that no counsel could contend against it.' *A History of the Criminal Law of England*, 3 vols. (London, 1883), 1: 382. In 1696 under 7–8 William III, c. 3 prisoners indicted for treason were allowed counsel for matters of fact as well as of law. In serious felony cases the defense's right to counsel was augmented throughout the eighteenth century, but it was not until 1836 that the right to counsel was extended to all aspects of trial for felony. For more on the development of counsel for the defense, see Beattie, *Crime and the Courts*, pp. 353–62; idem, 'Scales of Justice: Defense Counsel and the English Criminal Trial in the Eighteenth and Nineteenth Centuries,' *Law and History Review* 9 (1991): 221–67; Green, *Verdict According to Conscience*, chapter 7; Stephen Landsman, 'The Rise of the Contentious Spirit: Adversary Procedure in Eighteenth Century England,' *Cornell Law Review* 75 (1990): 498–609; Langbein, 'Criminal Trial Before the Lawyers,' pp. 282–3; idem, *The Origins of Adversary Criminal Trial* (Oxford, 2003); idem, 'The Prosecutorial Origins of Defense Counsel in the Eighteenth Century: The Appearance of Solicitors,' *Cambridge Law Journal* 58 (1999): 314–65; idem, 'Shaping the Eighteenth-Century Criminal Trial,' pp. 123–34.

45. Smith, *De Republica*, p. 114. François de la Rochefoucauld included an account of a defendant's testimony:

> The accused is able to speak as much as he wishes and to defend himself as best he can; the judge never interrupts him. I actually saw, in one case, the prisoner interrupt the judge three times, and all three times the judge stopped to let him explain himself.

A Frenchman's Year in Suffolk: French impressions of Suffolk life in 1784, trans. and ed. Norman Scarfe (London, 1988), p. 83.

46. Langbein, *Origins*, pp. 35–6.

47. Beattie, *Crime and the Courts*, pp. 344–5; Green, *Verdict According to Conscience*, pp. 273, 285–7; Langbein, 'Criminal Trial before the Lawyers,' pp. 284–300.

48. Langbein, 'Criminal Trial before the Lawyers,' p. 288.

49. *A Frenchman's Year*, p. 84. H. Misson corroborates Rochefoucauld's impression:

> One of the judges makes a discourse upon all that has been said, recapitulates the discourse pro and con, weighs and considers all things, draws

his conclusions, and declares to the jury, that conformably to the laws of the country they ought to bring it in so and so. *Memoirs and Observations in his Travels over England* (London, 1719), p. 328.

50. For a more extensive discussion of the relationship between the judge and the jury during the eighteenth century, see Beattie, *Crime and the Courts*, pp. 397, 413–15, 424–7; Green, *Verdict According to Conscience*, chapter 7; Hay, 'Property, Authority and the Criminal Law,' in *Albion's Fatal Tree*; Langbein, 'Albion's Fatal Flaws;' and Peter Linebaugh, '(Marxist) Social History and (Conservative) Legal History,' *New York University Law Review* 60 (1985): 212–43.

51. King, *Crime, Justice, and Discretion*, p. 223.

52. J.M. Beattie, *Policing and Punishment in London, 1660–1750: Urban Crime and the Limits of Terror* (Oxford, 2001), pp. 269–70. According to Smith, jurors sometimes had as many as eleven or twelve cases to consider. In such cases 'the inquest will say, my Lord, we pray you charge us with no more, it is ynough for our memorie.' *De Republica*, p. 114.

53. Beattie, *Crime and the Courts*, pp. 396–9. Most deliberations were brief, lasting only a few minutes. In more complicated cases, the jury might leave the courtroom to deliberate for fifteen to twenty minutes. Unlike petty juries on the assize circuits, Old Bailey juries continued to withdraw from the courtroom to deliberate until 1738. Beattie, *Policing and Punishment*, p. 272.

54. Langbein, 'Criminal Trial before the Lawyers,' p. 276; Green, *Verdict According to Conscience*, p. 272.

55. For more on jury discretion, see Beattie, *Crime and the Courts*, chapters 7 and 8; Cockburn, *Introduction*; Cockburn and Green, *Twelve Good Men and True*; Green, *Verdict According to Conscience*, especially chapter 7; Cynthia Herrup, 'Law and Morality in Seventeenth-Century England,' *Past and Present* 106 (1985); idem, *The Common Peace*; King, *Crime, Justice, and Discretion* (1985): 102–23; and idem, 'Decision Makers and Decision Making.'

56. Beattie, *Crime and the Courts*, p. 140. Petty larceny was usually punished with whipping while other misdemeanors carried a fine. Those who could not pay the fine served a term in the county gaol or house of correction.

57. William Blackstone justified 'pious perjury' as an adjustment for inflation. *Commentaries*, vol. 4, p. 239. For more on the practice, see Beattie, *Crime and the Courts*, pp. 424–5.

58. Beattie, *Crime and the Courts*, pp. 91–9, 406, 420, 424–30.

59. King, *Crime, Justice, and Discretion*, chapters 7–8.

60. Wrightson, 'Two Concepts of Order: Justices,' in *An Ungovernable People*.

61. Green, *Verdict According to Conscience*, p. 287; Green, 'Retrospective' in *Twelve Good Men and True*, pp. 394–5.

62. King, *Crime, Justice, and Discretion*, pp. 231–4.

63. Langbein, 'Criminal Trial before the Lawyers,' p. 289.

64. If the judge disagreed with the jury's verdict, he might re-instruct the jury and send them out to reconsider their decision.

65. King, *Crime, Justice, and Discretion*, p. 252.

66. Beattie, *Policing and Punishment*, pp. 344–5.

67. Some prisoners made a motion in arrest of judgment while others requested a pardon. Some women asked for a suspension of judgment because of pregnancy. If a prisoner appeared to be insane, a judge would grant a respite. Some prisoners claimed the benefit of clergy, the privilege of exemption from

trial by a secular court allowed to or claimed by clergymen arraigned for felony. By the eighteenth century a clergyable offence exempted a prisoner from sentence which, in the case of certain offenses, might be pleaded on first conviction by everyone who could read. The number of clergyable offenses had shrunk by the eighteenth century and the privilege was abolished altogether in 1827. On pregnancy and respite, see James Oldham, 'On Pleading the Belly: A History of the Jury of Matrons,' *Criminal Justice History* 6 (1985): 1–64. On the benefit of clergy, Beattie, *Crime and the Courts*, pp. 88–9, 141–6, 167–81, 451–8, 474–7, and 509–10.

68. Blackstone defined a reprieve as 'the withdrawal of the sentence for an interval of time.' *Commentaries*, vol. 4, p. 394. Green outlines the origins of the pardon in *Verdict According to Conscience*, p. 24. He distinguishes between pardons of course, 'granted automatically, for slaying in self-defense, through accident or through insanity, as though the defendant had done no wrong' and pardons of grace granted by the king 'usually for a price' which 'absolved a person of a wrongdoing, or at least insured the person against prosecution. In addition to the judge, members of the jury or even the prosecutor could recommend a convicted felon for a pardon. Langbein, 'Criminal Trial before the Lawyers,' p. 297.

69. Blackstone, *Commentaries*, vol. 4, p. 394.

70. J.M. Beattie, 'The Cabinet and the Management of Death at Tyburn after the Revolution of 1688–1689,' in *The Revolution of 1688–1689: Changing Perspectives*, ed. Lois Schwoerer (Cambridge, 1992), pp. 218–21.

71. Transportation was a feature of the English legal system by the late seventeenth century: 4,500 convicted felons were sent to the colonies between 1655 and 1699. For more on pardons, see Beattie, *Crime and the Courts*, pp. 430–49; Sharpe, *A County Study*, p. 147; Sir Leon Radzinowicz, *A History of English Criminal Law and its Administration from 1750*, 4 vols. Vol. 1: *The Movement for Reform 1750–1833* (New York, 1948), pp. 114–16.

72. Beattie, *Crime and the Courts*, pp. 430–6. For more on the factors that affected the pardoning of criminals during the eighteenth century, see King, *Crime, Justice, and Discretion*, chapter 9. On pardons in the late eighteenth century, see Gatrell, *Hanging Tree*.

73. Langbein, *Origins*.

74. Beattie, 'The Cabinet and the Management of Death,' pp. 224–9; and idem, *Policing and Punishment*, chapter 9.

75. *Statutes of the Realm*, vol. 8, pp. 168–9. Blackstone traced the recommendation to admit witnesses for the defense to Mary's reign and then to 31 Eliz c. 4.

76. Blackstone, *Commentaries*, vol. 4, p. 353.

77. *Ibid.*

78. *Statutes of the Realm*, vol. 4, part 2, p. 1135. The penultimate chapter in the history of the sworn testimony of defense witnesses took place in 1696 with passage of the Treason Act (7–8 William III, c. 3) which allowed defendants counsel as well as 'lawfull witnesse or witnesses who shall then bee upon Oath for his and their just defence in that behalfe.' *Statutes of the Realm*, vol. 7, p. 6.

79. The Act made returning to England before the end of the term of transportation a capital crime. Beattie explains the government's sponsorship of the Transportation Act and the implications of the initiative in 'The Cabinet and

the Management of Death,' pp. 231–3; and idem, *Policing and Punishment*, pp. 333–5 and chapter 9.

80. Beattie, *Crime and the Courts*, pp. 503–5. This was not the government's first attempt to design alternative, non-capital punishments. During Elizabeth's reign a conditional pardon was granted in exchange for work on the galleys while under James I convicts were conscripted into foreign military service. Baker, 'Criminal Courts and Procedure,' in *Crime in England*, p. 45. 5 Ann c. 6 (1706) allowed judges to sentence those convicted of clergyable offenses to hard labor and imprisonment in a house of correction. Beattie discusses the history of the Transportation Act in chapter 9 of *Crime and the Courts*. He traces the role played by William Thomson (1678–1739) in the construction and enforcement of this legislation in *Policing and Punishment*, chapter 9.

81. Beattie, *Crime and the Courts*, pp. 506–13; idem, *Policing and Punishment*, pp. 432–48.

82. Beattie, *Crime and the Courts*, pp. 513–19; idem, *Policing and Punishment*, pp. 448–62.

83. Beattie, *Crime and the Courts*, p. 509 and King, *Crime, Justice, and Discretion*, chapters 8 and 9.

84. Beattie, *Crime and the Courts*, pp. 513–19.

85. For more on the emergence of counsel for the prosecution, see Beattie, *Crime and the Courts*, pp. 352–6; Langbein, 'Criminal Trial before the Lawyers,' pp. 311–12; idem, 'The Prosecutorial Origins of Defense Counsel;' and idem, *Origins*.

86. Langbein, *Origins*, pp. 2–7.

87. *Ibid.*, pp. 113–15.

88. *Ibid.*, pp. 145–58.

89. *Ibid.*, pp. 170–2.

90. Standard trial practice began with the prosecution's examination of witnesses against the defendant followed by the defendant's cross-examination of them. The defendant then presented witnesses in his defense who were subsequently cross-examined by the prosecution. *The Complete Juryman: or, A Compendium of Laws relating to Jurors* (London, 1752), p. 158.

91. Langbein, 'Shaping the Eighteenth Century Criminal Trial,' pp. 123–33; Beattie, *Crime and the Courts*, pp. 374–5.

92. William Eden, *Principles of Penal Law* (London, 1771), p. 219. Rochfoucault's comments quoted above date from 1784 and give a similar 'conversational' impression.

93. Langbein, *Origins*, p. 169.

94. Beattie, 'Scales of Justice,' p. 227; King, *Crime, Justice, and Discretion*, p. 228.

95. Beattie, p. 228; King, *Crime, Justice, and Discretion*, pp. 227–8; May, *Bar and the Old Bailey*, p. 35. Langbein describes the methodological difficulties in quantifying the presence of counsel at the Old Bailey in *Origins*, pp. 168–70.

96. Langbein, *Origins*, p. 256.

97. *Ibid.*, p. 257.

98. *Ibid.*, pp. 311–14, 319–21.

99. Beattie, *Crime and the Courts*, pp. 361–2; King, *Crime, Justice, and Discretion*, pp. 227–8.

100. Beattie, p. 361.

101. Langbein, *Origins*, pp. 266–73.

102. Langbein, *Origins*, pp. 258–61.
103. *Ibid.*, p. 109.
104. Langbein details the effect of the adversarial trial on the role of the judge in *ibid.*, pp. 321–31.
105. Walker, 'Insanity before 1800.'
106. Edward Coke, *The Third Part of the Institutes of the Laws of England* (London, 1670), p. 6.
107. Some examples of manuals for justices of the peace include *The Mirrour of Justices*, ed. William Robinson, attributed to Andrew Horne (d. 1328) (Washington, DC, 1903); Anthony Fitzherbert, *The Newe Boke of Justices of the Pleas* (London, 1538); and Michael Dalton, *The Countrey Justice* (London, 1618). An example from the eighteenth century is Richard Burn, *The Justice of the Peace, and Parish Officer* (London, 1758).
108. For more on the history of idiocy, see David Wright and Ann Digby, eds., *From Idiocy to Mental Deficiency: Historical Perspectives on People with Learning Disabilities* (New York, 1996).
109. Hale, *Pleas of the Crown*, vol. 1, p. 30.
110. *Ibid.*
111. *Ibid.*, p. 31.
112. *Ibid.*
113. John Brydall, *Non Compos Mentis: or, the Law Relating to Natural Fools, Mad Folks, and Lunatic Persons* (London, 1700).
114. *Ibid.*, p. 68.
115. *Ibid.*, p. 69.
116. Blackstone, *Commentaries*, vol. 4, p. 21.
117. *Ibid.*, p. 25. The statute also allowed justices of the peace to apprehend and to restrain anyone considered a 'rogue' or a 'vagabond'. The justices could then send the prisoner by a vagrant pass to his home and appropriate his land and goods to pay any expenses incurred in the process. The passage of the statute did not override the rights of the prisoner's relations or friends to take over his or her custody and care.
118. Bracton, *Laws and Customs*, vol. 2, p. 424. Discussions of the will and criminal intent appear in vol. 2, pp. 23, 100, 289–90, and 384. For a comprehensive discussion of the law relating to suicide, see Michael MacDonald and Terence Murphy, *Sleepless Souls: Suicide in Early Modern England* (Oxford, 1990), pp. 20, 21–2.
119. *Ibid.*, vol. 4, p. 308.
120. Anthony Platt and Bernard Diamond, 'The Origins and Development of the "Wild Beast" Concept of Mental Illness and its Relation to Theories of Criminal Responsibility,' *Journal of the History of the Behavioral Sciences* 1 (1965): 355–67.
121. Walker, 'Insanity before 1800,' pp. 28–9; Platt and Diamond, ' "Wild-Beast" and Criminal Responsibility.'
122. Walker, *Crime and Insanity*, vol. 1, pp. 42–4; MacDonald, *Mystical Bedlam*, pp. 123–6.
123. Hurnard, *The King's Pardon*, pp. 159–79. Barbara Hanawalt, ed., *Crime in East Anglia in the Fourteenth Century: Norfolk Gaol Delivery Rolls, 1307–1316* (Norfolk, 1976), case #80, p. 30 and #469, p. 79. Between 1558 and 1642 very few cases involving criminal insanity came to court on the Home Circuit

Assizes; those that did come to trial involved serious crimes such as grand larceny, arson, and murder. When a defendant was found to be clearly and obviously insane, the jury dismissed the case with an acquittal or ruled that the offender should be incarcerated indefinitely. Cockburn, *Calendar of Assize Records: Surrey Indictments, Elizabeth I* (London, 1980), Assi 35/14/2, case #610, p. 109; idem, *Calendar of Assize Records: Surrey Indictments, James I* (London, 1982), Assi 35/51/7, case #238, p. 40; idem, *Calendar of Assize Records: Essex Indictments, James I* (London, 1982), Assi 35/53/2, case #676, p. 105; idem, *Assize Records: Essex, James I*, Assi 35/53/1, case #621, p. 96; idem, *Calendar of Assize Records: Kent Indictments, Charles I* (London, 1995), 35/81/4, case #1748, p. 369; and Sharpe, *A County Study*, p. 131.

124. For more on the care lunatics in the early modern period, see, Jonathan Andrews, Asa Briggs, Roy Porter, Penny Tucker, and Keir Waddington, *The History of Bethlem* (London, 1997); Jonathan Andrews and Andrew Scull, *Customers and Patrons of the Mad-Trade: The Management of Lunacy in Eighteenth-Century London* (Berkeley, 2003); and idem, *Undertaker of the Mind: John Monro and Mad-Doctoring in Eighteenth-Century England* (Berkeley, 2001).

125. For examples of such cases, see Rushton, 'Lunatics and Idiots.' Other examples of the treatment of lunatics are found in the correspondence of the board of Greencloth which committed 41 persons to Bridewell and Bethlem between 1670 and 1751. LS 13/104 fols. 46, 89–90.

126. Ida Macalpine and Richard Hunter, *George III and the Mad-Business* (London, 1969), pp. 310–13.

127. *Ibid.*, p. 310.

128. Henry Clifford, *Old Bailey Sessions Papers* [hereafter *OBSP*], January 1688.

129. Elizabeth Bennit, *OBSP*, January 1711.

130. *Gentlemen's Magazine*, 4 (1734), p. 509.

131. *Gentlemen's Magazine*, 32 (1762), p. 446.

132. William Hall, *OBSP*, October 1772, #782. Cases of obvious, uncontested insanity appeared in the Old Bailey at least once a year.

133. *Gentlemen's Magazine*, 29 (1759), p. 439.

134. Blackstone, *Commentaries*, vol. 4, p. 25. Hale warned that: 'Because there may be great fraud in this matter, yet if the crime be notorious, as *treason or murder*, the judge before such respite or judgment may do well to impanel a jury to inquire *ex officio* touching such insanity, whether it be real or counterfeit.' *Pleas of the Crown*, vol. 1, p. 35. Emphasis in the original.

135. Robert Ogle, *OBSP*, June 1756, #271.

136. *Ibid.*

137. *Ibid.*

138. MacDonald, *Mystical Bedlam*, especially pp. 112–32. These descriptions of Ogle conform to early modern conceptions of insanity which defined as mad any behavior that violated the social order or proved self-destructive.

139. Hale, *Pleas of the Crown*, vol. 1, p. 30.

140. MacDonald, *Mystical Bedlam*, pp. 112–21; and Eigen 'Intentionality and Insanity.' The recognition of the signs of mental impairment reflects a widespread familiarity with mental illness which was the result of the close proximity in which people lived and the fact that, for the most part, in the seventeenth century the insane were not segregated from the rest of their community. The asylum movement which attempted to incarcerate

lunatics began at the end of the eighteenth century. For more on this move-ment, see Andrew Scull, *The Most Solitary of Afflictions: Madness and Society in Britain, 1700–1900* (New Haven, 1993).

141. Elizabeth Cole, *OBSP*, January 1709. Cole was found not guilty. Also see *The Cruel Mother, Being a strange and unheard of Account of one Mrs. Elizabeth Cole, a Child's Coat-Maker* ... (London, 1708). The association of childbirth with the onset of temporary insanity and the crime of infanticide is the subject of chapter 4.

142. Hannah Gill, *OBSP*, April 1719.

143. *Ibid.* Gill was acquitted.

144. Stephen Swate, *OBSP*, January 1708.

145. Samuel Prigg, *OBSP*, May 1746, #216.

146. *Ibid.* Prigg was convicted and sentenced to death.

147. Philip Gibson, *OBSP*, May 1751, #379. Gibson was found guilty, sentenced to death, and recommended for mercy.

148. The association of women, labor, and madness has been documented for the seventeenth century by Garthine Walker in *Crime, Gender, and Order*, pp. 148–9; and Keith Wrightson, 'Infanticide in Earlier Seventeenth-Century England,' *Local Population Studies* 15 (1975): 10–22. For more eighteenth-century examples, see John Monro's case book for 1766 published in Andrews and Scull, *Customers and Patrons of the Mad-Trade*. William Cowper was found not guilty and discharged. Assi 44/58.

149. Assizes, Northern Circuit, 1743: Assi 45/22/3/22.

150. Assizes, Northern Circuit, 1750: Assi 45/24/2/12.

151. *Ibid.*

152. *Ibid.*

153. Assizes, Northern Circuit, 1750: Assi 45/24/2/13.

154. *Ibid.* Barber was found guilty of threatening violent assault. He was fined and sentenced to three years in prison. His indictment charged him 'to remain in gaol 'till he finds surer sureties.' Assi 44/64.

155. Assizes, Northern Circuit, Assi 44/74.

156. Assizes, Northern Circuit, 1759: Assi 45/26/3/100. Similarly, Anne Hutchinson was committed for several misdemeanors against the peace in 1753. Four years later in 1757 the gaol delivery record pronounced that she 'hath also been strongly suspected not to have always the right use of her reason, but to be subject to fits of frenzy and lunacy whereby she cannot be permitted to go at large without manifest danger to his majesty's subjects.' Assi 44/72. An affidavit described John Windle as 'a very dangerous man' and urged his continued detention because he 'has not the right use of reason but [is] subject to fits of frenzy and lunacy.' Assi 45/26/1/156.

157. Richard Cooper, *OBSP*, May 1731. Cooper was found guilty and sentenced to death.

158. Edward Stafford, *OBSP*, July 1731. The jury brought in a verdict of lunacy.

159. Assizes, Northern Circuit, 1755: Assi 45/25/4/148c.

160. Assizes, Northern Circuit, 1783: Assi 45/34/4/196.

161. *Ibid.*

162. *Ibid.*

163. The word 'insane' was written beside Swift's name on the gaol delivery list and no indictment survives which suggests that the case did not go to trial.

164. Hale, *Pleas of the Crown*, vol. 1, p. 30.
165. *Ibid.*
166. John Newman, *OBSP*, June 1720. The jury found him guilty to the value of 10d and ordered him transported.
167. James Codner, *OBSP*, December 1720. The jury found him guilty to the value of 4s 6d and he was sentenced to be burned on the hand.
168. Richard Cooper, *OBSP*, May 1731. Cooper was found guilty and sentenced to death.
169. Charles Farrel, *OBSP*, June 1756, #268. Farrel was found guilty and sentenced to 'be imprisoned in his majesty's gaol of Newgate for one year and to find security for his good behaviour for a year after the expiration of the same.'
170. William Ward, *OBSP*, February 1772, #251. Ward was found guilty to the value of 10d and transported.
171. Jane Bartwick, *OBSP*, February 1716. The jury found Bartwick guilty to the value of 10d.
172. Joel Farringdon, *OBSP*, April 1731. Farringdon was acquitted for lack of evidence.
173. Ann Burger, *OBSP*, June 1756, #240.
174. *Ibid.* The jury found Burger guilty and branded her in the hand.
175. This number is based on a sample of 13 years between 1715 and 1800.
176. Susanne Winton, Reports on Criminals, Correspondence, June 1786: HO 47/4. The judge in James Husband's case from 1784 (HO 47/3) also noted that there was no 'surmise at the trial of any insanity.' The omission of this evidence supports my assertion that counsel hesitated to introduce evidence of mental states that was not clear-cut.
177. *The Cruel Mother. Being the Strange unheard of Account …* (London, 1708), p. 5.
178. Although they do not refer to sensibility, Thomas A. Green and Peter King discuss the discomforts of prosecutors and legal authorities with enforcing the harsh penalties prescribed by the 'bloody code.' King, *Crime, Justice, and Discretion*, pp. 325–33; and Green, *Verdict According to Conscience*, chapter 7.
179. Pierre Jean Grosley, *A Tour to London; or New Observations on England and its Inhabitants*. 2 vols. trans. from French by Thomas Nugent (London, 1772, originally published 1765), 2: 144.
180. For more on the English movement for legal reform in the eighteenth century, see Beattie, *Crime and the Courts*, chapters 9 and 10; Green *Verdict According to Conscience*, chapter 7; and Radzinowicz, *English Criminal Law*, Vol. 1.
181. Henry Fielding, *An Enquiry into the Causes of the late Increase of Robbers* (1751), in *An Enquiry into the Causes of the late Increase of Robbers and Related Writings*, ed. Malvin Zirker (New York, 1988), p. 154.
182. *Ibid.*
183. *Ibid.*
184. Samuel Johnson, *Rambler*, #114, Saturday, 20 April 1751, in *The Yale Edition of the Works of Samuel Johnson*, 16 vols. Vol. 4: *The Rambler*, ed. W.J. Bates and Albrecht B. Strauss (New Haven, CT, 1969), p. 245.
185. *Ibid.*
186. *Ibid.*, p. 246.
187. Blackstone, *Commentaries*, vol. 4, p. iii.

188. Blackstone, *Commentaries*, vol. 4, p. 3.
189. *Ibid.*
190. *Ibid.*, vol. 4, p. 19.
191. William Paley, *Principles of Moral and Political Philosophy* (London, 1785), p. 411.
192. *Ibid.*
193. *Ibid.*
194. For more on the debate about capital punishment and public execution, see Randall McGowen, 'Civilizing Punishment: The End of the Public Execution in England,' *Journal of British Studies* 33 (1994): 257–82.
195. Martin Madan, *Thoughts on Executive Justice* (London, 1785), p. 13.
196. *Ibid.*, p. 138.
197. *Ibid.*, p. 139.
198. *Ibid.*, pp. 137–8.
199. *Ibid.*, p. 137.
200. *Ibid.*, p. 138.
201. *Ibid.*, pp. 50–1.
202. Eden, *Principles*, p. 291.
203. *Ibid.*, p. 14.
204. *Ibid.*, p. 15.
205. *Ibid.*, p. 21.
206. *Ibid.*, pp. 292–3.
207. *Ibid.*, p. 29.
208. *Ibid.*
209. Manasseh Dawes, *An Essay on Crimes and Punishments with a View of, and Commentary upon Beccaria, Rousseau, Voltaire, Montesquieu, Fielding and Blackstone* (London, 1782), p. 3.
210. *Ibid.*, p. 40
211. *Ibid.*, p. 54.
212. *Ibid.*, p. 9.
213. *Ibid.*, p. 11.
214. *Ibid.*, p. 71.
215. *Ibid.*, p. 3. As a transitive verb the word compassionate means 'to regard or treat with compassion; to pit, commiserate (a person, or his distress, etc.)'
216. *Ibid.*, p. 4.

3 Old Excuses, New Meanings: 'Temporary Phrenzy,' Necessity, Passion, and Compulsion

1. Raymond Martin and John Barresi, *The Naturalization of the Soul: Self and Personal identity in the Eighteenth Century* (New York, 2000).
2. G.J. Barker-Benfield, *The Culture of Sensibility: Sex and Society in Eighteenth-Century Britain* (Chicago, 1992), pp. 3–9, 15–36; John Mullan, *Sentiment and Sociability: The Language of Feeling in the Eighteenth Century* (Oxford, 1988), pp. 201–40; and Ann Jessie Van Sant, *Eighteenth-century Sensibility and the Novel: the Senses in Social Context* (Cambridge, 1993).
3. Studies of the self assign the biological, social, and psychological components of such an entity varying degrees of importance. Jerrold Seigel,

'Problematizing the Self,' in *Beyond the Cultural Turn: New Directions in the Study of Culture and Society*, ed. Victoria E. Bonnell and Lynn Hunt (Berkeley, 2000), pp. 281–314.

4. Martin and Barresi, *Naturalization of the Soul*, pp. 1–2.

5. For more on the discussion of the existence of a true self in the eighteenth century, see Martin and Barresi, *Naturalization of the Soul*; Felicity Nussbaum, *The Autobiographical Subject: Gender and Ideology in Eighteenth-Century England* (Baltimore, 1989); Christine Roulston, *Virtue, Gender, and the Authentic Self in Eighteenth-Century Fiction: Richardson, Rousseau, and Laclos* (Gainesville, 1998); and Patricia Meyer Spacks, *Imagining a Self: Autobiography and Novel in Eighteenth-Century England* (Cambridge, MA, 1976).

6. John Locke, *An Essay Concerning Human Understanding* (1689), ed. P.H. Nidditch (Oxford, 1975), p. 341.

7. For more on seventeenth-century philosophy, see *Philosophy, Science, and Religion in England, 1640–1700*, ed. Richard Kroll, Richard Ashcroft, and Perez Zagorin (Cambridge, 1992).

8. Locke, *Essay Concerning Human Understanding*, ed. Nidditch, p. 342. Chapter 27, 'Of Identity and Diversity,' was added to the second edition published in 1694.

9. David Hume, *A Treatise of Human Nature* (1739), ed. David Fate Norton and Mary J. Norton (Oxford, 2000), p. 137.

10. *Ibid.*, p. 138.

11. Patricia Meyer Spacks argues that his autobiography represents Hume's belief in a stable self; Felicity Nussbaum contests this interpretation. Spacks, *Imagining a Self*, pp. 13–15 and Nussbaum, *The Autobiographical Subject*, p. 8.

12. Nussbaum, *Autobiographical Subject*, p. 38. This debate was not limited to philosophy nor to England. Similar themes run through Laurence Sterne's *Tristram Shandy*, William Godwin's work, as well as that of Jean-Jacques Rousseau, Denis Diderot, Choderlos Laclos, among other French authors.

13. One could argue that the novel evolved as a forum best suited to explore and develop ideas about identity, subjectivity, and selfhood. For more on identity and the self and eighteenth-century literature, see John Bender, *Imagining the Penitentiary: Fiction and the Architecture of the Mind in Eighteenth-Century England* (Chicago, 1987); Stephen Cox, 'The Stranger Within Thee': *Concepts of the Self in Late-Eighteenth Century Literature* (Pittsburgh, 1980); Deidre Shanna Lynch, *The Economy of Character: Novels, Market Culture, and the Business of Inner Meaning* (Chicago, 1998); Michael Mascuch, *Origins of the Individualist Self: Autobiography and Self-Identity in England, 1591–1791* (Palo Alto, CA, 1996); John Preston, *The Created Self: The Reader's Role in Eighteenth-Century Fiction* (New York, 1970); Roulston, *Virtue, Gender and the Authentic Self*; Spacks, *Imagining a Self*; and Dennis Todd, *Imagining Monsters: Miscreations of the Self in Eighteenth-Century England* (Chicago, 1995).

14. George Starr, *Defoe and Casuistry* (Princeton, 1971), p. v.

15. Defoe's interest in crime is the subject of much literary criticism including Ian A. Bell, *Defoe's Fiction* (London, 1985); idem, *Literature and Crime in Augustan England* (London, 1991); Lincoln Faller, *Defoe and Crime: A New Kind of Writing* (Cambridge, 1993); idem, *Turn'd to Account: The Forms and Functions of Criminal Biography in Late Seventeenth and Early Eighteenth-Century England* (Cambridge, 1987); John Richetti, *Popular Fiction before Richardson: Narrative*

Patterns, 1700–1739 (Oxford, 1969); Starr, *Defoe and Casuistry*; and Ian Watt, *The Rise of the Novel: Studies in Defoe, Richardson and Fielding* (Berkeley, 1957).

16. Daniel Defoe, *Moll Flanders* (New York, 1981), pp. 114–15.

17. *Ibid.*, p. 115.

18. *Ibid.*, p. 168.

19. *Ibid.*, p. 169.

20. *Ibid.*

21. *Ibid.*

22. William Alderman, 'Shaftesbury and the Doctrine on Benevolence in the Eighteenth Century,' *Transactions of the Wisconsin Academy of Sciences, Arts and Letters* 26 (1931): 137–59.

23. Anthony Ashley Cooper, 3rd Earl of Shaftesbury, *Characteristicks of Men, Manners, Opinions, Times* (1711), 2 vols., ed. Philip Ayres (Oxford, 1999), 1: 260.

24. *Ibid.*, vol. 2, p. 137.

25. William Alderman, 'Shaftesbury and the Doctrine of Moral Sense,' *PMLA* 46 (1931): 1087–94; John K. Sheriff, *The Good-Natured Man: The Evolution of a Moral Ideal, 1660–1800* (University, AL, 1982); and Ernest Lee Tuveson, *The Imagination as a Means of Grace: Locke and the Aesthetics of Romanticism* (Berkeley, 1960).

26. Shaftesbury, *Characteristicks*, ed. Ayres, vol. 1, p. 166.

27. *Ibid.*, pp. 166–7.

28. *Ibid.*, p. 167.

29. It is ironic that while Shaftesbury implies that women lacked self-control, the agent of that control, the 'correctrice,' was presumably female.

30. Shaftesbury, *Characteristicks*, ed. Ayres, vol. 1, p. 167.

31. For more on gender and the language of sentiment, see John Barrell, 'Sad Stories: Louis XVI, George III, and the Language of Sentiment,' in *Refiguring Revolutions: Aesthetics and Politics from the English Revolution to the Romantic Revolution*, ed. Kevin Sharpe and Steven N. Zwicker (Berkeley, 1998), pp. 75–6.

32. Shaftesbury, *Characteristicks*, ed. Ayres, vol. 1, p. 67.

33. *Ibid.*, p. 167.

34. *Ibid.*, pp. 167–8.

35. For Shaftesbury's influence on shaping conceptions of the appropriate behavior of the English elite, see Lawrence E. Klein, *Shaftesbury and the Culture of Politeness: Moral Discourse and Cultural Politics in Early Eighteenth-Century England* (Cambridge, 1994).

36. Karen Halttunen, 'Humanitarianism and the Pornography of Pain in Anglo-American Culture,' *American Historical Review* 100 (1995), particularly pp. 303–10; and Janet Todd, *Sensibility: An Introduction* (London, 1986), pp. 21–3. On the Scottish Enlightenment and the moral sense, see Gladys Bryson, *Man and Society: The Scottish Inquiry of the Eighteenth Century* (Princeton, 1945); R.H. Campbell and Andrew S. Skinner, eds., *The Origins and Nature of the Scottish Enlightenment* (Edinburgh, 1982); David Daiches, Peter Jones, and Jean Jones eds., *A Hotbed of Genius: The Scottish Enlightenment, 1730–1790* (Edinburgh, 1982); and John Dwyer, *Virtuous Discourse: Sensibility and Community in Late Eighteenth-Century Scotland* (Edinburgh, 1987).

37. Adam Smith, *The Theory of Moral Sentiments* (1759), ed. D.D. Raphael and A.L. Macfie (Oxford, 1976), p. 25.

38. *Ibid.*, p. 9.

39. James Boswell, *Boswell's Life of Johnson* (1791), 6 vols., ed. George Birkbeck Hill, (Oxford, 1934), 2 : 440.
40. Smith, *Moral Sentiments*, ed. Raphael and Macfie, p. 152.
41. *Ibid.*, p. 244.
42. *Ibid.*
43. *Ibid.*, p. 245.
44. *Ibid.*, p. 152.
45. *Ibid.*, p. 244.
46. *Ibid.*
47. *Ibid.*, p. 245.
48. *Ibid.*, p. 244.
49. *Ibid.*, p. 24.
50. *Ibid.*
51. Samuel Johnson, *Rambler*, #7, Tuesday, 10 April 1750, on the *Yale Edition of the Works of Samuel Johnson*, 16 vols. Vol. 3, *The Rambler*, eds. W.J. Bates and Albrecht B. Strauss (New Haven, 1969), p. 38.
52. *Ibid.*
53. Johnson, *Rambler*, #151, Tuesday, 27 August 1751, in *Yale Edition*, vol. 5, p. 42.
54. Johnson, *Rambler*, #8, Saturday, 14 April 1750, in *Yale Edition*, vol. 3, p. 42.
55. *Ibid.*, p. 46.
56. Johnson, *Rambler* #70, Saturday, 17 November 1750, in *Yale Edition*, vol. 4, p. 6. Although the first printing numbered only 500, *Rambler* essays were often reprinted in full.
57. Johnson, *Rambler*, #7, in *Yale Edition*, vol. 3, p. 37.
58. Smith, *Moral Sentiments*, ed. Raphael and Macfie, p. 237.
59. *Ibid.*, pp. 25–6.
60. *Ibid.*, p. 241.
61. Adela Pinch, *Strange Fits of Passion: Epistemologies of Emotion, Hume to Austen* (Palo Alto, CA, 1996), p. 2.
62. Barrell, 'Sad Stories,' in *Refiguring Revolutions*, p. 76; Halttunen, 'Humanitarianism and the Pornography of Pain,' pp. 304–5; Todd, *Sensibility*, chapter 1; Mullan, *Sentiment and Sociability*; Johnson, *Rambler*, #70, in *Yale Edition*, vol. 4, p. 3.
63. Todd, *Sensibility*, p. 9. The 'era of sensibility' dated from the end of the seventeenth century until the beginning of the nineteenth.
64. Pinch, *Epistemology*, p. 11.
65. Todd, *Sensibility*, p. 2.
66. For a fuller analysis of Mackenzie's *The Man of Feeling*, see R.F. Brissenden, *Virtue in Distress: Studies in the Novel of Sentiment from Richardson to Sade* (New York, 1974); Mullan, *Sentiment and Sociability*; and Todd, *Sensibility*.
67. Henry Mackenzie, *The Man of Feeling* (New York, 1958), p. 37.
68. For a discussion of sympathy, pity, and visual perception, see Van Sant, *Eighteenth-Century Sensibility*, chapter 2.
69. Todd, *Sensibility*, p. 13.
70. Van Sant, *Eighteenth-Century Sensibility*, pp. 16–59.
71. Richard Steele, *The Christian Hero: Or, No Principles but those of Religion Sufficient to make a Great Man*, ed. Rae Blanchard (Oxford, 1932), pp. xvii–xxiii.
72. This section on the religious origins of sensibility summarizes R.S. Crane's important article, 'Suggestions Towards a Genealogy of the "Man of Feeling," '

English Literary History 1 (1934): 205–30. For more on the Cambridge Platonists, *see Philosophy, Science, and Religion*, ed. Kroll, Ashcroft, and Zagorin. For more on Latitudinarianism, see Martin I.J. Griffin, Jr., *Latitudinarianism in the Seventeenth-Century Church of England* (New York, 1992) and *Philosophy, Science, and Religion*, ed. Kroll, Ashcroft, and Zagorin.

73. Crane, 'Suggestions Towards a Genealogy,' pp. 221–7.

74. Steele was not alone. Moralists, preachers, other cultural observers such as Timothy Nourse, *A Discourse Upon Nature and Faculties of Man* (1686, 1697), Thomas Woodcock, *Art of Knowing One-Self or an Enquiry into the Sources of Morality* (1694, 1698), and W. Ayloffe *Government of the Passions* (1700) preceded him in carving out the main premises of his anti-Stoic position.

75. Steele, *Christian Hero*, p. 77.

76. *Ibid.*

77. *Ibid.*

78. *Ibid.*, p. 78.

79. *Ibid.*, p. 9.

80. *Ibid.*, p. 8.

81. For a detailed history of the SRM and their religious campaign for moral reform, see Dudley Bahlman, *The Moral Revolution of 1688* (New Haven, CT, 1957) and Garnet Portus, *Caritas Anglicana Or An Historical Inquiry into those Religious and Philanthropical Societies that flourished in England between the years 1678 and 1740* (London, 1912). More recently scholars have tried to interpret the significance of the Societies in Restoration culture. See T.C. Curtis and W.A. Speck, 'The Societies for the Reformation of Manners: A Case Study in the Theory and Practice of Moral Reform,' *Literature and History* 3 (1976): 45–64; and Robert Shoemaker, 'Reforming the City: The Reformation of Manners Campaign in London, 1690–1738,' in *Stilling the Grumbling Hive: The Response to Social and Economic Problems in England, 1689–1750*, ed. Lee Davison, Tim Hitchcock, Tim Keirn, and Robert Shoemaker (New York, 1992), pp. 99–115.

82. Barker-Benfield, *Culture of Sensibility*, p. 57.

83. Barbara Benedict, *Framing Feeling: Sentiment, and Style in English Prose Fiction, 1745–1800* (New York, 1994), pp. 15–18.

84. Barker-Benfield, *Culture of Sensibility*, pp. 58–62; Benedict, *Framing Feeling*, pp. 23–5.

85. Barker-Benfield, *Culture of Sensibility*, p. 74.

86. Mullan, *Sentiment and Sociability*, chapter 2, especially, pp. 57–62.

87. *Ibid.*, p. 61.

88. *Ibid.*

89. Roulston, *Virtue, Gender, and the Authentic Self*, pp. 12–14.

90. *Ibid.*, chapter 1, especially, pp. 2, 17.

91. Mullan, *Sentiment and Sociability*, p. 83.

92. Samuel Richardson, *Clarissa or, the History of A Young Lady*, ed. Angus Ross, (London, 1985), p. 1019.

93. Roulston, *Virtue, Gender, and the Authentic Self*, p. 67.

94. Richardson, *Clarissa*, p. 1253.

95. For more on rape trials in early modern England, see J.M. Beattie, *Crime and the Courts in England, 1660–1800* (Princeton, 1986), pp. 124–32 and Miranda Chaytor, 'Husband(ry): Narratives of Rape in the Seventeenth Century,' *Gender and History* 7 (1995): 378–407.

96. Richardson, *Clarissa*, pp. 1254–5.
97. Spacks, *Imagining a Self*, p. 12.
98. Johnson, *Rambler*, #70, in *Yale Edition*, vol. 4, p. 5.
99. *Ibid.*, p. 3.
100. *Ibid.*, p. 6.
101. Barker-Benfield's *Culture of Sensibility*, pp. 161–7. My own research verifies the prevalence of these themes in the printed materials circulating in the eighteenth century.
102. Mullan, *Sentiment and Sociability*, p. 61.
103. Matthew Hale, *The History of the Pleas of the Crown*, 2 vols. (London, 1736), 1 : 32.
104. William Blackstone, *Commentaries on the Laws of England*, 4 vols. Vol. 4: *Of Public Wrongs* (1769), Introduction by Thomas A. Green (Chicago, 1979), p. 25.
105. *Ibid.* For more on the legal history of the excuse of drunkenness, see David McCord, 'The English and American History of Voluntary Intoxication to Negate *Mens Rea*,' *Journal of Legal History* 11 (1990): 372–95 and R. U. Singh, 'The History of the Defense of Drunkenness in English Criminal Law,' *Law Quarterly Review* 49 (1933): 528–46.
106. For more on the culture of drinking, see Peter Clark, *The English Alehouse: A Social History 1200–1830* (London, 1983); T.G. Coffey, 'Beer Street: Gin Lane: Some Views of Eighteenth-Century Drinking,' *Quarterly Journal for the Study of Alcoholism* 34 (1966): 662–92. For a discussions of gender and honor in early modern England, see Garthine Walker, *Crime, Gender, and Social Order in Early Modern England* (Cambridge, 2003), esp. pp. 33–9, 230–3.
107. Assizes, Northern Circuit, 1740: Assi 45/21/4/83. Thwaites was found not guilty of felony. Assi 44/55.
108. Hannah Hore, *OBSP*, October 1750, #636. Hore was found guilty and sentenced to transportation; McDaniel was acquitted. Assizes, Northern Circuit, 1752: Assi 44/24/4/98. Assi 44/67. According to the *Oxford English Dictionary* fuddle means 'to drink, liquor, "booze" '; 'to stupefy, muddle, confuse.' One who is fuddled is 'intoxicated; also, muddled.'
109. No verdict was recorded on Richardson's indictment. Assizes, Northern Circuit, 1756: Assi 45/25/4/129. Assi 44/73; Johnson was found guilty and sentenced to death by hanging. Assizes, Northern Circuit, 1768: Assi 45/29/1/88. Assi 44/83.
110. James Cartwright, *OBSP*, July 1772, #520. Cartwright was found guilty and sentenced to transportation.
111. Assizes, Northern Circuit, 1728: Assi 45/18/5/34.
112. This description of drunkenness contrasts sharply with Michael Dalton's in *The Countrey Justice* (London, first edition 1618, 1655 edition used here). Dalton's advice manual for justices of the peace, reprinted throughout the seventeenth and eighteenth centuries, defined someone as drunk when 'the same legs which carry a man into the house cannot carry him out again.' (p. 29).
No indictment survives for the Heavysides case. A missing indictment could indicate loss or damage, or it might suggest that the grand jury did not find sufficient evidence for trial. For more on indictment, see J.H. Baker, 'Criminal Courts and Procedure at Common Law, 1550–1800,' in *Crime in England*, ed. J.S. Cockburn (Princeton, 1977) pp. 18–20; and J.S. Cockburn,

Calendar of Assize Records, Home Circuit Indictments, Elizabeth I and James I. Vol. 1: *Introduction* (London, 1985).

113. Assizes, Northern Circuit, 1756: Assi 45/26/1/153. Wharton was acquitted. Assi 44/72.

114. Assizes, Northern Circuit, 1796: Assi 45/39/1/142. Wardle was found guilty, fined, and imprisoned in the house of correction 'for 12 months or until fine paid.' Assi 44/111.

115. Assizes, Northern Circuit, 1742: Assi 45/22/2/48G.

116. Foster was found not guilty of felony. He was found guilty of misdemeanor and fined 10 shillings. Assizes, Northern Circuit, 1742: Assi 44/57.

117. Assizes, Northern Circuit, 1768: Assi 45/29/1/78C. Heron was found guilty of the reduced charge of simple felony. Assi 44/83.

118. Assizes, Northern Circuit, 1750: Assi 45/24/3/16C. The final outcome of this case is unknown. According to the gaol book, Clark was removed to Wales by a writ of Habeas Corpus. Assi 42/5.

119. John Moer, *OBSP*, January 1716. Moer was acquitted.

120. Assizes, Northern Circuit, 1743: Assi 45/22/4/48B.

121. *Ibid.*

122. No indictment survives for this case. Perhaps the victim decided not to press charges any further because he couldn't be bothered, or maybe he initiated legal proceedings as a means of urging Harwood not to engage in such unlawful behavior in the future. Perhaps Elizabeth and William disagreed about the severity of the crime, or it is possible that the complainant received some compensation from the accused in exchange for dropping the case. Robert Shoemaker discusses how the early stages of the legal process were used to reach negotiated settlements in *Prosecution and Punishment: Petty Crime and the Law in London and Rural Middlesex, 1660–1725* (Cambridge, 1991).

123. For more on character, see J.M. Beattie, 'Crime and the Court in Surrey 1736–1753,' in *Crime in England*, pp. 155–86; Cockburn, *Introduction*; Peter King, 'Decision-Makers and Decision-Making in English Criminal Law, 1750–1800,' *The Historical Journal* 27 (1984): 26–49; idem, *Crime, Justice, and Discretion in England, 1740–1820* (Oxford, 2000).

124. For more on the alehouse, see Clark, *The English Alehouse*. For an overview of English leisure time, see Robert Malcolmson, *Popular Recreations in English Society, 1700–1850* (Cambridge, 1973).

125. Assizes, Northern Circuit, 1758: Assi 45/29/1/42. The final outcome of this case is unknown because no indictment survives, but Coultherd's name was found on a jail delivery list for 1768, ten years after the depositions were taken. Assi 44/83.

126. Assizes, Northern Circuit, 1758: Assi 45/26/2/95G. Purchas survived the attack which probably explains the dismissal of the case. 'Upon consent of the prosecutor, Edward Purchas, and on reading the affidavit of Nathaniel Bayley and Richard Lambert, surgeons, ordered that Ricarby's recognizance to answer be discharged.' Assi 42/7.

127. Cynthia Herrup discusses seventeenth-century appeals to the doctrine of universal human depravity in 'Law and Morality in Seventeenth-Century England,' *Past and Present* 106 (1985): 110–11; idem, *The Common Peace: Participation and the Criminal Law in Seventeenth-Century England* (Cambridge, 1987).

128. Robert Stephenson was found guilty of manslaughter. The depositions are found in Assizes, Northern Circuit, 1737: Assi 45/21/2/53–57; the verdict is

recorded on the indictment found in Assi 44/52. No indictment was found in Downham's case, but the gaol delivery states: 'Joseph Downham, committed the 6th day of October, 1762, for not finding sufficient sureties for his keeping the peace to Alice Downham his wife.' Northern Circuit, 1763: Assi 45/27/1/12.

129. Jonathan White, 'The "Slow but Sure Poyson": The Representation of Gin and its Drinkers, 1736–1751,' *Journal of British Studies* 42 (2003): 35–64. For more on addiction prior to the eighteenth century, see Jessica Warner, 'Resolv'd to drink no more': Addiction as a Preindustrial Construct,' *Journal of Studies on Alcohol* 55 (1994): 685–91. Eighteenth-century addiction is discussed in J. Hirsh, 'Enlightened Eighteenth-Century Views of the Alcohol Problem,' *Journal of the History of Medicine* 4 (1949): 230–6; J.S. Madden, 'Samuel Johnson's Alcohol Problem,' *Medical History* 11 (1967): 141–9; Roy Porter, 'The Drinking Man's Disease: The "Pre-History" of Alcoholism in Georgian Britain,' *British Journal of Addiction* 80 (1985): 385–96; Keith Rix, 'James Boswell (1740–1795) "No Man is more easily hurt with wine than I am",' *Journal of Alcoholism* 10 (1975): 73–7; and idem, 'John Coakley Lettsom and Some Effects of Hard Drinking,' *Journal of Alcoholism* 11 (1976): 98–113.

130. Elizabeth Lawler, *OBSP*, May 1718. Lawler was found guilty to the value of 10d. She was sentenced to transportation for seven years.

131. Nathaniel Parkhurst, *OBSP*, April 1715. The writers of the *OBSP* associated the crime with Packhurst's drinking rather than lunacy. 'It appearing that he had been drinking with company, from four in the afternoon, to the time of the crime committed, the jury brought him in guilty of willful murder and the Statute of Stabbing.' The Statute of Stabbing 1 Jac. 1, c. 8 (1604) made it a capital, non-clergyable offense to 'stab, or thrust, so as the person or persons so stabbed or thrust shall thereof die within … six months then next following, although it cannot be proved that the same was done of malice forethought.' Leon Radzinowicz, *A History of English Criminal Law and its Administration from 1750*, 4 vols. Vol. 1: *The Movement for Reform 1750–1833* (New York, 1948), 1: 630, 695.

132. Sarah Hatchet, *OBSP*, August 1726.

133. *Ibid*. Hatchet was found guilty. According to the OED, Geneva refers to 'a spirit distilled from grain, and flavoured with the juice of juniper berries. In the shortened form gin, the name chiefly denotes a spirit of British manufacture, originally an imitation of the Dutch spirit, and usually flavoured not with juniper but with some substitute, but the words are sometimes used indiscriminately.'

134. William Smithson, *OBSP*, December 1778, #65.

135. *Ibid*.

136. Smithson was found guilty of theft and was sentenced to navigation for three years. Navigation, enforced labor on England's river system, replaced transportation in the years during and after the American Revolution. For more on alternative punishments that developed in response to the suspension of transportation, see Beattie, *Crime and the Courts*, pp. 538–40, 546–8, 560–5. Thomas Erskine revisited the link between physical injury and insanity in his defense of James Hadfield in 1800. Erskine's arguments are the focus of chapter 6 below.

137. For a comprehensive study of the economic realities of early modern life see Keith Wrightson's *Earthly Necessities: Economic Lives in Early Modern Britain* (New Haven, 2000).

138. The *Penitential of Theodore*, 23: 18–19, in *Ancient Laws and Institutes of England*, ed. B. Thorpe (London, 1840), p. 290.

139. Other medieval ecclesiastical texts that discuss the treatment of poverty include The *Confessional and Penitential of Ecgberht*. Legal codes that comment on the legal treatment of poverty include the Laws of King Aethelred, from the tenth century, II Canute from the eleventh century, and the Laws of Henry I from the twelfth century.

140. Britton, *The Pleas of the Crown*, 2 vols., ed. Francis Morgan Nichols (Oxford, 1865), 1 : 42. Britton is a thirteenth-century legal text commissioned by Edward I. Its authorship is contested. Some have attributed it to John le Breton, Bishop of Hereford (d. 1275); Nichols speculates that it was written by a different John le Breton who served as a justice for the county of Norfolk, or an anonymous clerk employed in the legal service of the Crown.

141. The circumstances that legitimated a plea of poverty are clarified in Britton's chapter on larceny. He referred to the poor in relation to 'small thefts, as of sheaves of corn in harvest, or of pigeons or poultry.' In cases of petty larceny Britton recommended that the authorities set the offender's punishment in accordance with the offender's character.

> If the thieves are not found to be otherwise of bad character, and the thing stolen is under the value of twelve pence, they shall be put in the pillory for an hour in the day, and be not admissible to make oath on any jury or inquest, or as witnesses.

However, 'if these petty thieves are persons of bad character, or if they have offended out of mere wickedness, and not through want,' then the rather mild discipline of the pillory was to be replaced with the loss of an ear and the defendants were to 'be rendered infamous for ever.' Britton, *Pleas of the Crown*, vol. 1, p. 61.

142. The case of *Robert Reniger v Anthony Fogossa* came before the Court of Exchequer during the Easter Term, 1550–1551. The case concerned a dispute over the disposal of 1693 kintals of green woad. *Edmund Plowden, English Reports*, vol. 75 (London, 1907), pp. 1–33.

143. *Ibid.*, vol. 75, p. 30.

144. Francis Bacon, *The Elements of the Common Laws of England*, 2 vols. (London, 1630), 1 : 29. Mention of poverty in manuals for justices of the peace can be found in Andrew Horne, *The Mirrour of Justices*, ed. William Robinson (Washington, DC, 1903), p. 212 and Dalton's, *Countrey Justice*, pp. 255–6.

145. Hale, *Pleas of the Crown*, vol. 1, p. 54.

146. Blackstone, *Commentaries*, vol. 4, p. 27. Emphasis in the original. In cases of 'particular hardship' Blackstone allowed that a royal pardon could 'soften the law and ... extend mercy.' *Commentaries*, vol. 4, p. 32.

147. Hale, *Pleas of the Crown*, vol. 1, p. 54; Blackstone, *Commentaries*, vol. 4, p. 32.

148. Thomas Welsh, *OBSP*, January 1746, #40. Welsh was found guilty and sentenced to transportation.

149. William Smith, *OBSP*, September 1750, #501. Smith was found guilty and sentenced to death.

150. Valentine Dudden, *OBSP*, October 1772, #770. Dudden was found guilty and sentenced to transportation.

151. Other defendants addressed only their lack of a criminal intent without mentioning mental compulsion. In May 1719 Mary Time 'pleaded that she did not take them with a felonious intent; but wanting a little money to buy her shoes, offered to pawn the spoon, and designed to redeem it again and

put it in its proper place.' Mary Time, *OBSP*, May 1719. The jury found Time guilty to the value of 10d and sentenced her to transportation. In 1746 Peter Swan confessed to stealing, but said, 'I took these things out of mere necessity, out of no design to wrong her.' Peter Swan, *OBSP*, February 1746, #112. Swan was found guilty and sentenced to transportation for seven years.

152. Assizes, Northern Circuit, 1749: Assi 45/24/2/4. Mary Atkinson was found not guilty. Assizes, Northern Circuit, 1750: Assi 44/64.

153. Assizes, Northern Circuit, 1756: Assi 45/25/4/148D. George Taylor was found not guilty. Assizes, Northern Circuit, 1756: Assi 44/71.

154. These defenses seem to play on the 'preparation defense' usually brought by single women accused of infanticide by implying that poverty prevented this fundamental parental obligation. Infanticide is the subject of chapter 4.

155. Edward Meredith, *OBSP*, May 1751, #387. Meredith stole twelve moidores (Portuguese or Brazilian gold coins), three 36 shilling pieces, and seven guineas.

156. *Ibid.* Meredith was found guilty and sentenced to transportation.

157. Assizes, Northern Circuit, 1758: Assi 45/26/2/73. For more on the relationship between love and insanity, see Michael MacDonald, *Mystical Bedlam: Madness, Anxiety, and Healing in Seventeenth-Century England* (Cambridge, 1981), pp. 88–98.

158. *The Case and Memoirs of the late Reverend Mr. James Hackman, and of his Acquaintance with the late Miss Martha Reay: With a Commentary on his Conviction* (London, 1779), p. 12.

159. *Ibid.*, p. 13. For more on Hackman's case, see John Brewer, *A Sentimental Murder: Love and Madness in the Eighteenth Century* (New York, 2004); and for more on Hackman's case, see Michael MacDonald and Terence R. Murphy, *Sleepless Souls: Suicide in Early Modern England* (Oxford, 1990), pp. 191–2, 194–5.

160. Assizes, Northern Circuit, 1764: Assi 45/27/2/66. The outcome of this case is not known. For a discussion on murder, male honor, and excuse, see Davis, *Fiction in the Archives*, chapter 2 and Walker, *Crime, Gender and Social Order*, pp. 116–38.

161. Richard Grantham, *OBSP*, July 1721. Grantham was found guilty of manslaughter and burned in the hand.

162. John Garton, *OBSP*, September 1722. Garton was acquitted.

163. William Platten, *OBSP*, April 1761, #154. Platten was acquitted.

164. Assizes, Northern Circuit, 1729: Assi 45/18/6/57. Platton was found guilty. Assi 44/47.

165. Assizes, Northern Circuit, 1737: Assi 45/21/2/57.

166. Hale and Blackstone detail various sorts of compulsion that parallel those discussed by defendants. Hale, *Pleas of the Crown*, vol. 1, pp. 42–52 Blackstone, *Commentaries*, vol. 4, pp. 28–31.

167. Richard and Timothy Young, *OBSP*, October 1731. Both men were found guilty of felony and sentenced to transportation.

168. Assizes, Northern Circuit, 1740: Assi 45/21/4/35. The outcome of this case is not known.

169. Ann and Humphrey Jones, *OBSP*, March 1721. Ann was acquitted; Humphrey was found guilty and sentenced to transportation.

170. Ann Dunkerton, *OBSP*, December 1750, #71–#72. Dunkerton was acquitted. Catherine Butler, *OBSP*, April 1751, #347. Butler was acquitted.

171. John Turner, *OBSP*, May 1736, #32–#33. Descriptions of women as sinful temptresses were common in the seventeenth century. For more, see Frances Dolan, *Dangerous Familiars: Representations of Crime in England, 1500–1700* (Ithaca, 1994); and Peter Lake, 'Deeds against Nature: Cheap Print, Protestantism and Murder in Early Seventeenth-Century England,' in *Culture and Politics in Early Stuart England*, eds. Kevin Sharpe and Peter Lake (Palo Alto, CA, 1993), pp. 257–83.

172. Assizes, Northern Circuit, 1733: Assi 45/19/4/22. Pearson was found guilty and sentenced to hang. Assi 44/49.

173. Assizes, Northern Circuit, 1765: Assi 45/28/1/128. Pease is an old spelling for peas or any leguminous plants. Tunstill was found not guilty. Assi 44/80.

174. Mary Pollard, *OBSP*, January 1749, #102. Pollard was found guilty to 39 shillings and transported.

175. Robert Sparrow, *OBSP*, January 1756, #100. Sparrow was found guilty and transported.

176. Simon Devereaux, 'The City and the Sessions Paper: "Public Justice" in London, 1770–1800,' *Journal of British Studies* 35 (1996): 468. This concern for public justice is also reflected in the efforts to compile the complete and accurate state trials.

177. *Ibid.*, pp. 490–501.

178. The literature on domestic service is vast. The presence of domestic servants in the eighteenth-century household is examined in Bridget Hill, *Servants: English Domestics in the Eighteenth Century* (Oxford, 1996); Paula Humfrey, 'Female Servants and Women's Criminality in Early Eighteenth-Century London,' in *Criminal Justice in the Old World and the New: Essays in Honour of J.M. Beattie*, ed. Greg T. Smith, Allyson N. May, and Simon Devereaux et al. (Toronto, 1998), pp. 58–84; D.A. Kent, 'Ubiquitous But Invisible: Female Domestic Servants in Mid Eighteenth-Century London,' *History Workshop Journal* 28 (1989): 111–28; Graham Mayhew, 'Life-cycle Service and the Family Unit in Early Modern Rye,' *Continuity and Change* 6 (1991): 201–26; Tim Meldrum, *Domestic Service and Gender, 1660–1760: Life and Work in the London Household* (New York, 2000); Patty Seleski, 'Women, Work, and Cultural Change in Eighteenth- and Early Nineteenth-Century London,' in *Popular Culture in England, c. 1500–1850*, ed. Tim Harris (New York, 1995), pp. 143–67.

179. Watt, *Rise of the Novel*, p. 175. Watt discusses the expansion of privacy in the domestic sphere on pp. 188–207. For more on privacy, see Patricia Meyer Spacks, *Privacy: Concealing the Eighteenth-Century Self* (Chicago, 2003).

180. Barker-Benfield, *Culture of Sensibility*, pp. 165–8 and Tim Meldrum, 'Domestic Service, Privacy, and the Eighteenth-Century Metropolitan Household,' *Urban History* 26 (1999): 27–31.

4   Bodies of Evidence, States of Mind: Infanticide, Emotion, and Sensibility

1. Mark Jackson, *New-Born Child Murder: Women, Illegitimacy and the Courts in Eighteenth-Century England* (Manchester, 1996), pp. 133–4. Jackson points out that a drop in convictions accompanied a rise in grand jury dismissals of

accused women and findings of natural death or stillbirth by coroner's juries. The term infanticide, is, as Jackson has argued, vague. Almost all of the cases discussed here involved the death of a newborn infant and none refers to the death of a child older than one year of age. The drop in convictions for infanticide is described in J.M. Beattie, *Crime and the Courts in England, 1660–1800* (Princeton, 1986), pp. 113–24; Peter Hoffer and N.E.H. Hull, *Murdering Mothers: Infanticide in England and New England, 1558–1803* (New York, 1981), pp. 65–91; and R.W. Malcolmson, 'Infanticide in the Eighteenth Century,' in *Crime in England 1550–1800*, ed. J.S. Cockburn (London, 1977), pp. 196–8.

2. Beattie, *Crime in the Courts*, pp. 120–4; Jackson, *New-Born Child Murder*, pp. 133–50.

3. 21 Jac. 1, c. 27 reads as follows:
'An act to prevent the destroying and murthering of bastard children.

   Whereas, many lewd women that have been delivered of bastard children, to avoid their shame, and to escape punishment, do secretly bury or conceal the death of their children, and after, if the child be found dead, the said women do alledge that the said child was born dead; whereas it falleth out sometimes (although hardly it is to be proved) that the said child or children were murthered by the said women, their lewd mothers, or by their assent or procurement:

   II. For the preventing therfore of this great mischief, be it enacted by the authority of this present parliament, that if any woman after one month next ensuing the end of this session of parliament be delivered of any issue of her body, male or female, which being born alive, should by the laws of this realm be a bastard, and that she endeavour privately, either by drowning or secret burying thereof, or any other way, either by herself or the procuring of others, so to conceal the death thereof, as that it may not come to light, whether it were born alive or not, but be concealed: in every such case the said mother so offending shall suffer death as in case of murther, except such mother can make proof by one witness at the least, that the child (whose death was by her so intended to be concealed) was born dead.'

4. On single women, see Amy Froide, *Never Married: Singlewomen in Early Modern England* (Oxford, forthcoming); Amy Froide and Judith Bennett, eds., *Singlewomen in the European Past, 1250–1800* (Philadelphia, 1999); Bridget Hill, *Women Alone: Spinsters in England, 1660–1850* (New Haven, 2001); and Olwen Hufton, 'Women Without Men: Widows and Spinsters in Britain and France in the Eighteenth Century,' *Journal of Family History* 9 (1984): 355–76.

5. On the medical presence in the courtroom, see Michael Clark and Catherine Crawford, eds., *Legal Medicine in History* (Cambridge, 1994) and Thomas Forbes, *Surgeons at the Bailey: English Forensic Medicine to 1878* (New Haven, 1985). Mark Jackson examines the growing medical discourse surrounding infanticide in *New-Born Child Murder*, especially pp. 60–110.

6. J.A. Sharpe, *Crime in Early Modern England* (New York, 1999), p. 157.

7. Adela Pinch, *Strange Fits of Passion: Epistemologies of Emotion, Hume to Austen* (Palo Alto, 1996), p. 11.

8. John Barrell, 'Sad Stories: Louis XVI, George III, and the Language of Sentiment,' in *Refiguring Revolutions: Aesthetics and Politics from the English Revolution to the Romantic Revolution*, ed. Kevin Sharpe and Steven N. Zwicker (Berkeley, 1998), p. 75.

9. *Ibid.*, pp. 75–98, especially 76.

10. Married men appeared as a significant but small minority of the defendants in cases of infanticide. Obviously, the explanation for their crimes did not rest on a biological vulnerability to insanity brought on by pregnancy and birth. Instead, an evaluation of intent in these murder trials usually rendered an acquittal: married parents who killed their children were almost always automatically declared insane, their crimes explained as irrational and unintended. For more on men and infanticide, see my article 'Beyond "lewd women" and "wanton wenches": Infanticide and Child Murder in the Long Eighteenth Century,' in *Writing British Infanticide: Child Murder and the Rise of the Novelist*, ed. Jennifer Thorn (Newark, 2003), pp. 45–69.

11. Although the statute forced reason onto single women accused of infanticide, this is not to say that insanity was never associated with single women who killed their infants in the seventeenth century. Garthine Walker points out that in addition to the image of the 'unnatural mother,' accounts of infanticide in the seventeenth century sometimes depicted the mother as a 'victim of feminine frailty.' *Crime, Gender, and Order in Early Modern England* (Cambridge, 2003), pp. 148–9. In 'Infanticide in Earlier Seventeenth-Century England,' *Local Population Studies* 15 (1975): 10–22, Keith Wrightson examines several cases in which the single woman's mental imbalance was taken into account in the legal proceedings.

12. The children of married women were not automatically charged on the parish; married women who had a bastard child were seldom exposed as long as the child had a legal father.

13. Matthew Hale, *History of the Pleas of the Crown*, 2 vols. (London, 1736), 1: 36.

14. *Ibid.*

15. *Ibid.*

16. *Ibid.*

17. Hale's exception, inconsistently applied, reflects the belief in the connection between women's child bearing and insanity. The eighteenth-century trials examined here and in chapter 2 provide a history of the acceptance of this link by the nineteenth century. See Shelley Day, 'Puerperal Insanity: the Historical Sociology of a Disease' (PhD diss., Cambridge University, 1985) and Roger Smith, *Trial by Medicine: Insanity and Responsibility in Victorian Trials* (Edinburgh, 1981), pp. 143–60.

18. Mary Dixon, *OBSP*, July 1735, #108.

19. *Ibid.*

20. *Ibid.*

21. Hale, *Pleas of the Crown*, vol. 1, p. 36.

22. Laura Gowing describes how knowledge about the birthing process was controlled by married women and suggests the impact this had on single women in 'Secret Births and Infanticide in Seventeenth-Century England,' *Past and Present* 156 (1997): 87–115; and in 'Ordering the Body: Illegitimacy and Female Authority in Seventeenth-century England,' in *Negotiating Power in Early Modern Society*, ed. Michael Braddick and John Walter (Cambridge, 2001), pp. 43–62.

23. Beattie, *Crime in the Courts*, pp. 120–4 and Malcolmson 'Infanticide,' pp. 197–8.

24. A biggin is a child's bonnet or head covering. Elizabeth Turner, *OBSP*, June 1734, #21.

25. Jackson, *New-Born Child Murder*, pp. 113–28.
26. William Blackstone, *Commentaries on the Laws of England*: Vol. 4 *Of Public Wrongs* (Chicago, 1979), p. 198. John Beattie argues that a rejection of the 'crudity' of the statute of 1624, its presumption of guilt, and the way the offense was 'formulated and punished' accounted for the drop in the accusation and conviction rate. *Crime and the Courts*, p. 124. Mark Jackson gives a detailed explication of the statute and changing laws of evidence and standards of proof in *New-Born Child Murder*, pp. 145–51.
27. Although the preparation defense was the most common, some women also claimed the child was stillborn or that the child had died during or immediately after birth. These other defenses did not exclude a preparation defense.
28. William Hunter, 'On the Uncertainty of the Signs of Murder, in the Case of Bastard Children,' *Medical Observations and Inquiries* 6 (1784), p. 271.
29. *Ibid.*, p. 268.
30. *Ibid.*, pp. 272–3.
31. *Ibid.*, p. 278.
32. *Ibid.*, p. 279.
33. *Ibid.*, pp. 288–9.
34. Bernard Mandeville (1670–1731) first described the reasons a generally virtuous woman might commit infanticide. *Fable of the Bees: or, Private Vices, Publick Benefits* (1714), 2 vols., ed. F.B. Kaye (Oxford, 1924), 1: 71–6.
35. Hunter, 'On the Uncertainty,' p. 270.
36. *Ibid.*, p. 269.
37. Thomas Laqueur, 'Bodies, Details, and the Humanitarian Narrative,' in *The New Cultural History*, ed. Lynn Hunt (Berkeley, 1989), pp. 176–204.
38. For more on this, see Frances Dolan, *Dangerous Familiars: Representations of Crime in England, 1500–1700* (Ithaca, 1994) and Peter Lake, 'Deeds Against Nature: Cheap Print, Protestantism, and Murder in Seventeenth-Century England,' in *Culture and Politics in Early Stuart England*, ed. Kevin Sharpe and Peter Lake (Stanford, 1993), pp. 264–5.
39. Conviction rates were high in the years immediately after passage of the act of 1624 and even in the late seventeenth and early eighteenth centuries. By the middle of the 1720s, however, Beattie notes 'a striking shift in attitudes' toward the women accused of infanticide. Beattie, *Crime and the Courts*, pp. 118–19, 122. Mark Jackson's findings for the Northern Circuit qualify Beattie's conclusions. Jackson suggests that prosecutions may not have fallen at the same rate all over the country. Jackson's conclusion, based on depositions rather than indictments and trial transcripts, shows that suspicion of the crime persisted throughout the eighteenth century and undermines evidence of public sympathy for those women accused of infanticide. Jackson, *New-Born Child Murder*, pp. 13–14.
40. This study begins in 1714 when the complete set of microfilmed records of the Old Bailey begins; the study ends in 1803 with the repeal of the statute of 1624 under Lord Ellenborough's (1750–1818), *Offences Against the Person Act* (43 Geo. III, c. 58).
41. The number of verdicts is greater than the number of trials because there were several cases with two or more defendants. Of the 20 women found guilty, only one, Ann Terry (1744), was certainly pardoned and transported to the colonies for life. Others may have been pardoned, but this information is not consistently noted in the *OBSP*.

42. The pleas in this sample included any allusion to emotional turmoil that might compromise mental capacity and influence behavior. I considered this language from anyone participating in the courtroom discussion.

43. Mary Radford's trial was the 22nd case of infanticide tried at the Old Bailey between 1714 and 1723. No language of emotion was introduced to excuse the crime and no insanity pleas were made in the first nine years of the sample. The frequency of the language increased thereafter. The second instance of such language of emotion was in Pleasant Bateman's successful use of the insanity defense just a month after Radford's conviction in February 1723.

44. The ninth case that introduced language of emotion before 1745 was Ann Terry's conviction in May 1744. Terry's pardon might be seen to herald a changing reception of the defense of insanity.

45. In light of the increasing acceptance of pleas of the mind in the latter half of the eighteenth century, Jane Cornforth's conviction in 1774 seems strange. But compared to other insanity defenses, it is not surprising that her plea was unsuccessful. Cornforth's insanity was introduced at her trial by Mary Jarvis, the mistress of the workhouse where Jane was brought after the crime was discovered. None of the seven witnesses who appeared on her behalf corroborated Cornforth's insanity. No one made any mention of her mental capacity before, during, or after the crime.

46. The tests for idiocy were set out by Anthony Fitzherbert (1470–1538) in *La Nouvelle Natura Brevium* (London, 1534), 233. b. According to Fitzherbert an idiot would be unable to count to 20, name his parents, or state his own age. 'But if he knows letters, or can read by the instruction of another, then he is no idiot.' For more on the diagnosis and treatment of idiocy in early modern England, see Michael MacDonald, *Mystical Bedlam: Madness, Anxiety, and Healing in Seventeenth-Century England* (Cambridge, 1981); Richard Neugebauer, 'Treatment of the Mentally Ill in Medieval and Early Modern England: A Reappraisal,' *Journal of the History of the Behavioural Sciences* 14 (1978): 158–69; Peter Rushton, 'Lunatics and Idiots: Mental Disability, the Community, and the Poor Law in North-East England, 1600–1800,' *Medical History* 32 (1988): 34–50; and David Wright and Anne Digby, eds., *From Idiocy to Mental Deficiency: Historical Perspectives on People with Learning Disabilities* (New York, 1996).

47. Mary Radford, *OBSP*, January 1723. Radford was sentenced to death.

48. Sarah Allen, *OBSP*, October 1737, #3. Allen was found guilty and sentenced to death.

49. Ann Terry, *OBSP*, May 1744, #251. Ann Terry was found guilty and sentenced to death. She was later pardoned and transported to the colonies.

50. Pleasant Bateman, *OBSP*, February 1723. Bateman was acquitted.

51. Elizabeth Ambrook, *OBSP*, January 1735, #11. Ambrook was found guilty and sentenced to death.

52. Sarah Hunter, *OBSP*, June 1769, #366. Hunter was acquitted.

53. Elizabeth Parkins, *OBSP*, April 1771, #275. Parkins was acquitted. When the court asked the overseer, Thomas Stevenson, if Parkins was 'in her right senses,' he opined, 'I did not think so, I will assure you.'

54. Mary Shrewsbury, *OBSP*, February, 1737, #23. Shrewsbury was found guilty.

55. Isabella Buckham, *OBSP*, December 1755, #33. Buckham was acquitted.

56. Pleasant Bateman, *OBSP*, February 1723.

57. Diana Parker, *OBSP*, September 1794, #505. Parker was acquitted.

58. Hannah Perfect, *OBSP*, February 1747, #129. Perfect was acquitted.
59. Elizabeth Harris, *OBSP*, May 1781, #284. Harris was acquitted.
60. Elizabeth Jarvis, *OBSP*, July 1800, #90. Jarvis was acquitted.
61. Hunter, 'On the Uncertainty,' p. 272.
62. *Ibid.*, p. 273.
63. Smith, *Trial by Medicine*, p. 147.
64. Janet Todd, *Sensibility: An Introduction* (London, 1986), p. 13.
65. Ann Jessie Van Sant, *Eighteenth-Century Sensibility and the Novel: the Senses in Social Context* (Cambridge, 1993), pp. 16–59.
66. This was Lord Ellenborough's bill, which became the *Offenses Against the Person Act* (43 Geo. III, c. 58). This 'Act for the further prevention of malicious shooting, stabbing, cutting, wounding, and poisoning, and also the malicious setting fire to buildings; and also for repealing a certain Act, made in the first year of the late King James the first, intituled, An act to prevent the destroying and murthering of bastard children, and for substituting other provisions in lieu of the same' passed in June 1803. Ellenborough's act claimed to:

   > relieve the judges from the difficulties they labour under in respect to the trial of women indicted for child-murder, in the case of bastards. At present the judges were obliged to strain the law for the sake of lenity, and to admit the slightest suggestion that the child was still-born as evidence of the fact. Upon this point, the law, as it now stands, is so severe in the constructive view towards the mother of a bastard child, supposed to have been murdered after its birth, that in case of such child being found dead, or being made away with, the proof of the mother having previously concealed her pregnancy, is to be taken as sufficient to convict for murder. T.C. Hansard, *The Parliamentary History of England from the Earliest Period to the Year 1803*, 36 Vols. (London, 1820), 36: 1245.

67. The attempts to repeal the statute of 1624 in the 1770s are discussed in Jackson, *New-Born Child Murder*, pp. 158–77.

5 'An indulgence given to great crimes?' Sensibility, Compassion, and Law Reform

1. Peter King, 'Decision-Makers and Decision-Making in English Criminal Law, 1750–1800,' *The Historical Journal* 27 (1984): 26–49; idem, *Crime, Justice, and Discretion in England, 1740–1820* (Oxford, 2000).
2. Assizes, Northern Circuit, 1763: Assi 45/27/1/82. For more on the pre-trial process, see J.M. Beattie, *Crime and the Courts in England 1660-1800* (Princeton, 1986), pp. 267–81; King, *Crime, Justice, and Discretion in England, 1740–1820*, chapters 2–4.
3. The role of the judge in eighteenth-century trials is described in chapter 2.
4. Samuel Prigg, *OBPS*, May 1746, #216.
5. *Ibid.*
6. *Ibid.*
7. *Ibid.* For more on melancholy, see chapter 3.
8. Matthew Hale, *The History of the Pleas of the Crown*, 2 vols. (London, 1736), 1: 30.
9. Hale, *The History of the Pleas of the Crown*, 1: 30.

10. For more on the development of defense counsel, see the discussion in chapter 2 and the works cited there.

11. Thomas Simkins, *OBSP*, October 1751, #607. Simkins was acquitted.

12. Lucy Booth, *OBSP*, October 1751, #610. Booth was found guilty to the value of 10d.

13. Christopher Wade, *OBSP*, December 1755, #52. Wade was convicted and sentenced to death.

14. Daniel Dwite, *OBSP*, February 1756, #165.

15. *Ibid.* Emphasis in the original. Dwite was acquitted.

16. *Ibid.*

17. Thomas Jacocks, *OBSP*, September 1766, #470. Jacocks was found guilty, sentenced to death, and recommended for pardon.

18. *Ibid.*

19. Samuel Toy, *OBSP*, February 1756, case #144. Toy was found guilty to the amount of 10d and sentenced to transportation for seven years.

20. James Aldridge, *OBSP*, December 1765, #18. Aldridge was found guilty and sentenced to death.

21. Peter Deal, *OBSP*, January 1766, #105. Deal was found guilty to the value of 10d and whipped.

22. William Smithson, *OBSP*, December 1778, #65.

23. *Ibid.*

24. *Ibid.* Smithson does not seem to have retained counsel, so I speculate that these questions come from the judge in his capacity as the prisoner's advocate although they could have been asked by the prosecuting attorney.

25. *Ibid.*

26. *Ibid.*

27. *Ibid.* Smithson was found guilty and sentenced to navigation for three years. Navigation, enforced labor on England's river system, replaced transportation in the years during and after the American Revolution.

28. William Blackstone, *Commentaries on the Laws of England*, 4 vols. Vol. 4: *Of Public Wrongs* (1769) (Chicago, 1979), p. 191.

29. Beattie, *Crime and the Courts*, pp. 79–80, 87–9, 91–6.

30. For more on provocation, see Jeremy Horder, *Provocation and Responsibility* (Oxford, 1992); idem, 'Pleading Involuntary Lack of Capacity,' *Cambridge Law Journal* 52 (1993): 298–318.

31. James Mutter, *OBSP*, October 1751, #566. Mutter was found guilty of manslaughter and branded.

32. Antonio de Silva, *OBSP*, May 1761, #183.

33. *Ibid.* De Silva was found guilty of manslaughter.

34. Joseph Brice, *OBSP*, June 1761, case #199.

35. *Ibid.*

36. *Ibid.*

37. The language of the mind in this case reached further than descriptions of the victim and the defendant. Two witnesses explained their inability to give clear and accurate evidence by referring to their 'confusion.' Bower Church said he could not identify the person coming from the crime scene because 'Upon my word, I was in such confusion I do not know whether I went upon my hands or my head; I cannot tell who he was.' Edward Terry told the court

that he could not recollect Jasper's exact words because 'he spoke very low, I was in a confusion, seeing the wound he had received.' In a lengthy exchange the prosecuting attorney pressed Terry for an accurate recollection. Terry reiterated that 'he [Jasper] said something very low, but I being in a confusion, am not perfect in the words.'

38. Ryder presided at the sessions held in October 1754, April 1755, October 1755, and April 1756. His use of shorthand enabled him to record many of the trials' details. Ryder's Notebook and Assize Diary were transcribed from the shorthand by K.L. Perrin. Copies of the transcriptions are in Lincoln's Inn Library and at the University of Chicago Law Library. John Langbein has written extensively about Ryder's Notebook and his Assize Diary. For more on these source, their reliability, and their uses for legal historians, see 'Shaping the Eighteenth-Century Trial: A View from the Ryder Sources,' *University of Chicago Law Review* 50 (1983): 1–136.

39. Notes made by Dudley Ryder on cases at the Old Bailey, 1754–1756 [hereafter Ryder Notebook], p. 11.

40. Ryder Notebook, p. 12.

41. *Ibid.*

42. Ogle was found 'not of sound mind and memory.' Robert Ogle, *OBSP*, June 1756. Ogle's first appearance in April in front of Ryder did not make it into the *OBSP*.

43. Ryder notebook, p. 49. This trial did not make it into the *OBSP*, so it is impossible to compare Ryder's notes with the trial record.

44. Notes made by Dudley Ryder on cases at the Home Circuit assizes, 1754–55 [hereafter Ryder Assize Diary], p. 4.

45. Ryder Assize Diary, p. 4.

46. *Ibid.*

47. *Ibid.*, p. 28. Ryder referred incorrectly to the prisoner's 'disposal' according to 12 Anne, c. 22. It was 13 Anne, 2, c. 23 that allowed two justices of the peace 'to restrain and confine' a lunatic found 'furiously mad' and 'dangerous to be permitted to go abroad.'

48. Peter Duinby, *OBSP*, case #185, April 1755. Duinby was found guilty and sentenced to transportation.

49. Although the transcription of Ryder's notebook by K.L. Perrin reads Quinby and Thomson, the *OBSP* has the defendant's name as Duinby and the witness as Tompson. Ryder Notebook, pp. 27–8.

50. In Lloyd Davys' drunkenness case from October 1754, Ryder stressed a comment by the prosecution's only witness who admitted that 'he was drunk and did not know whether he fell upon the prisoner or the prisoner on him.' Ryder again emphasized the prisoner's comment that both he and the witness 'hand in hand both in liquor fell down together. There were [a] vast number of people passing and re-passing.' Although he made no mention of drunkenness in his notes on the case, Ryder did report telling the jury: 'I thought there was no ground to find him guilty on this single evidence, and the jury found him not guilty.' The presentation of the case ended abruptly when some of the witnesses failed to appear, and Ryder adjourned the trial to the next sessions. Ryder Notebook, pp. 17–18.

51. In 1782 the Southern Department of the Secretary's Office became the Home Department with its own Principal Secretary. The Home Office handled

domestic affairs. Before the establishment of the Home Office, these matters were handled by the State Office, Domestic whose records are found in the State Papers. M.S. Giuseppi, *A Guide to the Manuscripts preserved in the Public Record Office*, 2 vols. (London, 1924), 2: 2, 98, 103. For more on the pardoning process and pardon petitions, see Beattie, *Crime and the Courts*, pp. 430–49; idem, *Policing and Punishment in London, 1660–1750: Urban Crime and the Limits of Terror* (Oxford, 2001), pp. 346–69, 452–6. The Home Office records discussed here are the subject of extensive discussion in King, *Crime, Justice, and Discretion*, pp. 297–333. For more on these sources and an analysis of their relationship to the debate about the capital punishment, see V.A.C. Gatrell, *The Hanging Tree: Execution and the English People, 1770–1868* (Oxford, 1994).

52. Beattie, *Crime and the Courts*, p. 432.
53. James Husband, Reports on Criminals, Correspondence, November 1784: HO 47/3.
54. Decima Chapple, Reports on Criminals, Correspondence, June 1786: HO 47/4.
55. *Ibid.*
56. Amelia Gill, Reports on Criminals, Correspondence, June 1787: HO 47/6.
57. Eleanor Hyde, Reports on Criminals, Correspondence, June 1784: HO 47/3.
58. James Askoe, Reports on Criminals, Correspondence, February 1787: HO 47/6.
59. Samuel Aderton, Reports on Criminals, Correspondence, August 1788: HO 47/7.
60. Susanne Winton, Reports on Criminals, Correspondence, June 1786: HO 47/4.
61. *Ibid.* The judge in James Husband's case described above also noted that there was no 'surmise at the trial of any insanity.'
62. Thomas Davis, Reports on Criminals, Correspondence, June 1787: HO 47/6.
63. Joseph King, Reports on Criminals, Correspondence, March 1788: HO 47/7.
64. John Wood, Reports on Criminals, Correspondence, September 1784: HO 47/3.
65. Thomas Truss, Reports on Criminals, Correspondence, May 1784: HO 47/3.
66. Joseph Smith, Reports on Criminals, Correspondence, June 1788: HO 47/7.
67. William Baker, Reports on Criminals, Correspondence, 1788: HO 47/7.
68. Robert Williams, Reports on Criminals, Correspondence, January–November 1785: HO 47/2.
69. James Oakes, Reports on Criminals, Correspondence, July 1785: HO 47/3.
70. William Smith, Reports on Criminals, Correspondence, 1786, HO 47/5.
71. John Carney, Reports on Criminals, Correspondence, March 1784: HO 47/1. Later in the letter Carney expressed his 'hopes [that] some attention will be paid to his claim for mercy being but young and inexperienced in life.'
72. John Hewitt, Reports on Criminals, Correspondence, November 1784: HO 47/1.
73. John Lenney, Reports on Criminals, Correspondence, August 1784: HO 47/1.
74. Francis Danger, Reports on Criminals, Correspondence, March 1786: HO 47/4. The *Oxford English Dictionary* defines 'distress' as 'the sore pressure or strain of adversity, trouble, sickness, pain, or sorrow: anguish or affliction

affecting the body, spirit, or community.' When used in the plural, distresses refer to 'a sore trouble, a misfortune or calamity that presses hardly.'

75. Francis Coath, Reports on Criminals, Correspondence, April 1786: HO 47/4.
76. Joseph Partridge, Reports on Criminals, Correspondence, 1786: HO 47/5.
77. Peter Ogier, Reports on Criminals, Correspondence, October 1786: HO 47/5. The judge reiterated the assertion common to the testimony recorded in the *OBSP* that the prisoner had 'affirmed that he always intended to redeem the things whenever he could get a little money.' The judge's comment 'that he had actually redeemed and replaced a few articles, the very morning before he was detected' suggests that the judge believed the prisoner and thought this behavior reduced criminal intent.
78. John Smith, Reports on Criminals, Correspondence, January 1787: HO 47/6.
79. Luke Hoyle, Reports on Criminals, Correspondence, 1786: HO 47/5.
80. John Smith, Reports on Criminals, Correspondence, June 1784: HO 47/3.
81. Thomas Bax, Reports on Criminals, Correspondence, March 1786: HO 47/4.
82. The judge's insistence that Bax receive some, albeit mitigated, punishment is consistent with the eighteenth-century judicial trend to impose some penalty on those convicted of manslaughter instead of simply branding them on the hand.
83. William Rose, Reports on Criminals, Correspondence, March 1784: HO 47/1, pp. 69–70. In a similar case from 1786, William Sketley wrote on behalf of Robert Scattergutt explaining that 'it must have been extreme poverty that made him swerve from that line of rectitude' to steal two geese, but that this was an 'offense that arose more from accident, than premeditated intention.' Robert Scattergutt, Reports on Criminals, Correspondence, January 1786: HO 47/5.
84. Ryder Notebook, p. 7
85. *Ibid.*, pp. 18–21.
86. *Ibid.*, p. 21.
87. *Ibid.*, p. 22.
88. Ryder Assize Diary, p. 5.
89. *Ibid.*
90. John Smith, Reports on Criminals, Correspondence, January 1787: HO 47/6.
91. James Askoe, Reports on Criminals, Correspondence, February 1787: HO 47/6.
92. John Jacob, Reports on Criminals, Correspondence, June 1785: HO 47/2.
93. George Owen, Reports on Criminals, Correspondence, January 1785: HO 47/3.
94. Matthew Barker, Reports on Criminals, Correspondence, September 1784: HO 47/1.
95. *Ibid.* Similarly in a letter on behalf of George Owen from 1785, the petitioner apologized for writing a second letter explaining, 'my compassion is so strongly excited by his wretched family.' George Owen, Reports on Criminals, Correspondence, January 1785: HO 47/3.
96. *Ibid.*
97. Thomas Davis, Reports on Criminals, Correspondence, October 1787: HO 47/6. In a similar case Abraham Sanguinete petitioned for pardon because 'he has the misfortune by times of being insane occasioned from a violent fever.' The judge who presided at his trial in Cambridge in 1788 urged, 'I should be much concerned to discourage any sentiments of mercy that his majesty may

be inclined to entertain for him.' Abraham Sanguinete, Reports on Criminals, Correspondence, July 1788: HO 47/7.

98. Henry Fielding, *An Enquiry into the Causes of the late Increase of Robbers* (1751), in *An Enquiry into the Causes of the late Increase of Robbers and Related Writings*, ed. Malvin Zirker (New York, 1988), p. 154.

99. For more on changes in early modern methods of punishment, see Michel Foucault, *Discipline and Punish: The Birth of the Prison*, translated by Alan Sheridan (New York, 1977). Michael Ignatieff applies Foucault's theories to his study of the history and development of solitary confinement and its ultimate failure in *A Just Measure of Pain: The Penitentiary in the Industrial Revolution, 1750–1850* (New York, 1978). For a qualification of Ignatieff's approach, see Margaret DeLacy, *Prison Reform in Lancashire, 1700–1850* (Palo Alto, 1986). In *The Fabrication of Virtue, English Prison Architecture, 1750–1840* (Cambridge, 1982) Robin Evans relates the debates about prison reform to the architecture of the prison. His book includes a discussion of the forces of rehabilitation believed to be unleashed by isolation.

100. Samuel Johnson, *Rambler*, #70, Saturday, 17 November 1750, in *The Yale Edition of the Works of Samuel Johnson*, 16 vols. Vol. 4: *The Rambler*, ed. W. J. Bates and Albrecht B. Strauss (New Haven, 1969), p. 5.

101. *Ibid.*, p. 6.

102. *Ibid.*, pp. 5–6.

103. Johnson, *Rambler* #110, Saturday, 6 April 1751, in *Yale Edition*, ed. Bates and Strauss, vol. 4, pp. 224–5.

104. Several English writers, including Thomas Bray and Bernard Mandeville, had called for the separation of prisoners in the early eighteenth century. Ignatieff, *A Just Measure*, pp. 52–4.

105. Beattie, *Crime and the Courts*, pp. 569–76; Ignatieff, *A Just Measure*, chapters 3 and 4; Evans, chapter 4.

106. Manasseh Dawes, *An Essay on Crimes and Punishments with a View of, and Commentary upon Beccaria, Rousseau, Voltaire, Montesquieu, Fielding and Blackstone* (London, 1782), p. 5.

107. *Ibid.*, p. 67.

108. William Paley, *Principles of Moral and Political Philosophy* (London, 1785), p. 409.

109. For more about Hanway, see Stephen James Taylor, *Jonas Hanway: Founder of the Marine Society: Charity and Policy in Eighteenth-century Britain* (London, 1985).

110. Jonas Hanway, *Solitude in Imprisonment* (London, 1776), p. 4. All emphasis in the original.

111. *Ibid.*, pp. 75, 100.

112. *Ibid.*, p. 38.

113. *Ibid.*, p. 27.

114. *Ibid.*, p. 50

115. *Ibid.*, p. 52.

116. *Ibid.*, p. 102.

117. *Ibid.*, p. 142.

118. *Ibid.*

119. Hanway, *Solitude in Imprisonment*, p. 105.

120. *Ibid.*, p. 88.

121. *Ibid.*, pp. 74, 44.
122. *Ibid.*, p. 42. In the *OED* affliction is 'the action of inflicting grievous pain or trouble.'
123. *Ibid.*, p. 109.
124. *Ibid.*, p. 103.
125. *Ibid.*, p. 107.
126. *Ibid.*, p. 32.
127. John Brewster, *On the Prevention of Crimes, and on the Advantages of Solitary Imprisonment* (London, 1792), p. 4.
128. *Ibid.*, pp. 7, 26.
129. *Ibid.*, p. 15.
130. *Ibid.*, p. 16.
131. *Ibid.*, p. 17.
132. *Ibid.*, p. 27, emphasis in the original.
133. *Ibid.*
134. *Ibid.*, p. 28.
135. William Godwin, *Enquiry Concerning Political Justice and its Influence on Morals and Happiness*, 3 volumes (1798), ed. F.E.L. Priestly (Toronto, 1946) 2: 386–7. Evans summarizes the debates about solitary confinement in *Fabrication of Virtue*, pp. 67–76 and 187–92.
136. Josiah Dornford, *Nine Letters ... on the state of the city prisons and prisoners ...* (London, 1786), p. 35.
137. For more on the implementation of and retreat from solitary confinement, see Delacy, *Prison Reform*, Evans, *Fabrication of Virtue*, and Ignatieff, *A Just Measure.*
138. Brewster, *Prevention of Crimes*, p. 27
139. *Ibid.*, p. 11.

6 The End of Excuse? James Hadfield and the Insanity Plea

1. John Barrell, *Imagining the King's Death: Figurative Treason, Fantasies of Regicide, 1793–1796* (Oxford, 2000); idem, 'Imagining the King's Death: The Arrest of Richard Brothers,' *History Workshop* 37 (1994): 1–32; idem, 'Imaginary Treason, Imaginary Law: the State Trials of 1794,' in *The Birth of Pandora and the Division of Knowledge*, ed. John Barrell (Philadelphia, 1992), pp. 119–44; idem, 'Sad Stories: Louis XVI, George III, and the Language of Sentiment,' in *Refiguring Revolutions: Aesthetics and Politics from the English Revolution to the Romantic Revolution*, ed. Kevin Sharpe and Steven N. Zwicker (Berkeley, 1998), pp. 75–98; and F.K. Prochaska, 'English State Trials in the 1790's: A Case Study,' *Journal of British Studies* 13 (1973): 63–82.
2. Richard Moran has done the most detailed scholarship on the Hadfield case in 'The Origin of Insanity as a Special Verdict: The Trial for Treason of James Hadfield (1800),' *Law and Society Review* 19 (1985): 487–519; idem, 'The Modern Foundation for the Insanity Defense: The Cases of James Hadfield (1800) and Daniel McNaughten (1843),' *The Annals of the American Academy of Political and Social Science* 477 (1985): 31–42.

3. Joel Eigen, *Witnessing Insanity: Madness and Mad-Doctors in the English Court* (New Haven, 1995); Roger Smith, *Trial by Medicine: Insanity and Responsibility in Victorian Trials* (Edinburgh, 1981); and Nigel Walker, *Crime and Insanity in England*, 2 vols. Vol. 1: *The Historical Perspective* (Edinburgh, 1967).
4. Moran, 'The Origin of Insanity,' and idem, 'The Modern Foundation.' Others who have written about the case include Alan Dershowitz, 'The Origins of Preventive Confinement in Anglo-American Law – Part I: The English Experience,' *University of Cincinnati Law Review* 43 (1974): 1–60; Ida Macalpine and Richard Hunter, *George III and the Mad-Business* (New York, 1969); idem, *Three Hundred Years of Psychiatry: A History Presented in Selected English Texts* (Oxford, 1963); and J.M. Quen, 'James Hadfield and Medical Jurisprudence of Insanity,' *New York State Journal of Medicine* 69 (1969): 1221–6.
5. Moran, 'The Origin of Insanity,' p. 517.
6. My interpretation of the Hadfield trial takes inspiration from an unpublished paper by Scott Brophy (Philosophy, Hobart and William Smith Colleges) presented at the University of Miami's Annual Interdisciplinary Symposium in Medieval, Renaissance, and Baroque Studies in February 1993. Brophy's paper, 'Changing Conceptions of Insanity in the Anglo-American Legal Tradition,' asserted that the Hadfield case foreshadowed many of the M'Naughten Rules and limited the kind of exculpatory evidence that could be presented at trial.
7. *Bells Weekly Messenger*, May 18, 1800, p. 158.
8. *Ibid.*
9. *Ibid.* The campaign in Flanders (1793–1795) was part of the Austrian-Netherlands campaigns. It was launched in response to a French attack from the direction of Antwerp. The Duke of York, George III's second son, was appointed to command the force of 6,500 men in February 1793. The campaign was a failure until Austrian troops attacked the French in March. The Battle at Lincelles was fought on August 18, 1793 five miles from Lisle as the British troops made their way to Dunkirk. The troops were unprepared, the army was not supplied with the appropriate ammunition, and the insistence on Dunkirk and the defense of the straits of Dover undermined British cooperation with their allies.
10. *Ibid.* Hadfield's explanation for his crime as a means of hastening his own death is revealing. Although this kind of explanation recurs in the legal record, it has not yet been the focus of a detailed study.
11. Part of the Republican movement and inspired by the French Revolution, the London Corresponding Society (LCS) formed in 1792 to campaign for English parliamentary reform. Its members called themselves corresponding because it was illegal to form a national organization. The government responded to the LCS with harsh oppressive measures. Although the LCS was eventually driven underground, it was with it that the political tradition of working-class organization was born. The Independent Order of Odd Fellows was a fraternal and benevolent secret society that originated in England in the eighteenth century. Some Odd Fellow lodges moved towards a working-class membership and may have formed the basis on which the later benefit societies were founded. Benefit societies were co-operative associations in which the members, by the regular payment of dues, became entitled to

financial aid in case of illness, old age, or injury. Life insurance and burial expenses were sometimes provided.

12. *Bells Weekly Messenger*, May 18, 1800, p. 158.
13. *Ibid.*
14. *Ibid.*
15. The others present were the Earl of Chatham, Prime Minister William Pitt, the speaker of the House of Commons, the attorney general and solicitor general, and two barristers, Messrs. King and Ford.
16. *Bell's Weekly Messenger*, May 18, 1800, p. 159.
17. *Ibid.*
18. *Ibid.*, p. 158.
19. *London Times*, May 17, 1800, p. 3 and *Morning Post and Gazetteer*, May 16, 1800, p. 2.
20. *Morning Post and Gazetteer*, June 19, 1800, p. 4. After a career at sea, Thomas Erskine returned to England and read for the bar. He became a prominent barrister, a member of parliament, and eventually, lord chancellor. Serjeant Best later became a judge in King's Bench.
21. Mitford, a barrister of the Inner Temple, wrote *A Treatise on the Pleadings in Suits in the Court of Chancery by English Bill*, which was reprinted several times in England and America. Mitford became a member of parliament in 1788, solicitor general for England in 1793, and attorney general in 1799. In February 1801 Sir John Mitford was chosen speaker of the House of Commons, and a year later was appointed lord chancellor of Ireland and was made a peer of the United Kingdom as Baron Redesdale.
22. T.B. Howell, ed., *A Complete Collection of State Trials and Proceedings for High Treason and Other Crimes and Misdemeanors*, 34 vols. (London, 1820), 27: 1284.
23. *Ibid.*
24. *Ibid.*, 1285, 1292.
25. *Ibid.*, 1292.
26. *Ibid.*, 1287.
27. *Ibid.*, 1286.
28. *Ibid.*, 1288.
29. *Ibid.*
30. *Ibid.*, 1286.
31. *Ibid.*, 1287.
32. *Ibid.*
33. Edward Arnold's unsuccessful attempt to murder Lord Onslow in 1723 resulted in his conviction in 1724. Arnold's insanity plea failed, but thanks to a reprieve, arranged for him by Onslow, he spent the next 30 years of his life in the gaol at Southwark.
34. Howell, ed., *State Trials*, vol. 27, 1289.
35. *Ibid.*
36. *Ibid.*, 1290.
37. *Ibid.*
38. *Ibid.*, 1291.
39. Howell, ed., *State Trials*, vol. 27, 1292.
40. *Ibid.*
41. *Ibid.*, 1290.

42. *Ibid.*, 1294, 1297.
43. *Ibid.*, 1294.
44. *Ibid.*, 1296.
45. *Ibid.*, 1301.
46. *Ibid.*, 1304–5.
47. *Ibid.*, 1308, 1309. The treatment of suspects indicted for treason was dictated by the Treason Act of 1696 (7–8 William III, c. 3).
48. *Ibid.*, 1309.
49. *Ibid.*, 1310.
50. *Ibid.*, 1311–12.
51. *Ibid.*, 1312, 1313.
52. Like Shaftesbury's correctrice, cited in chapter 3, reason is gendered female.
53. *Ibid.*, 1313.
54. *Ibid.*, 1313–14.
55. *Ibid.*, 1314–15. For this reason Erskine dismissed Lord Ferrers' claim to insanity because 'I cannot allow the protection of insanity to a man who only exhibits violent passions and malignant resentments, *acting upon real circumstances*; who is impelled to evil from no morbid delusions.'
56. *Ibid.*, 1317.
57. *Ibid.*, 1319.
58. *Ibid.*, 1314.
59. *Ibid.*, 1319.
60. *Ibid.*, 1320–1.
61. *Ibid.*, 1321.
62. *Ibid.*, 1322.
63. *Ibid.*, 1325.
64. *Ibid.*, 1328.
65. *Ibid.*, 1329.
66. *Ibid.*, 1331.
67. *Ibid.*, 1334. Alexander Crichton, the author of the *Inquiry into the Nature and Origin of Mental Derangement* (London, 1798), later became a physician to Tsar Alexander I and headed the civil medical department in Russia.
68. *Ibid.*, 1353.
69. *Ibid.*, 1356. William Garrow served on the team that prosecuted Hadfield, but in the Old Bailey trials he often acted as defense counsel, presenting an insanity defense. Besides his work as a lawyer, Garrow also served as a judge, attorney general, and baron of the exchequer. David Lemmings reconstructs Garrow's career in *Professors of the Law: Barristers and English Legal Culture in the Eighteenth Century* (Oxford, 2000). Allyson May examines his work at the Old Bailey in *The Bar and the Old Bailey, 1750–1850* (Chapel Hill, 2003).
70. *Ibid.*
71. The debate of these bills took place on June 30 and July 11, 1800. For a full text, see *Parliamentary History*, vol. 35, pp. 389–93.
72. William Cobbett, *The Parliamentary History of England from the earliest period to the year 1803*, 36 vols. (London, 1820), 35: 390.
73. *Parliamentary History*, vol. 35, p. 392.
74. *Parliamentary History*, vol. 35, p. 392.
75. *Ibid.*, p. 393.

76. Moran, 'The Origin of Insanity,' p. 516. In 1802 Hadfield was accused of murdering a fellow patient, Benjamin Swain, by knocking him on the head. Hadfield was cleared of the charges. Hadfield escaped from Bethlem with another patient, John Dunlop, in 1804. They were captured in Dover waiting to cross the channel into France.
77. Howell, ed., *State Trials*, vol. 27, pp. 1312–13.
78. *Ibid.*, 1313.
79. *Ibid.*
80. Francis Parr, *OBSP*, January 1787, #158, p. 228.
81. Howell, ed., *State Trials*, vol. 27, 1290.
82. John Simpson, *OBSP*, April 1786, #360, p. 600.
83. William Edwards, *OBSP*, October 1784, #943, p. 1259.
84. Richard Crutcher, *OBSP*, September 1797, #542, p. 532.
85. Henry Piers, *OBSP*, April 1800, #315, p. 279.
86. Francis Parr, *OBSP*, January 1787, #158, p. 228.
87. *Ibid.*
88. The Scottish plea of diminished responsibility provided an alternative to the uneven development of the insanity defense in England. For more on this topic, see R.A. Houston, *Madness and Society in Eighteenth-Century Scotland* (Oxford, 2000); and Walker, *Crime and Insanity*.
89. Quen, 'James Hadfield and Medical Jurisprudence,' pp. 1221–6.
90. Matthew Hale, *The History of the Pleas of the Crown*, 2 vols. (London, 1736), 1: 30.
91. Francis Parr, *OBSP*, January 1787, #158, p. 228.
92. John Simpson, *OBPS*, April 1786, #360, p. 601.
93. Howell, ed., *State Trials*, vol. 27, 1356.
94. Karen Halttunen, *Murder Most Foul: The Killer and the American Gothic Imagination* (Cambridge, MA, 1998), pp. 214–40.
95. For the former interpretation, see Eigen, *Witnessing Insanity*; Smith, *Trial by Medicine*; and Walker, *Crime and Insanity*. For the latter, see Moran, 'The Origin of Insanity,' and idem, 'The Modern Foundation.'

7   From Self to Subject

1. John Langbein, *The Origins of Adversary Criminal Trial* (Oxford, 2003), pp. 20–1.
2. J.M. Beattie, *Crime and the Courts in England, 1660–1800* (Princeton, 1986), pp. 350–2; and Langbein, *Origins*, pp. 50–1.
3. J.A. Sharpe, ' "Last Dying Speeches": Religion, Ideology, and Public Execution in Seventeenth-Century England,' *Past and Present* 107 (1985): 144–67.
4. Samuel Prigg, *OBSP*, May 1746, #216.
5. Charles Taylor, *Sources of the Self: The Making of the Modern Identity* (Cambridge, 1989), p. 3.
6. Joel Eigen, Witnessing *Insanity: Madness and Mad-Doctors in the English Court* (New Haven, 1995); and Martin Weiner, *Reconstructing the Criminal: Culture, Law and Policy in England, 1830–1914* (Cambridge, 1990).
7. Karen Halttunen, *Murder Most Foul: the Killer and the American Gothic Imagination* (Cambridge, MA, 1998); Michel Foucault, *Discipline and Punish:*

The Birth of the Prison, translated by Alan Sheridan (New York, 1977); and Wiener, *Reconstructing the Criminal: Culture, Law, and Policy in England*.

8. Dror Wahrman's work, based on literary sources that represent mostly middling and elite notions of self and identity, argues that during the eighteenth-century a 'crisis of confidence in categories of difference' contributed to a 're-anchoring of notions of identity in what may be seen as more 'modern' essentializing foundations.' See his 'The English Problem with Identity in the American Revolution,' *American Historical Review* 106 (2001): 1236–62; idem, 'Gender in Translation: How the English Wrote Their *Juvenal*, 1644–1815,' *Representations* 65 (1999): 1–41; idem, 'On Queen Bees and Being Queens: A Late-Eighteenth-Century "Cultural Revolution"?' in *The Age of Cultural Revolutions: Britain and France, 1750–1820* (Berkeley, 2002), pp. 251–80; and his *The Invention of the Modern Self* (New Haven, 2004).

9. Judith Walkowitz, *Prostitution and Victorian Society: Women, Class, and the State* (Cambridge, 1980); and Wiener, *Reconstructing the Criminal*.

10. Jonas Hanway, *Solitude in Imprisonment* (London, 1776), pp. 4, 75.

11. For more on the colonial subject, see Antoinette Burton, *At the Heart of Empire: Indians and the Colonial Encounter in Late-Victorian Britain* (Berkeley, 1998); idem, *Burdens of History: British Feminists, Indian Women and Imperial Culture, 1865–1915* (Chapel Hill, NC, 1994); idem, *Gender, Sexuality, and Colonial Modernities* (New York, 1999); Mrinalini Sinha, *Colonial Masculinity: The 'Manly Englishman' and the 'Effeminate Bengali' in the Late Nineteenth Century* (Manchester, 1995); and Ann Stoler, *Carnal Knowledge and Imperial Power: Race and the Intimate in Colonial Rule* (Berkeley, 2002).

Selected Bibliography

Alderman, William. 'Shaftesbury and the Doctrine on Benevolence in the Eighteenth Century.' *Transactions of the Wisconsin Academy of Sciences, Arts and Letters* 26 (1931): 137–59.

Alderman, William. 'Shaftesbury and the Doctrine of Moral Sense.' *PMLA* 46 (1931): 1087–94.

Alschuler, A.W. 'Plea Bargaining and its History.' *Columbia Law Review* 79 (1979): 1–43.

Amussen, Susan D. ' "The part of a Christian man": The Cultural Politics of Manhood in Early Modern England.' In *Political Culture and Cultural Politics in Early Modern England: Essays Presented to David Underdown*, ed. Susan D. Amussen and Mark A. Kishlansky. Manchester, 1995, pp. 213–33.

Andrew, Donna T. *Philanthropy and Police: London Charity in the Eighteenth Century*. Princeton, 1989.

Andrews, Jonathan and Andrew Scull. *Customers and Patrons of the Mad-Trade: The Management of Lunacy in Eighteenth-Century London*. Berkeley, 2003.

Andrews, Jonathan and Andrew Scull. *Undertaker of the Mind: John Monro and Mad-Doctoring in Eighteenth-Century England*. Berkeley, 2001.

Andrews, Jonathan, Asa Briggs, Roy Porter, Penny Tucker, and Keir Waddington. *The History of Bethlem*. London, 1997.

Armstrong, Nancy. *Desire and Domestic Fiction: A Political History of the Novel*. Oxford, 1987.

Arnold, John H. 'The Historian as Inquisitor: The Ethics of Interrogating Subaltern Voices.' *Rethinking History* 2, 3 (1998): 379–86.

Bahlman, Dudley. *The Moral Revolution of 1688*. New Haven, 1957.

Baker, J.H. *Legal Records and the Historian*. London, 1978.

Barker-Benfield, G.J. *The Culture of Sensibility: Sex and Society in Eighteenth-Century Britain*. Chicago, 1992.

Barrell, John. 'Imaginary Treason, Imaginary Law: The State Trials of 1794.' In *The Birth of Pandora and the Division of Knowledge*, ed. John Barrell. Philadelphia, 1992, pp. 119–44.

Barrell, John. 'Imagining the King's Death: The Arrest of Richard Brothers.' *History Workshop* 37 (1994): 1–32.

Barrell, John. *Imagining the King's Death: Figurative Treason, Fantasies of Regicide, 1793–1796*. Oxford, 2000.

Barrell, John. 'Sad Stories: Louis XVI, George III, and the Language of Sentiment.' In *Refiguring Revolutions: Aesthetics and Politics from the English Revolution to the Romantic Revolution*, ed. Kevin Sharpe and Steven N. Zwicker. Berkeley, 1998, pp. 75–98.

Barry, Jonathan. 'Literacy and Literature in Popular Culture: Reading and Writing in Historical Perspective.' in *Popular Culture in England, c. 1500–1850*, ed. Tim Harris. New York, 1995, pp. 69–94.

Beattie, J.M. 'The Cabinet and the Management of Death at Tyburn after the Revolution of 1688–1689.' In *The Revolution of 1688–1689: Changing Perspectives*, ed. Lois Schwoerer. Cambridge, 1992, pp. 218–33.

Beattie, J.M. *Crime and the Courts in England, 1660–1800*. Princeton, 1986.

Beattie, J.M. *Policing and Punishment in London, 1660–1750: Urban Crime and the Limits of Terror*. Oxford, 2001.

Beattie, J.M. 'Scales of Justice: Defense Counsel and the English Criminal Trial in the Eighteenth and Nineteenth Centuries.' *Law and History Review* 9 (1991): 221–67.

Beier, A.L. *Masterless Men: The Vagrancy Problem in England 1560–1640*. London, 1985.

Bell, Ian A. *Literature and Crime in Augustan England*. London, 1991.

Bender, John. *Imagining the Penitentiary: Fiction and the Architecture of the Mind in Eighteenth-Century England*. Chicago, 1987.

Benedict, Barbara. *Framing Feeling: Sentiment, and Style in English Prose Fiction, 1745–1800*. New York, 1994.

Brewer, John. *A Sentimental Murder: Love and Madness in the Eighteenth Century*. New York, 2004.

Brewer, John. *The Pleasures of the Imagination: English Culture in the Eighteenth Century*. New York, 1997.

Brewer, John and John Styles, eds. *An Ungovernable People? The English and their Law in the Seventeenth and Eighteenth Centuries*. London, 1980.

Brissenden, R.F. *Virtue in Distress: Studies in the Novel of Sentiment from Richardson to Sade*. New York, 1974.

Brock, Helen. 'The Many Facets of Dr. William Hunter (1718–1783).' *History of Science* 23 (1994): 387–408.

Brooks, Peter and Paul Gewirtz, eds. *Law's Stories: Narrative and Rhetoric in the Law*. New Haven, 1996.

Bryson, Anna. *From Courtesy to Civility: Changing Codes of Conduct in Early Modern England*. Oxford, 1998.

Bryson, Gladys. *Man and Society: The Scottish Inquiry of the Eighteenth Century*. Princeton, 1945.

Burton, Antoinette. Introduction to *Gender, Sexuality, and Colonial Modernities*, ed. Antoinette Burton. New York, 1999, pp. 1–16.

Bynum, W.F. and Roy Porter, eds. *William Hunter and the Eighteenth-Century Medical World*. Cambridge, 1985.

Campbell, R.H. and Andrew S. Skinner, eds. *The Origins and Nature of the Scottish Enlightenment*. Edinburgh, 1982.

Capp, Bernard. *Astrology and the Popular Press: English Almanacs, 1500–1800*. London, 1979.

Capp, Bernard. 'Popular Literature.' In *Popular Culture in Seventeenth-Century England*, ed. Barry Reay. London, 1985, pp. 198–243.

Chaytor, Miranda. 'Husband(ry): Narratives of Rape in the Seventeenth Century.' *Gender and History* 7 (1995): 378–407.

Clark, Michael and Catherine Crawford, eds. *Legal Medicine in History*. Cambridge, 1994.

Clark, Peter. *The English Alehouse: A Social History 1200–1830*. London, 1983.

Cockburn, J.S. *Calendar of Assize Records, Home Circuit Indictments, Elizabeth I and James I. Introduction*. London, 1985.

Cockburn, J.S. 'Early Modern Assize Records as Historical Evidence.' *The Journal of the Society of Archivists* 5 (1975): 215–31.

Cockburn, J.S. *A History of English Assizes from 1558 to 1714*. Cambridge, 1972.

Cockburn, J.S. 'The Northern Assize Circuit.' *Northern History* 3 (1968): 118–30.

Cockburn, J.S. 'Seventeenth-Century Clerks of Assize-Some Anonymous Members of the Legal Profession.' *American Journal of Legal History* 13 (1969): 315–32.

Cockburn, J.S. 'Trial by the Book? Fact and Theory in the Criminal Process, 1558–1625.' In *Legal Records and the Historian*, ed. J.H. Baker. London, 1978, pp. 60–79.

Cockburn, J.S., ed. *Crime in England, 1550–1800*. Princeton, 1977.

Cockburn, J.S. and Thomas A. Green, eds. *Twelve Good Men and True: The Criminal Trial Jury in England, 1200–1800*. Princeton, 1988.

Coffey, T.G. 'Beer Street, Gin Lane: Some Views of Eighteenth-Century Drinking.' *Quarterly Journal for the Study of Alcoholism* 34 (1966): 662–92.

Collinson, Patrick. *The Religion of the Puritans*. Oxford, 1982.

Collinson, Robert. *The Story of Street Literature: Forerunner of the Popular Press*. London, 1973.

Cox, Stephen. *'The Stranger Within Thee': Concepts of the Self in Late-Eighteenth Century Literature*. Pittsburgh, 1980.

Crane, R.S. 'Suggestions Towards a Genealogy of the "Man of Feeling." ' *English Literary History* 1 (1934): 205–30.

Cressy, David. *Literacy and the Social Order: Reading and Writing in Tudor and Stuart England*. Cambridge, 1980.

Cressy, David. 'Literacy in Context: Meaning and Measurement in Early Modern England.' In *Consumption and the World of Goods*, ed. John Brewer and Roy Porter. London, 1993, pp. 305–19.

Curtis, T.C. and W.A. Speck. 'The Societies for the Reformation of Manners: A Case Study in the Theory and Practice of Moral Reform.' *Literature and History* 3 (1976): 45–64.

Daiches, David, Peter Jones, and Jean Jones, eds. *A Hotbed of Genius: The Scottish Enlightenment, 1730–1790*. Edinburgh, 1982.

Damrosch, Leo. *Sorrows of the Quaker Jesus: James Naylor and the Puritan Crackdown on the Free Spirit*. Cambridge, MA, 1996.

Davis, Natalie. *Fiction in the Archives: Pardon Tales and Their Tellers in Sixteenth-Century France*. Palo Alto, 1987.

Day, Shelley. 'Puerperal Insanity: The Historical Sociology of a Disease.' PhD diss., Cambridge University, 1985.

DeLacy, Margaret. *Prison Reform in Lancashire, 1700–1850*. Palo Alto, 1986.

Dershowitz, Alan. 'The Origins of Preventive Confinement in Anglo-American Law – Part I: The English Experience.' *University of Cincinnati Law Review* 43 (1974): 1–60.

Devereaux, Simon. 'The City and the Sessions Paper: 'Public Justice' in London, 1770–1800.' *Journal of British Studies* 35 (1996): 466–503.

Dolan, Frances E. *Dangerous Familiars: Representations of Crime in England, 1500–1700*. Ithaca, 1994.

Dolan, Frances E. "Gentlemen, I Have One Thing More to Say": Women on Scaffolds in England, 1563–1680.' *Modern Philology: A Journal Devoted to Research in Medieval and Modern Literature* 92, 2 (1994): 157–78.

Donagan, Barbara. 'Godly Choice: Puritan Decision Making in Seventeenth-Century England.' *Harvard Theological Review* 76 (1983): 307–34.

Donagan, Barbara. 'Providence, Chance, and Explanation: Some Paradoxical Aspects of Puritan Views of Causation.' *Journal of Religious History* 11 (1981): 385–403.

Donagan, Barbara. 'Understanding Providence: The Difficulties of Sir William and Lady Waller.' *Journal of Ecclesiastical History* 39 (1988): 433–44.

Duden, Barbara. *Disembodying Women: Perspectives on Pregnancy and the Unborn.* Translated by Lee Hoinacki. Cambridge, MA, 1993.

Dwyer, John. *Virtuous Discourse: Sensibility and Community in Late Eighteenth-Century Scotland.* Edinburgh, 1987.

Eigen, Joel. 'Delusion in the Courtroom: The Role of Partial Insanity in Early Forensic Testimony.' *Medical History* 35 (1991): 25–49.

Eigen, Joel. ' "I Answer as a Physician": The Assertion of Opinion over Fact in Pre-McNaughtan Insanity Trials.' In *Legal Medicine in History*, ed. Catherine Crawford and Michael Clark. Cambridge, 1994, pp. 167–99.

Eigen, Joel. 'Intentionality and Insanity: What the Eighteenth-Century Juror Heard.' In *The Anatomy of Madness: Essays in the History of Psychiatry.* 3 vols. Vol. 2: *Institutions and Society*, ed. William Bynum, Roy Porter, and Michael Shepherd. London, 1985, pp. 34–51.

Eigen, Joel. *Witnessing Insanity: Madness and Mad-Doctors in the English Court.* New Haven, 1995.

Evans, Robin. *The Fabrication of Virtue: English Prison Architecture, 1750–1840.* Cambridge, 1982.

Ewick, Patricia and Susan Silbey, eds. *The Common Place of Law: Stories from Everyday Life.* Chicago, 1998.

Faller, Lincoln B. *Crime and Defoe: A New Kind of Writing.* Cambridge, 1993.

Faller, Lincoln B. *Turned to Account: The Forms and Functions of Criminal Biography in Late Seventeenth- and Early Eighteenth-Century England.* Cambridge, 1987.

Farber, Daniel and Suzanna Sherry. 'Telling Stories Out of School: An Essay on Legal Narratives.' *Stanford Law Review* 65 (1993): 807–57.

Fessler, A. 'The Management of Lunacy in Seventeenth-Century England: An Investigation of Quarter-Sessions Records.' *Proceedings of the Royal Society of Medicine* 49 (1956): 901–7.

Fletcher, Anthony and John Stevenson. Introduction to *Order and Disorder in Early Modern England*, ed. Anthony Fletcher and John Stevenson. Cambridge, 1985, pp. 1–40.

Forbes, Thomas. *Surgeons at the Bailey: English Forensic Medicine to 1878.* New Haven, 1985.

Foucault, Michel. *Discipline and Punish: The Birth of the Prison.* Translated by Alan Sheridan. New York, 1977.

Foyster. Elizabeth A. *Manhood in Early Modern England. Honour, Sex and Marriage.* London, 1999.

Froide, Amy. *Never Married: Singlewomen in Early Modern England.* Oxford, forthcoming.

Froide, Amy and Judith Bennett, eds. *Singlewomen in the European Past, 1250–1800.* Philadelphia, 1999.

Gallagher, Catherine and Thomas Laqueur, eds. *The Making of the Modern Body: Sexuality and Society in the Nineteenth Century.* Berkeley, 1987.

Gaskill, Malcolm. *Crime and Mentalities in Early Modern England.* Cambridge, 2000.

Gaskill, Malcolm. 'The Displacement of Providence: Policing and Prosecution in Seventeenth- and Eighteenth-Century England.' *Continuity and Change* 11 (1996): 341–74.

Gaskill, Malcolm. 'Reporting Murder: Fiction in the Archives in Early Modern England.' *Social History* 23 (1998): 1–30.

Gatrell, V.A.C. *The Hanging Tree: Execution and the English People, 1770–1868.* Oxford, 1994.

Gibson, Marion. *Reading Witchcraft: Stories of Early English Witches.* New York, 1999.

Gladfelder, Hal. *Criminality and Narrative in Eighteenth-Century England: Beyond the Law.* Baltimore, 2001.

Glassey, Lionel. *Politics and the Appointment of Justices of the Peace, 1675–1720.* Oxford, 1979.

Goldstein, Jan Ellen. *Console and Classify: The French Psychiatric Profession in the Nineteenth Century.* With a new Afterword. Chicago, 2001.

Gowing, Laura. *Domestic Dangers: Women, Words, and Sex in Early Modern London.* Oxford, 1996.

Gowing, Laura. 'Ordering the Body: Illegitimacy and Female Authority in Seventeenth-Century England.' In *Negotiating Power in Early Modern Society*, ed. Michael Braddick and John Walter. Cambridge, 2001, pp. 43–62.

Gowing, Laura. 'Secret Births and Infanticide in Seventeenth-Century England.' *Past and Present* 156 (1997): 87–115.

Green, Thomas A. *Verdict According to Conscience: Perspectives on the English Criminal Trial Jury, 1200–1800.* Chicago, 1985.

Greenwald, Gary I. and Maria White Greenwald. 'Medicolegal Progress in Inquest of Felonious Deaths: Westminster, 1761–1866.' *Journal of Legal Medicine* 2, 2 (1981): 193–264.

Greenwald, Maria White and Gary I. Greenwald. 'Coroner's Inquests. A Source of Vital Statistics: Westminster, 1761–1866.' *Journal of Legal Medicine* 4, 1 (1983): 51–86.

Griffin, Martin I.J., Jr. *Latitudinarianism in the Seventeenth-Century Church of England.* New York, 1992.

Grossberg, Michael. *A Judgment for Solomon: The d'Hauteville Case and Legal Experience in Antebellum America.* Cambridge, 1996.

Grossman, Jonathan. *The Art of Alibi: English Law Courts and the Novel.* Baltimore, 2002.

Grupp, Stanley. 'Some Historical Aspects of the Pardon in England.' *American Journal of Legal History* 7 (1963): 51–62.

Halttunen, Karen. 'Humanitarianism and the Pornography of Pain in Anglo-American Culture.' *American Historical Review* 100 (1995): 303–34.

Halttunen, Karen. *Murder Most Foul: The Killer and the American Gothic Imagination.* Cambridge, MA, 1998.

Hariman, Robert, ed. *Popular Trials: Rhetoric, Mass Media, and the Law.* Tuscaloosa, 1990.

Harris, Michael. 'Trials and Criminal Biographies: A Case Study in Distribution.' In *Sale and Distribution of Books from 1700*, ed. Robin Myers and Michael Harris. Oxford, 1982, pp. 1–36.

Hay, Douglas. 'Property, Authority, and the Criminal Law.' In *Albion's Fatal Tree: Crime and Society in Eighteenth-Century England*, ed. Douglas Hay, Peter Linebaugh, John G. Rule, E.P. Thompson, and Cal Winslow. New York, 1975, pp. 17–63.

Hay, Douglas. 'War, Dearth and Theft in the Eighteenth Century: The Record of the English Courts.' *Past and Present* 95 (1982): 117–60.

Hay, Douglas and Nicholas Rogers. *Eighteenth-Century English Society: Shuttles and Swords.* Oxford, 1997.

Hay, Douglas, Peter Linebaugh, John G. Rule, E.P. Thompson, and Cal Winslow, eds. *Albion's Fatal Tree: Crime and Society in Eighteenth-Century England.* New York, 1975.

Herrup, Cynthia. *The Common Peace: Participation and the Criminal Law in Seventeenth-Century England.* Cambridge, 1987.

Herrup, Cynthia. *A House in Gross Disorder: Sex, Law, and the 2nd Earl of Castlehaven.* Oxford, 1999.

Herrup, Cynthia. 'Law and Morality in Seventeenth-Century England.' *Past and Present* 106 (1985).

Hill, Bridget. *Servants: English Domestics in the Eighteenth Century.* Oxford, 1996.

Hill, Bridget. *Women Alone: Spinsters in England, 1660–1850.* New Haven, 2001.

Hindle, Steve. *The State and Social Change in Early Modern England, c. 1550–1640.* London, 2000.

Hirsh, J. 'Enlightened Eighteenth-Century Views of the Alcohol Problem.' *Journal of the History of Medicine* 4 (1949): 230–6.

Hitchcock, Tim, Peter King, and Pamela Sharpe, eds. *Chronicling Poverty: The Voices and Strategies of the English Poor, 1640–1840.* London, 1997.

Hoffer, Peter and N.E.H. Hull, *Murdering Mothers: Infanticide in England and New England, 1558–1803.* New York, 1981.

Horder, Jeremy. 'Pleading Involuntary Lack of Capacity.' *Cambridge Law Journal* 52 (1993): 298–318.

Horder, Jeremy. *Provocation and Responsibility.* Oxford, 1992.

Houston, R.A. *Literacy in Early Modern Europe: Culture and Education, 1500–1800.* London, 1988.

Houston, R.A. *Madness and Society in Eighteenth-Century Scotland.* Oxford, 2000.

Houston, R.A. 'Legal Protection of the Mentally Incapable in Early Modern Scotland.' *Journal of Legal History* 24 (2003): 165–86.

Houston, R.A. 'Madness and Gender in the Long Eighteenth Century.' *Social History* 27 (2003): 309–26.

Hufton, Olwen. 'Women Without Men: Widows and Spinsters in Britain and France in the Eighteenth Century.' *Journal of Family History* (1984): 355–76.

Humfrey, Paula. 'Female Servants and Women's Criminality in Early Eighteenth-Century London.' In *Criminal Justice in the Old World and the New: Essays in Honour of J.M. Beattie,* ed. Greg T. Smith, Allyson N. May, and Simon Devereaux. Toronto, 1998, pp. 58–84.

Hunnisett, R.F. 'The Importance of Eighteenth-Century Coroners' Bills.' In *Law, Litigants and the Legal Profession,* ed. E.W. Ives and A.H. Manchester. London, 1983, pp. 126–39.

Hunnisett, R.F. 'Pleas of the Crown and the Coroner.' *Bulletin of the Institute of Historical Research* 32 (1959): 117–37.

Hunt, William. *The Puritan Moment: The Coming of Revolution in an English County.* Cambridge, MA, 1983.

Hunter, Michael. *Science and Society in Restoration England.* Cambridge, 1981.

Hurnard, Naomi. *The King's Pardon for Homicide before A.D. 1307.* Oxford, 1969.

Ignatieff, Michael. *A Just Measure of Pain: The Penitentiary in the Industrial Revolution, 1750–1850.* New York, 1978.

Ingram, Martin. 'Communities and Courts: Law and Disorder in Early-Seventeenth-Century Wiltshire.' In *Crime in England, 1550–1800*, ed. J.S. Cockburn. Princeton, NJ, 1977, pp. 110–34.

Innes, Joanna and John Styles. 'The Crime Wave: Recent Writing on Crime and Criminal Justice in Eighteenth-Century England.' *Journal of British Studies* 25 (1986): 380–435.

Jackson, Mark. *New-Born Child Murder: Women, Illegitimacy and the Courts in Eighteenth-Century England*. Manchester, 1996.

Jordanova, Ludmilla. *Sexual Visions: Images of Gender in Science and Medicine between the Eighteenth and the Twentieth Centuries*. Madison, 1989.

Kent, D.A. 'Ubiquitous But Invisible: Female Domestic Servants in Mid Eighteenth-Century London.' *History Workshop Journal* 28 (1989): 111–28.

King, Peter. *Crime, Justice, and Discretion in England, 1740–1820*. Oxford, 2000.

King, Peter. 'Decision-Makers and Decision-Making in English Criminal Law, 1750–1800.' *The Historical Journal* 27 (1984): 26–49.

King, Peter. 'Edward Thompson's Contribution to Eighteenth-Century Studies: The Patrician–Plebeian Model Re-examined.' *Social History* 21 (1996): 215–28.

Klein, Lawrence E. *Shaftesbury and the Culture of Politeness: Moral Discourse and Cultural Politics in Early Eighteenth-Century England*. Cambridge, 1994.

Knott, Sarah. 'Sensibility and the American War of Independence.' *American Historical Review* 109 (2004): 19–40.

Korobkin, Laura Hanft. *Criminal Conversations: Sentimentality and Nineteenth-Century Legal Stories of Adultery*. New York, 1998.

Kroll, Richard, Richard Ashcroft, and Perez Zagorin, eds. *Philosophy, Science, and Religion in England, 1640–1700*. Cambridge, 1992.

Lake, Peter. 'Popular Form, Puritan Content? Two Puritan Appropriations of the Murder Pamphlet from Mid-Seventeenth-Century London.' In *Religion, Culture and Society in Early Modern Britain*, ed. Anthony Fletcher and Peter Roberts. Cambridge, 1994, pp. 313–34.

Lake, Peter. 'Protestantism, Arminianism and a Shropshire Axe-Murder.' *Midland History* 15 (1990): 37–64.

Landau, Norma. *The Justices of the Peace, 1679–1760*. Berkeley, 1984.

Landau, Norma., ed. *Law, Crime, and English Society, 1660–1830*. Cambridge, 2002.

Landsman, Stephen. 'The Rise of the Contentious Spirit: Adversary Procedure in Eighteenth Century England.' *Cornell Law Review* 75 (1990): 498–609.

Langbein, John. '*Albion's* Fatal Flaws.' *Past and Present* 98 (1983): 96–120.

Langbein, John. 'The Criminal Trial before the Lawyers.' *The University of Chicago Law Review* 45 (1978): 263–316.

Langbein, John. *The Origins of Adversary Criminal Trial*. Oxford, 2003.

Langbein, John. *Prosecuting Crime in the Renaissance: England, Germany, France*. Cambridge, MA, 1974.

Langbein, John. 'The Prosecutorial Origins of Defense Counsel in the Eighteenth Century: The Appearance of Solicitors.' *Cambridge Law Journal* 58 (1999): 314–65.

Langbein, John. 'Shaping the Eighteenth-Century Criminal Trial: A View from the Ryder Sources.' *The University of Chicago Law Review* 50 (1983): 1–136.

Langbein, John. 'Understanding the Short History of Plea Bargaining.' *Law and Society Review* 13 (1979): 261–72.

Laqueur, Thomas. 'Bodies, Details, and the Humanitarian Narrative.' In *The New Cultural History*, ed. Lynn Hunt. Berkeley, 1989, pp. 176–204.

Laqueur, Thomas W. 'Crowds, Carnival and the State in English Executions 1604–1868,' in *The First Modern Society: Essays in English History in Honour of Lawrence Stone*, ed. A.L. Beier, David Cannadine and James Rosenheim. Cambridge, 1989.

Liddle, A. Mark. 'State, Masculinities and Law: Some Comments on Gender and English State-Formation.' *British Journal of Criminology* 36, 3 (1996): 361–81.

Linebaugh, Peter. *The London Hanged: Crime and Civil Society in the Eighteenth Century*. Cambridge, 1992.

Linebaugh, Peter. '(Marxist) Social History and (Conservative) Legal History.' *New York University Law Review* 60 (1985): 212–43.

Lynch, Deidre Shanna. *The Economy of Character: Novels, Market Culture, and the Business of Inner Meaning*. Chicago, 1998.

Macalpine, Ida and Richard Hunter, *George III and the Mad-Business*. New York, 1969.

Macalpine, Ida and Richard Hunter, eds. *Three Hundred Years of Psychiatry: A History Presented in Selected English Texts*. Oxford, 1963.

MacDonald, Michael. *Mystical Bedlam: Madness, Anxiety, and Healing in Seventeenth-Century England*. Cambridge, 1981.

MacDonald, Michael. 'Popular Beliefs about Mental Disorder in Early Modern England.' In *Heilberufe und Kranke im 17. und 18. Jahrhundert; die Quellen und Forschungssituation*, ed. W. Eckart and J. Geyer-Kordesch. Munster, 1982, pp. 148–73.

MacDonald, Michael and Terence Murphy. *Sleepless Souls: Suicide in Early Modern England*. Oxford, 1990.

Macfarlane, Alan. *The Justice and the Mare's Ale: Law and Disorder in Seventeenth-Century England*. Alan Macfarlane in collaboration with Sarah Harrison. New York, 1981.

Macfarlane, Alan, ed. *The Diary of Ralph Josselin, 1616–1683*. London, 1976.

Madden, J.S. 'Samuel Johnson's Alcohol Problem.' *Medical History* 11 (1967): 141–9.

Malcolmson, Robert. *Popular Recreations in English Society, 1700–1850*. Cambridge, 1973.

Martin, Raymond and John Barresi. *The Naturalization of the Soul: Self and Personal Identity in the Eighteenth Century*. New York, 2000.

Mascuch, Michael. *Origins of the Individualist Self: Autobiography and Self-Identity in England, 1591–1791*. Palo Alto, 1996.

May, Allyson. *The Bar and the Old Bailey, 1750–1850*. Chapel Hill, 2003.

Mayhew, Graham. 'Life-Cycle Service and the Family Unit in Early Modern Rye.' *Continuity and Change* 6 (1991): 201–26.

Maza, Sara. 'Stories in History: Cultural Narratives in Recent Works in European History.' *American Historical Review* 101 (1996): 1493–1515.

McCord, David. 'The English and American History of Voluntary Intoxication to Negate *Mens Rea*.' *Journal of Legal History* 11 (1990): 372–95.

McGowen, Randall. 'The Changing Face of God's Justice: The Debates over Divine and Human Punishment in Eighteenth-Century England.' *Criminal Justice History* 9 (1988): 63–98.

McGowen, Randall. 'Civilizing Punishment: The End of the Public Execution in England.' *Journal of British Studies* 33 (1994): 257–82.

McGowen, Randall. ' "He Beareth not the Sword in Vain": Religion and the Criminal Law in Eighteenth-Century England.' *Eighteenth Century Studies* 21 (1988): 192–211.

McGowen, Randall. 'A Powerful Sympathy: Terror, the Prison, and Humanitarian Reform in Early Nineteenth-Century Britain.' *Journal of British Studies* 25 (1986): 312–24.

McKenzie, Alan T. *Certain, Lively Episodes: The Articulation of Passion in Eighteenth-Century Prose.* Athens, 1990.

McKenzie, Andrea. ''Lives of the Most Notorious Criminals': Popular Literature of Crime in England, 1675–1775.' PhD diss., University of Toronto, 1999.

McKenzie, Andrea. 'Making Crime Pay: Motives, Marketing Strategies, and the Printed Literature of Crime in England, 1670–1770.' In *Criminal Justice in the Old World and the New: Essays in Honour of J. M. Beattie*, ed. Greg T. Smith, Allyson N. May, and Simon Devereaux. Toronto, 1998.

McKenzie, Andrea. 'Martyrs in Low Life? Dying "Game" in Augustan England.' *Journal of British Studies* 42 (2003): 167–205.

McKeon, Michael. *The Origins of the English Novel, 1600–1740.* Baltimore, 1987.

Meldrum, Tim. *Domestic Service and Gender, 1660–1760: Life and Work in the London Household.* New York, 2000.

Meldrum, Tim. 'Domestic Service, Privacy, and Eighteenth-Century Metropolitan Household.' *Urban History* 26 (1999): 27–31.

Mercer, Sarah. 'Crime in Late Seventeenth-Century Yorkshire: An Exception to a National Pattern?' *Northern History* 27 (1991): 106–19.

Micale, Mark S. *Approaching Hysteria: Disease and its Interpretations.* Princeton, 1995.

Micale, Mark S. and Robert L. Dietle, eds. *Enlightenment, Passion, Modernity: Historical Essays in European Thought and Culture.* Stanford, 2000.

Moran, Richard. 'The Modern Foundation for the Insanity Defense: The Cases of James Hadfield (1800) and Daniel McNaughten (1843).' *The Annals of the American Academy of Political and Social Science* 477 (1985): 31–42.

Moran, Richard. 'The Origin of Insanity as a Special Verdict: The Trial for Treason of James Hadfield (1800).' *Law and Society Review* 19 (1985): 487–519.

Morgan, Gwenda and Peter Rushton. *Rogues, Thieves, and the Rule of Law: The Problem of Law Enforcement in North-east England, 1718–1800.* London, 1998.

Morrill, John. *The Cheshire Grand Jury, 1625–1659.* Leicester, 1976.

Mullan, John. *Sentiment and Sociability: The Language of Feeling in the Eighteenth Century.* Oxford, 1988.

Neely, Carol. 'Recent Work in Renaissance Studies: Did Madness Have a Renaissance?' *Renaissance Quarterly* 44 (1991): 776–91.

Neugebauer, Richard. 'Treatment of the Mentally Ill in Medieval and Early Modern England: A Reappraisal.' *Journal of the History of the Behavioural Sciences* 14 (1978): 158–69.

Nussbaum, Felicity. *The Autobiographical Subject: Gender and Ideology in Eighteenth-Century England.* Baltimore, 1989.

Ober, William B. 'Infanticide in Eighteenth-Century England: William Hunter's Contribution to the Forensic Problem.' *Pathology Annual* 21 (1986): 311–19.

Oldham, James. 'On Pleading the Belly: A History of the Jury of Matrons.' *Criminal Justice History* 6 (1985): 1–64.

Oldham, James. 'Truth-Telling in the Eighteenth-Century English Courtroom.' *Law and History Review* 12, 1 (1994): 95–121.

Pinch, Adela. *Strange Fits of Passion: Epistemologies of Emotion, Hume to Austen.* Palo Alto, 1996.

Platt, Anthony and Bernard Diamond. 'The Origins and Development of the 'Wild Beast' Concept of Mental Illness and Its Relation to Theories of Criminal Responsibility.' *Journal of the History of the Behavioral Sciences* 1 (1965): 355–67.

Pocock, J.G.A. *Virtue, Commerce, and History: Essays on Political Thought and History, Chiefly in the Eighteenth Century.* Cambridge, 1985.

Porter, Roy. 'The Drinking Man's Disease: The "Pre-History" of Alcoholism in Georgian Britain.' *British Journal of Addiction* 80 (1985): 385–96.

Porter, Roy. *English Society in the Eighteenth Century.* London, 1982.

Porter, Roy. *Mind-Forg'd Manacles: A History of Madness in England from the Restoration to the Regency.* London, 1987.

Porter, Roy, ed. *Rewriting the Self: Histories from the Renaissance to the Present.* London, 1997.

Prest, Wilfrid. 'Judicial Corruption in Early Modern England.' *Past and Present* 133 (1991): 67–95.

Preston, John. *The Created Self: The Reader's Role in Eighteenth-Century Fiction.* New York, 1970.

Prochaska, F.K. 'English State Trials in the 1790's: A Case Study.' *Journal of British Studies* 13 (1973): 63–82.

Quen, J.M. 'James Hadfield and Medical Jurisprudence of Insanity.' *New York State Journal of Medicine* 69 (1969): 1221–6.

Rabin, Dana. 'Beyond "lewd women" and "wanton wenches": Infanticide and Child Murder in the Long Eighteenth Century.' In *Writing British Infanticide: Child Murder and the Rise of the Novelist,* ed. Jennifer Thorn. Newark, DE, 2003, pp. 45–69.

Rabin, Dana. 'Searching for the Self in Eighteenth-Century English Criminal Trials, 1730–1800.' *Eighteenth-Century Life* 27, 1 (2003): 85–106.

Radzinowicz, Leon. *A History of English Criminal Law and its Administration from 1750,* 4 vols. Vol. 1: *The Movement for Reform 1750–1833.* New York, 1948.

Raven, James, Helen Small, and Naomi Tadmor, eds. *The Practice and Representation of Reading in England.* Cambridge, 1996.

Redwood, John. *Reason, Ridicule and Religion: The Age of Enlightenment in England, 1660–1750.* Cambridge, MA, 1976.

Richetti, John. *Popular Fiction before Richardson: Narrative Patterns, 1700–1739.* Oxford, 1969.

Rivers, Isabel., ed. *Books and their Readers in Eighteenth-Century England.* Leicester, 1982.

Rix, Keith. 'James Boswell (1740–1795): "No Man is more easily hurt with wine than I am." ' *Journal of Alcoholism* 10 (1975): 73–7.

Rix, Keith. 'John Coakley Lettsom and Some Effects of Hard Drinking.' *Journal of Alcoholism* 11 (1976): 98–113.

Roulston, Christine. *Virtue, Gender, and the Authentic Self in Eighteenth-Century Fiction: Richardson, Rousseau, and Laclos.* Gainesville, 1998.

Rushton, Peter. 'Lunatics and Idiots: Mental Disability, the Community, and the Poor Law in North-East England, 1600–1800.' *Medical History* 32 (1988): 34–50.

Scull, Andrew T. *The Most Solitary of Afflictions: Madness and Society in Britain, 1700–1900.* New Haven, 1993.

Scull, Andrew T. *Museums of Madness: The Social Organization of Insanity in Nineteenth-Century England.* London, 1979.

Seaver, Paul. *Wallington's World: A Puritan Artisan in Seventeenth-Century London.* Palo Alto, 1986.

Seigel, Jerrold. 'Problematizing the Self.' In *Beyond the Cultural Turn: New Directions in the Study of Culture and Society*, ed. Victoria E. Bonnell and Lynn Hunt. Berkeley, 2000, pp. 281–314.

Seleski, Patty. 'Women, Work, and Cultural Change in Eighteenth and Early Nineteenth-Century London.' In *Popular Culture in England, c. 1500–1850*, ed. Tim Harris. New York, 1995, pp. 143–67.

Shapin, Steven. *A Social History of Truth: Civility and Science in Seventeenth-Century England*. Chicago, 1994.

Shapiro, Barbara. *A Culture of Fact: England 1550–1750*. Ithaca, 2000.

Shapiro, Barbara. *Probability and Certainty in Seventeenth-Century England: A Study of the Relationships between Natural Science, Religion, History, Law, and Literature*. Princeton, NJ, 1983.

Sharpe, J.A. *Crime in Seventeenth-Century England: A County Study*. Cambridge, 1983.

Sharpe, J.A. 'Domestic Homicide in Early Modern England.' *Historical Journal* 24, 1 (1981): 29–48.

Sharpe, J.A. 'Enforcing the Law in the Seventeenth-Century English Village,' in *Crime and the Law: The Social History of Crime in Western Europe since 1500*, ed. V.A.C. Gatrell, Bruce Lenman, and Geoffrey Parker. London, 1980, pp. 97–119.

Sharpe, J.A. ' "Last Dying Speeches": Religion, Ideology and Public Execution in Seventeenth-Century England.' *Past and Present* 107 (1985): 144–67.

Sharpe, J.A. *Crime in Seventeenth-Century England: A County Study*. Cambridge, 1983.

Shepard, Leslie. *The Broadside Ballad*. London, 1962.

Shepard, Leslie. *The History of Street Literature*. Newton Abbot, 1973.

Sheriff, John K. *The Good-Natured Man: The Evolution of a Moral Ideal, 1660–1800*. University, AL, 1982.

Shoemaker, Robert. *Prosecution and Punishment: Petty Crime and the Law in London and Rural Middlesex 1660–1725*. Cambridge, 1991.

Shoemaker, Robert. 'Reforming the City: The Reformation of Manners Campaign in London, 1690–1738.' In *Stilling the Grumbling Hive: The Response to Social and Economic Problems in England, 1689–1750*, ed. Lee Davison, Tim Hitchcock, Tim Keirn, and Robert Shoemaker. New York, 1992, pp. 99–115.

Singh, R.U. 'The History of the Defense of Drunkenness in English Criminal Law.' *Law Quarterly Review* 49 (1933): 528–46.

Singleton, Robert R. 'English Criminal Biography, 1651–1722.' *Harvard Library Bulletin* 18 (1970): 63–83.

Sinha, Mrinalini. *Colonial Masculinity: The 'manly Englishman' and the 'effeminate Bengali' in the Late Nineteenth Century*. Manchester, 1995.

Slack, Paul. *The Impact of Plague in Tudor and Stuart England*. London, 1985.

Slack, Paul. *Poverty and Policy in Tudor and Stuart England*. London, 1988.

Smith, Roger. *Trial by Medicine: Insanity and Responsibility in Victorian Trials*. Edinburgh, 1981.

Spacks, Patricia Meyer. *Imagining a Self: Autobiography and Novel in Eighteenth-Century England*. Cambridge, MA, 1976.

Spacks, Patricia Meyer. *Privacy: Concealing the Eighteenth-Century Self*. Chicago, 2003.

Spufford, Margaret. *Small Books and Pleasant Histories: Popular Fiction and Its Readership in Seventeenth-Century England*. Cambridge, 1981.

Stachniewski, John. *The Persecutory Imagination: English Puritanism and the Literature of Religious Despair*. Oxford, 1991.

Starr, George. *Defoe and Casuistry*. Princeton, 1971.

Starr, George. *Defoe and Spiritual Autobiography*. Princeton, 1965.

Stephen, James Fitzjames. *A History of the Criminal Law of England*. 3 vols. London, 1883.

Stoler, Ann. *Carnal Knowledge and Imperial Power: Race and the Intimate in Colonial Rule*. Berkeley, 2002.

Stone, Lawrence. 'Social Mobility in England, 1500–1700,' *Past and Present* 33 (1966): 16–55.

Suzuki, Akihito. 'Lunacy in Seventeenth- and Eighteenth-Century England: Analysis of Quarter Sessions Records (part one).' *History of Psychiatry* 2 (1991): 437–56.

Suzuki, Akihito. 'Lunacy in Seventeenth- and Eighteenth-Century England: Analysis of Quarter Sessions Records (part two).' *History of Psychiatry* 3 (1992): 29–44.

Taylor, Charles. *Sources of the Self: The Making of the Modern Identity*. Cambridge, MA, 1989.

Taylor, Stephen James. *Jonas Hanway: Founder of the Marine Society: Charity and Policy in Eighteenth-Century Britain*. London, 1985.

Thomas, Keith. 'Age and Authority in Early Modern England.' *Proceedings of the British Academy* 62 (1976): 205–48.

Thomas, Keith. *Man and the Natural World: A History of the Modern Sensibility*. New York, 1983.

Thomas, Keith. *Religion and the Decline of Magic*. New York, 1971.

Thompson, E.P. *Customs in Common: Studies in Traditional Popular Culture*. New York, 1993.

Thompson, E.P. 'Eighteenth Century English Society: Class Struggle Without Class.' *Social History* 10 (1978): 133–65.

Thompson, E.P. 'Patrician Society, Plebian Culture.' *Journal of Social History* 7 (1974): 382–405.

Thompson, E.P. *Whigs and Hunters: The Origins of the Black Act*. New York, 1975.

Todd, Dennis. *Imagining Monsters: Miscreations of the Self in Eighteenth-Century England*. Chicago, 1995.

Todd, Janet. *Sensibility: An Introduction*. London, 1986.

Tuveson, Ernest Lee. *The Imagination as a Means of Grace: Locke and the Aesthetics of Romanticism*. Berkeley, 1960.

Umphrey, Martha Merrill. 'The Dialogics of Legal Meaning: Spectacular Trials, the Unwritten Law, and Narratives of Criminal Responsibility.' *Law and Society Review* 33 (1999): 393–423.

Van Sant, Ann Jessie. *Eighteenth-Century Sensibility and the Novel: The Senses in Social Context*. Cambridge, 1993.

Vila, Anne C. *Enlightenment and Pathology: Sensibility in the Literature and Medicine of Eighteenth-Century France*. Baltimore, 1998.

Wahrman, Dror. 'The English Problem with Identity in the American Revolution.' *American Historical Review* 106 (2001): 1236–62.

Wahrman, Dror. 'Gender in Translation: How the English Wrote Their Juvenal, 1644–1815.' *Representations* 65 (1999): 1–41.

Wahrman, Dror. *The Invention of the Modern Self*. New Haven, CT, 2004.

Wahrman, Dror. 'On Queen Bees and Being Queens: A Late-Eighteenth-Century "Cultural Revolution"?' In *The Age of Cultural Revolutions: Britain and France, 1750–1820*, eds. Colin Jones and Dror Wahrman. Berkeley, 2002, pp. 251–80.

Walker, Garthine. *Crime, Gender, and Social Order in Early Modern England*. Cambridge, 2003.

Walker, Nigel. *Crime and Insanity in England*. 2 vols. Vol. 1: *The Historical Perspective*. Edinburgh, 1967.

Walker, Nigel. 'The Insanity Defense before 1800.' *The Annals of the American Academy of Political and Social Science* 477 (1985): 25–30.

Walkowitz, Judith. *Prostitution and Victorian Society: Women, Class, and the State*. Cambridge, 1980.

Walsham, Alexandra. *Providence in Early Modern England*. Oxford, 1999.

Warner, Jessica. "Resolv'd to drink no more": Addiction as a Preindustrial Construct.' *Journal of Studies on Alcohol* 55 (1994): 685–91.

Watt, Ian. *The Rise of the Novel: Studies in Defoe, Richardson and Fielding*. London, 1963.

Watt, Tessa. *Cheap Print and Popular Piety, 1550–1640*. Cambridge, 1991.

Weiner, Martin. *Reconstructing the Criminal: Culture, Law, and Policy in England, 1830–1914*. Cambridge, 1990.

Welsh, Alexander. *Strong Representations: Narrative and Circumstantial Evidence in England*. Baltimore, 1992.

Westfall, Richard S. *Science and Religion in Seventeenth-Century England*. Ann Arbor, 1958.

White, J.B. *Heracles' Bow: Essays on the Rhetoric and Poetics of the Law*. Madison, 1985.

White, Jonathan. 'The "Slow but Sure Poyson": The Representation of Gin and Its Drinkers, 1736–1751.' *Journal of British Studies* 42 (2003): 35–64.

White, Maria. 'Westminster Inquests.' Master's thesis, Yale University, 1980.

Wilkinson, David. *The Duke of Portland: Politics and Party in the Age of George III*. New York, 2003.

Williams, Raymond. *The Long Revolution*. London, 1961.

Wiltenburg, Joy. *Disorderly Women and Female Power in the Street Literature of Early Modern England and Germany*. Charlottesville, 1992.

Wood, Andy. *The Politics of Social Conflict: The Peak Country, 1520–1770*. New York, 1999.

Worden, Blair. 'Providence and Politics in Cromwellian England.' *Past and Present* 109 (1985): 55–99.

Wright, David and Ann Digby, eds. *From Idiocy to Mental Deficiency: Historical Perspectives on People with Learning Disabilities*. New York, 1996.

Wrightson, Keith. *Earthly Necessities: Economic Lives in Early Modern Britain*. New Haven, CT, 2000.

Wrightson, Keith. *English Society, 1580–1680*. New Brunswick, 1982.

Wrightson, Keith. 'Infanticide in Earlier Seventeenth-Century England.' *Local Population Studies* 15 (1975): 10–22.

Wrightson, Keith. 'The Social Order of Early Modern England: Three Approaches.' In *The World We Have Gained: Histories of Population and Social Structure*, ed. Lloyd Bonfield, Richard Smith, and Keith Wrightson. New York, 1986, pp. 177–202.

Index